Valuing Us All

Valuing Us All

Feminist Pedagogy and Economics

April Laskey Aerni and

KimMarie McGoldrick, Editors

Ann Arbor

THE UNIVERSITY OF MICHIGAN PRESS

Copyright © by the University of Michigan 1999
All rights reserved
Published in the United States of America by
The University of Michigan Press
Manufactured in the United States of America
⊗ Printed on acid-free paper

2002   2001   2000   1999   4   3   2   1

A CIP catalog record for this book is available from the British Library.

Library of Congress Cataloging-in-Publication Data

Valuing us all : feminist pedagogy and economics / April Laskey
   Aerni and KimMarie McGoldrick, editors.
      p.   cm.
   Includes bibliographical references and index.
   ISBN 0-472-09704-0 (acid-free paper) — ISBN 0-472-06704-4 (pbk:
acid-free paper)
      1. Feminist economics—Study and teaching (Higher)   2.
Economics—Study and teaching (Higher)   3. Feminism and education.
I. Aerni, April Laskey.   II. McGoldrick, KimMarie.
HQ1381   .V35   1999
330'.071'1—dc21   99-6459
                                                              CIP

Contents

Part 3. Alternative Pedagogies

Foreword

Marianne Ferber

Academics have long been critical of colleges of education, claiming that they put all the emphasis on how to teach while neglecting to make sure that teachers are adequately prepared what to teach. At the same time these academics, while for the most part preparing their students adequately what to teach have generally failed entirely to make sure that they receive some preparation for how to teach. This is all the more surprising in view of the fact that many of their students will have careers as instructors at colleges and universities. The situation has, however, recently been changing, especially among feminists, including feminist economists, who have become increasingly aware that many students do not learn well in the typical economics course, most notably in the large introductory economics classes. Further, there is considerable evidence that this is particularly true for women and minorities. Feminist critics assign some of the blame for the unsatisfactory outcomes on the content of the courses, and there is certainly room for improvement in that respect; but a growing number now recognize that there is also much room for improvements in teaching.

This book brings together much of what has been learned both about ways to enrich the content of economics courses, and about better ways to reach diverse students, with differing backgrounds, interests, and learning styles. For the most part the essays in this volume are still exploratory, but they raise many interesting questions and suggest useful ways instructors may be able to find some of the answers for themselves in their own classrooms. In addition, they provide a wealth of information about current work in this area. Therefore, this book should prove useful not only to instructors who are at the beginning of their careers, but also to the many senior faculty members who feel frustrated because after years of trying they still find it difficult to transmit either their enthusiasm for or the knowledge of their subject to most of their students.

As already suggested, critics of introductory economics courses do not concentrate solely on pedagogy. For some time now feminist economists and other critics of mainstream neoclassical economics have cast a jaundiced eye on the standard claim incorporated in most introductory texts that a clear distinction must be made between positive analysis, the proper province of scientists, which merely presents the results of objective research, and normative approaches. The latter should be avoided because they permit value judgments to intrude, most notably when it comes to policy issues. This view strikes feminists as disingenuous; for at the very least ideology influences what problems are selected for study, how research is operationalized, and how the results are interpreted (Blau 1981).

Beyond that feminists question the uncritical acceptance of efficiency and maximization of output as the proper goal of "rational economic man," while frequently disregarding the equally important issues of equity and quality of life. This ignores the crucial facts that satisfaction is determined by the distribution as well as by level of income and output and that work is not merely a means of acquiring purchasing power, but also a source of direct satisfaction. Finally, and equally important, while neoclassical theory of the family (Becker 1991) does recognize that "economic man" may be an altruist vis-à-vis his family, they fail to recognize that this altruism can and does extend, to a greater or lesser degree, to extended families, to the community, to the nation, and even to the world. Feminists are concerned that such a narrow view is not only unrealistic but also encourages students to believe that narrow self-interest is a legitimate goal, perhaps the only legitimate goal, of a rational person.

The authors represented in this volume do not tend to share these views. On the contrary, they emphasize equity as well as efficiency, cooperation as well as competition, and interdependence as well as independence. They also focus on preparing students to be informed citizens and caring members of the community as well as productive workers. These broader aims, like the new pedagogy, are expected to have greater appeal for many students, and particularly for members of groups that have traditionally been underrepresented among economics students.

Even some prominent neoclassical economists appear to view the traditional approach as narrow and unrealistic. For instance, Blank (1993, 133) says she was startled to realize that many economists "really believe all this stuff about individuals constantly making fully informed rational choices accounting for all expected lifetime costs and benefits" and believes that this goes a long way toward explaining why 99 out of 100 students in introductory courses are likely to find the economic approach sort of crazy, though perhaps interesting.

Given recent concerns about the decline in the number of undergraduate economics majors, and the even greater decline in the number of women among them, this volume, which should be helpful in counteracting this trend, is particularly timely. This is true even for those of us who do not bemoan the fact that fewer students now appear to be entering this field as a means of getting a business oriented education when they are unable to gain admittance to other, more business oriented departments. For economics, while it can be a useful preparation for some to make a better living will, when taught as envisioned here, provide an excellent background for everyone who expects to live as a useful member of a modern society.

REFERENCES

Becker, Gary S. 1981. *A Treatise on the Family.* Cambridge, MA: Harvard University Press.

Blank, Rebecca M. 1993. "What Should Mainstream Economists Learn from Feminist Theory?" In *Beyond Economic Man,* ed. Marianne A. Ferber and Julie A. Nelson, 133–43. Chicago: University of Chicago Press.

Blau, Francine D. 1981. "On the Role of Values in Feminist Scholarship." *Signs: Journal of Women in Culture and Society* 7 (spring): 538–40.

Preface

Ever since we began teaching economics we've been frustrated by the inconsistencies and contradictions between the traditional neoclassical material presented in introductory texts and our own philosophies and viewpoints as feminists. Over the years we've each found ways to integrate our feminist perspectives through a trial and error approach. Though this may have ultimately made our teaching more effective and our students more informed, we incurred great start-up costs and often felt as if we were working in a vacuum. Prior to the founding of the International Association for Feminist Economics (IAFFE), in 1990, there were few outlets for constructive discussions of a feminist pedagogical approach in economics. IAFFE has provided a platform for discussions of the challenges so many of us have faced in our attempts to develop more inclusive materials and alternative pedagogical approaches to be used in our classrooms.

Economics is clearly shaped by those who practice economics as well as the teachers of economics. To quote Diana Strassmann, editor of the journal *Feminist Economics:* "research in economic education has identified racial and gender bias in disciplinary training and socialization practices and biased disciplinary conventions in publication, employment, and promotion practices, all of which serve to reproduce the current disciplinary hierarchy" (*Feminist Economics* 1, no. 1: 3). If we are interested in providing alternative methods of analysis, a reformulation of economic assumptions, or a pattern of research considering topics never before addressed, then we also need to reconsider course content and the method by which economic knowledge is generated. It is in the economics classroom that we, as educators, can have the most influence on the next generation of potential economists.

If we agree that science is socially constructed, then the pedagogical approaches suggested by feminist theory would allow for the (re)formation of economic analysis. "As teachers and instructors, we are not simply purveyors of knowledge; we are also producers of knowledge.... In organizing syllabi, designing assignments, selecting readings, and evaluating student work, we participate in the production and institutionalization of knowledge, and science, in particular" (Ewick, *Gender and Society* 8, no. 1: 106). The development of feminist pedagogy in economics will allow us to address the contradiction of feminist research coupled with conservative/traditional teaching. Feminist pedagogy will also have many additional positive side effects because it suggests a variety of methods that engage students in learning, transfer authority from instructor to student, allow for considerations of process over output, and allow for topics not considered by mainstream economic models. As such, it provides opportunities for more of our students to be engaged in the gathering of economic knowledge. This should increase the appeal of the discipline to those students so often turned off by the standard lecture-based classroom.

The growth of IAFFE has provided a forum for feminist ideas in economics. Indeed, there is now a constantly increasing wealth of published research on feminist economics focusing to a considerable extent on (re)examining issues such as marriage, family, and labor markets, but also markets more generally, economic development, and many other subjects of interest to economists. Surprisingly, however, the amount of published work in the area of feminist pedagogy in economics is far from extensive. Despite the substantial degree of feminist work on the subject that is currently under way, whether it is concerned with course content or with teaching methods, applications of feminist pedagogy have been largely neglected by mainstream economic journals.

Since 1990, we and other feminist economists have organized sessions on pedagogy at the IAFFE annual conferences and under IAFFE sponsorship at other economics conferences. Within the last five years, teaching workshops have been developed and a network evolved of like-minded economists who shared the methodologies they employed to teach a more balanced curriculum. It was at these sessions and at the myriad informal discussions before, during, and after such gatherings that we identified a pressing need to find and publish research on integrating feminist pedagogy in economics. This book gathers some of the pioneering work that is available and thus provides a valuable resource for college faculty teaching economics in the United States.

This book has grown out of these multitudes of discussions. At the 1996 IAFFE summer conference April Aerni, Robin Bartlett, KimMarie McGoldrick, and Jean Shackelford discussed what appeared to be an ever growing interest in pedagogical sessions with a focus on integrating feminist pedagogy into economics. We also noted the relatively few sources outlining and describing methods of incorporating feminist pedagogy that economists could turn to that were economics specific. Continued discussions after the conference led us to ponder how we might contribute to this development and provide some model for potential methods on how this integration might proceed.

In August of that year the four of us met at Bucknell University to outline our own definition of feminist pedagogy and its application in economics and to develop a strategy for transmitting this information to our colleagues. During our intensive brainstorming sessions we realized that a simple paper describing the application of feminist pedagogy to economics would not be sufficient. Indeed, a book was needed that provided a model as well as a number of examples of the process if we really intended to foster this discussion.

During our meeting at Bucknell we came to the conclusion that feminist pedagogy dealt necessarily with both content and classroom methodologies. In our discussions it became clear that our definition of feminist pedagogy also provided a perfect outline for the book and helped us identify potential contributors working on integrating feminist content and those developing teaching strategies. Finally, we also developed the purpose and identified the target audience for the book.

Throughout 1997 KimMarie McGoldrick and April Aerni gathered essays from contributors and put together the book proposal, while the four of us began to write a draft of what is now the first essay. We soon realized that we could benefit from working with someone with an institutionalist background who had also been active in working on pedagogical issues. Thus, Margaret Lewis was added to the mix and the five of us wrote and rewrote the opening essay during the next year. Obviously, this book has been a cooperative project from the beginning and our ideas and writing have evolved as we read and discussed one another's work.

Although this book focuses more on integrating issues of gender into economics classes than on other issues such as race, ethnicity, class, and so forth, we recognize their importance. Even though we have called what we are doing feminist pedagogy, it is in many ways more accurately described as an attempt at developing a more inclusive curriculum. We envision the discipline of economics becoming more diverse both in the people who practice it and in the ideas which it encompasses. Clearly, making sure our work is inclusive is something that all feminists struggle with in the presentation of their research and teaching. We certainly agree that feminist pedagogy does and must include concerns related to teaching about race, class, nationality/imperialism and sexual orientation as well as gender, and that one feminist goal is to educate about and fight against hierarchy and oppression. Many of the essays in this book, however, are based on experiments by the authors in their own classrooms and thus often focus on a single aspect such as gender inclusivity.

The book has been divided into three parts: an overview, a section in which changes in content are discussed, and a section in which changes in teaching methodology and strategies are discussed. This organization corresponds to the two aspects of change we believe are necessary to move toward feminist pedagogy in economics. Many of the essays in the latter two parts of the book function as case studies and as such provide examples of what feminist economists are trying in their attempts to move toward a more inclusive classroom.

The first section of the book introduces our vision of feminist pedagogy, explains the importance of developing feminist pedagogy in economics, and proposes a model for achieving feminist pedagogy in economics. To this end the first essay defines what we mean by feminist pedagogy, develops a model for integrating more inclusive course content in economics classes and for employing more cooperative and community-oriented pedagogical practices, and outlines the main themes of this book. The benefits of feminist pedagogy, as well as some of the challenges it presents, are discussed in the second essay, by Jean Shackelford. This essay has become a classic since it was published in the *American Economic Review* in 1992 and has guided many of us in our understanding of feminist pedagogy as applied in economics. In the final essay in this section, Margaret Lewis uses an institutionalist framework to indicate how the transformation to feminist pedagogy can be achieved through the re-visioning of pedagogy, content, methodology, and definition in the economic classroom.

The second section of the book focuses on the course content path to a feminist pedagogy in economics. It begins by providing in the Feiner and Roberts essay documentation of the invisibility of some groups in economics texts. The essays by Lewis, Peterson, Aerni, Hoffman, and Strober discuss how course content is biased and provide examples of how content can be altered to be more inclusive. Finally, this section concludes with a report by Lage and Treglia on how altering the course content had an impact on students at one university.

The final section documents alternative pedagogies and strategies in the classroom. The gender gap in economic education is well documented and is demonstrated both by the small number of women students majoring in economics and the performance of women students in introductory economics courses. This section begins with Hirschfeld, Moore, and Brown exploring the reasons for performance differences. Ziegert's essay that follows addresses learning style differences. The work done by these authors, among others, suggests that alternative approaches to teaching economics benefits students because of their diverse learning styles. Thus, the remaining essays in this section provide alternative teaching methods that are consistent with the goals outlined by the application of feminist pedagogy to economics. McGoldrick discusses the use of service learning, Jacobsen the use of structured peer review in writing-intensive classes, Young the use of internships, McCormick teaching case studies, Rishi the use of e-mail discussion lists, and Bartlett the use of collaborative learning.

It is our hope that this book acts as a map for new teachers as they travel down the many roads to feminist pedagogy in economics. In addition, we anticipate that it will reinvigorate those who have had longer careers and provide them with fresh ideas in their pursuit of feminist pedagogy in economics. Finally, we believe that there is so much more work that needs to be done in incorporating feminist pedagogy into economics and hope that this book not only promotes conversation about this process but also stimulates additional research in this very important area of economic education.

This book would not have been possible without the help of many people and we would like to thank all our colleagues who contributed to this book especially Robin Bartlett (who first thought up the earliest version of the grid presented in the first essay), Jean Shackelford (for encouraging this project from the very beginning by organizing our first meeting at Bucknell and for her leadership as founder and first president of IAFFE), and Margaret Lewis (who always found a way over the many walls we ran into in developing our vision of feminist pedagogy in economics and in completing the first essay in this volume).

We also wish to thank IAFFE presidents Myra Strober, Marianne Ferber, and Barbara Bergmann. This project was initially intended to be one of the first in a series of volumes by IAFFE. But the book advanced faster than volunteer committees assessing a book series project could move and the IAFFE Board gave us their unofficial blessing, and we have since finished the project without their official involvement. Not enough thanks could be said to Marianne Ferber, who read a draft of every essay in this volume, gave copious editorial comments, and constantly provided guidance when it was needed.

Both our institutions, Nazareth College of Rochester and University of Richmond, have provided valuable resources necessary for the completion of this book, including secretarial work (thank you Janet Wiltshire) and a sabbatical for April 1997–98. Thank you to Ellen McCarthy at the University of Michigan Press for her enthusiasm and editorial assistance. Finally, we would like to thank Richard Aerni and Carol F. Jones, without whose support and patience this book would not have been possible.

PART 1

Introduction to Feminist Pedagogy

Toward Feminist Pedagogy in Economics

April Laskey Aerni, Robin L. Bartlett,
Margaret Lewis, KimMarie McGoldrick,
and Jean Shackelford

Given the growing feminist literature oriented to reconstructing economics, it is time for economic educators, especially feminist economics educators, to look at what they teach in their courses and how they teach them. If the goals of economics education include increasing students' understanding of the world and enabling them to participate fully as citizens in a democratic society, then the economics classroom must invite all students to take part.

This essay begins by describing evidence from the United States that suggests that content and teaching methods may influence the demographics of economics students. Next, it suggests a framework that will help economists evaluate to what extent their courses offer inclusive content and an inclusive learning environment. It explores connections among inclusive course content, a different learning environment, and a feminist pedagogy. Finally, it discusses the challenges of moving the economics classroom toward a feminist pedagogy and the potential transformation of the discipline itself.

Observations from the U.S. Experience

Recent declines in economics majors in the United States have caused concern among economics educators in the United States (Siegfried and Scott 1994; Committee on Economic Education 1996). The relationship between the declining number of economics majors in the United States and the underrepresentation of women and people of color in economics classrooms is largely one of simple mathematics. As U.S. data indicate, women and people of color comprise an increasing number of college students (U.S. Department of Education 1997). However, as documented over the last twenty years, the percentage of women receiving economics degrees has remained relatively stable, increasing just four percentage points from 1977– 78 to 1993–94 (Siegfried and Scott 1994; Siegfried 1995). Results from a

3

recent national survey of undergraduate teaching methods sent to over 3,000 economics instructors across the United States conducted by William Becker and Michael Watts (1996) support the authors' view that, given recent demographic changes and our own experiences, teachers of economics who want to foster a more inclusive classroom must look inside their classrooms rather than at such external factors, such as academic subject cycles and the business cycle.[1]

According to Becker and Watts, "the dominant profile of U.S. undergraduate economics teachers is a male (83 percent), Caucasian (89 percent), Ph.D. (86 percent) . . . who lectures to a class of students as he writes text, equations, and graphs on the chalk board, and who assigns students readings from a standard textbook. This picture is basically the same for all courses and at all institutions, despite the fact that teaching loads and class size vary considerably across the different types of institutions" (1996, 450). In particular, 83 percent of the classes in economics are taught with lectures (except at the upper level courses in doctoral institutions), 83 percent of class time is spent with professors writing on the board, and 83 percent of the time a textbook is the only assigned reading (1996, 450).

This sterile—but evidently standard pedagogy in the United States—no doubt, affects the content of and the examples used in economics courses. Marianne Ferber (1997, 1995) and Susan Feiner and Barbara Morgan (1987) have found that the neoclassical model dominates the content of the typical U.S. textbook, from which women and people of color are noticeably absent or marginalized. A recent indicator of course content suggests that it may be narrowing further, rather than broadening to include alternative economic explanations and analyses of the significant economic factors of gender, race, and class. At the 1997 Allied Social Science Association meetings, the U.S.-based National Council on Economic Education advanced voluntary content standards for precollege students that, to the extent that they are followed, would further narrow the content of precollege and most college introductory economics courses.[2] These standards focus narrowly on a choice-theoretic model premised on the scarcity definition of economics and fail to explore many important issues, including the significance of gender, race, and class in the U.S. economy. Since the authors of these standards are prominent postsecondary economic educators, we may assume that their recommendations reflect a large segment of U.S. mainstream thinking concerning which basic economic concepts are critical for an informed citizenry.

Course content is not the only concern for those interested in dismantling the economics classroom's exclusivity. Becker and Watts's profile suggests that most U.S. economics instructors lecture to their classes from the text, even though many researchers have concluded that lectures are effective for only a small proportion of today's U.S. college students and that, even for those students, active learning environments provide a more effective education (see, e.g., Belenky, Clinchy, Goldberger, and Tarule 1992; Johnson, Johnson, and Smith 1991; Tobias 1990; Treisman 1992). Scholars also note that students may turn away from certain disciplines because, at present, the classroom tends to constitute a competitive environment, devoid of any sense of community or relevance to students' lives (see, e.g., Tobias 1990; Bartlett 1995). This atmosphere is often reinforced by the limited scope of material in the standard economics texts.

While economics educators have yet to explore possible connections between the underrepresentation of women and nonwhites in economics classrooms and the decline in economics majors, the authors believe that these two trends are closely related and, more importantly, that to reverse them teachers of economics must examine how their classrooms might be excluding increasing numbers of college students. In other words, if economics instructors want to attract and retain a more diverse group of students in their courses, they must find ways to make their classrooms more inclusive.

A Framework for a More Inclusive Classroom

The framework proposed here emphasizes two elements necessary for a more inclusive classroom. The first describes how course content might evolve as the economic experiences of all economic actors are incorporated, thereby making the subject of economics relevant for all students. The second describes how the classroom environment would have to change to foster an effective learning community for all students.

The model for making course content more inclusive draws on the works of Peggy McIntosh (1983a, b, 1990), Sue Rosser (1990), Marilyn Schuster and Susan Van Dyne (1985) and Frances Maher and Mary Kay Thompson Tetreault (1994), all of whom suggest that disciplinary content become more inclusive by proceeding through a series of interactive phases. For brevity, the authors present an adapted, eclectic version of these feminist phase-theory models with gender inclusiveness as its primary focus. This model, however, can and must be expanded to include other traditionally neglected sources of identity and diversity, such as race, class, ethnicity, sexual orientation, nationality, and geographic location, for the analysis of economic activity to be realistic and inclusive.

Phases of Making Course Content More Inclusive

1. Teaching the Received Neoclassical Canon (Womenless Economics)

2. Finding and Adding Members of Here-to-fore Underrepresented Groups

3. Challenging Core Concepts and Proposing Alternatives

4. Redefining and Reconstructing Economics to Include Us All

In the first phase economics is taught as if gender is not relevant for understanding economic activity, presenting individuals as nongendered "homogeneous globule(s) of desire" (Veblen 1993, 138) rather than as diverse actors influenced by cultural and biophysical factors. In addition, unlimited wants in a constrained world are assumed to motivate these "globules of desire," and these individuals are assumed to make rational economic decisions. Thus this economics is implicitly constructed as though all people were white men, although, as feminist economists have argued, these models are generally unrealistic even for this group (England 1993; Nelson 1996).

Neoclassical concepts and theories dominate the phase 1 course. Content focuses largely on abstract theories, grounded in a choice-theoretic framework, with the purpose of learning to "think like economists." Concrete examples, if presented at all, come after the theoretical explication and are used to demonstrate that the choice-theoretic model can indeed be used to explain a variety of situations, such as a person's decision either to specialize in housework or to participate in the labor market, to have children, or to obtain a divorce. Unfortunately, these applications are often inappropriate, particularly for analyzing the nonmarket work done by women, and consequently ignore this large segment of economic activity. In addition, markets and the state are foregrounded, thereby emphasizing stories about those who have the most economic power and are the most visible in existing economic and political systems. Moreover, competition, which is pivotal for achieving efficiency in the neoclassical model, tends to be valued as the most socially desirable behavior, while ignoring the usefulness of such other types of behavior, as altruism, cooperation, reciprocity, and redistribution.[3]

As feminist economists well know, the phase 1 course, with its neoclassical content, is not inclusive, since it is neither descriptive of nor relevant to many students' lives. Following feminist phase theories, a common response is to move into phase 2 by finding and discussing prominent women economists and by investigating and questioning the underrepresentation of women in economic analysis. At this stage, however, members of underrepresented groups still tend to be viewed as "other," and not as a "normal" part of the discipline. Sociologist Margaret Andersen (1987) observed that many social science texts added separate chapters on gender but do not incorporate gender into the rest of the text, which results in devoting only one or two days to these topics. This, of course, marginalizes the role gender plays in understanding economic activity.

Even when women as a group are considered in many parts of the course, they may end up being viewed simply as problems and anomalies rather than worthy of equal consideration with men as a group. Further difficulties arise when the course continues to employ exclusively the neoclassical analytical framework; its limitations in fully understanding the economic activities of women (and many men) quickly become apparent as the universal assumptions of rational behavior and competition and the market metaphor are recognized as not being appropriate or complete. At this point in phase 2 "the gender . . . biases of the disciplines are unveiled . . . [so that] we get the beginnings of the challenge to the core concepts of the disciplines" (Dugger 1990, 12). This unmasking of the false universality of neoclassical concepts and neoclassical economics' portrayal of women provide the catalyst for moving to the next phase.

In phase 3 women's economic experiences are increasingly recognized and seriously discussed. More appropriate information is introduced through the collection of new, more inclusive data. In addition, some economists may modify existing neoclassical theories to account for diverse experiences; altering constraints, adding more variables, or including historical and institutional analyses may lead to better explanations. Other economists may go further and turn to alternative paradigms. Feminist and other heterodox economists, as well as noneconomic scholars, challenge the existing neoclassical orthodoxy and question disciplinary boundaries and hierarchies.

The move to phase 4, an economics that is redefined and reconstructed to include us all, is currently under way as feminist economists, among others, recognize the limitations of currently accepted economic models to explain adequately the diversity of economic behavior. In this final phase instructors draw on critiques and alternative explanations from phase 3 and continue to revision course content. Viewed no longer as merely an abstract academic exercise for training students how to "think like economists," economics is now seen as a concrete way to understand the world in which we live. Only in this phase may economics be expected to provide useful information for citizens who wish to engage in social action. Although it remains difficult today to imagine all the details of a phase 4 course, some features can be identified:

> A phase 4 course will present alternative theories and use varied methodologies.

> It will encourage interaction among theory, empirical observation, and practice.

> It will be broad and multidisciplinary in content.

> It will be multicultural and reflect the experiences of all economic actors.

A course with these features would have more relevance to the lives and experiences of students than most of today's economics courses. Reductionist universal explanations designed to fit all people and all economic institutions for all time would no longer be uncritically accepted. An economics with competing theories and explanations weighed against evidence, and conclusions based on the experiences of different groups of people, will not only help students to understand the complexity of the economy, but it will also better prepare them to participate in it.

Course content is only one of the two elements that must change if the classroom is to become truly inclusive, the learning environment must also change. In the feminist phase theory tradition a model for a more inclusive classroom environment proceeds through several phases, from one in which students learn on their own with the instructor and the text as the sole authorities to one in which instructors and students learn from one another in a cooperative/collaborative environment, with the instructor, text, and students sharing authority. These three classroom environments are outlined here.

Phases of Making the Learning Environment More Inclusive

1. Individual Learning

2. Group Learning

3. Learning Communities

In the individual learning environment students listen passively as the instructor delivers lectures and narrates various economic stories with or without the usual props. Instructors expect students to interpret these stories individually and assess them on their individual understanding, as demonstrated in exercises, homework, and examinations. Alternatively, students can learn more actively, albeit still individually, as instructors solicit participation by asking questions, inviting discussion, or having students give presentations. Thus, lecture/discussion and the Socratic method are both possibilities within the individual learning environment.[4] The key characteristic in both is that students are solely responsible for their own learning and that the instructor and text are the sole authorities (Kenneth Bruffee 1993); the "sage-on-the-stage" determines the course material and evaluates whether or not students have adequately mastered it.

Instructors who are aware that many students learn more effectively in nonindividualized and noncompetitive environments are likely to find the phase 1 learning environment uncomfortable and ineffective for many of their students. In response, they may decide to introduce group-based pedagogical strategies in order to make the classroom more collaborative and cooperative.

In this second type of environment students learn from one another by working together in groups. These groups may or may not be structured, and they may meet occasionally or on a day-to-day basis. They can be constructed haphazardly with little rhyme or reason, or they can be more carefully constructed so that students' talents and capabilities complement each other. Structured cooperative groups, where the instructor defines the educational task and gives students roles to play within the group to keep them on task (Johnson, Johnson, and Smith 1991), seem to be effective as are teams, where students voluntarily choose to take a course alone or as a member of a team (Bartlett 1995). In the latter, team members perform each course assignment as a unit, and their work is evaluated by having one student, randomly selected, take the test or make the presentation. The important distinctions between group learning environments and individual ones are that students learn from one another as well as from the instructor, and that students' understanding of the material is evaluated by the students as well as by the instructor. Thus, in a group learning environment, the professor "allows students, through open dialogue and conversation, to compare, contrast and connect their ideas with those of others toward achieving a greater understanding of the subject. The result of this process is that students are actively engaged in the production of knowledge, as opposed to being the passive recipients of teacher imparted 'truth' " (Shackelford 1992, 571).

As students become more active participants in the construction of knowledge, instructors may recognize the opportunity for transforming the classroom into a learning community. This is a desirable move for teachers interested in valuing the experiences and concerns of all classroom participants. In such a phase 3 course instructor and students become "co-learners," sharing authority and evaluating one another. Together, they examine existing economic models based on individual and collective life experiences, critically assessing the applicability of these models to the world in which they all live. By recognizing the authority and needs of instructors and students, the learning environment may not only be reorganized but also expanded beyond the classroom's walls, so that students and teachers interact as co-learners within a broader community. This could include just the academic institution or the community within which the institution is located. As Gordon Wells, Gen Ling Chang, and Ann Maher (1990) discuss, learning communities within an institution involve reorganizing course material or even an entire curriculum around a particular theme, issue, or group. Cooperative learning is central to this learning process, and pedagogical strategies such as service learning (McGoldrick, 1998), oral histories and fieldwork take the instructor and students beyond the institution into the communities around them.

In learning communities combinations of pedagogical activities, such as keeping journals, doing case studies and learning outside the classroom walls, together with more traditional lectures and group exercises, encourage better understanding of the economic activities of a diverse population. Further, such a learning environment provides students (and instructors) with knowledge, skills, and strategies for active participation in the world.

Exploring the Intersections of Course Content and Learning Environments

A more inclusive classroom thus involves moving away from one in which the instructor lectures on neoclassical economics and toward a more community-oriented learning environment that explores a redefined and reconstructed economics. As the instructor recognizes the limitations of both neoclassical course content and hierarchical pedagogical practices, the question becomes how the interplay between changing course content and changing learning environments moves the classroom toward a more inclusive learning community and a more inclusive economics.

The squares of figure 1 illustrate the various combinations of course content and learning environments that might occur in an economics classroom. The vertical axis of figure 1 depicts four progressive phases of course content: Teaching the Neoclassical Canon, Finding and Adding,

Fig. 1. A More Inclusive Model of Course Content and Learning Environments

		Learning Environments		
		Phase 1 *Individual*	Phase II *Groups*	Phase III *Learning Communities*
Course Contents	Phase I The Received Neoclassical Cannon	1 Sage-on-the-Stage/ Neoclassical	2 Guide-on-the-Side/ Neoclassical	3 Co-Learners/ Neoclassical
	Phase II Finding and Adding Women	4 Sage-on-the-Stage/ Find-and-Add	5 Guide-on-the-Side/ Find-and-Add	6 Co-Learners/ Find-and-Add
	Phase III Challenging and Proposing	7 Sage-on-the-Stage/ Challenge	8 Guide-on-the-Side/ Challenge	9 Co-Learners/ Challenge
	Phase IV Redefined and Reconstructed	10 Sage-on-the-Stage/ Redefined	11 Guide-on-the-Side/ Redefined	12 Co-Learners/ Redefined

Challenging and Proposing, and Redefining and Reconstructing. As the instructor incorporates more inclusive course content, materials move from the neoclassical canon to a richly descriptive and critical multicultural, multi-methodological, multidisciplinary and continuously evolving economics. The horizontal axis of figure 1 indicates three types of successively more inclusive learning environments: Individual, Groups, and Learning Communities. As the instructor's pedagogical practices evolve, the classroom moves away from an individualized learning environment to a classroom with more group-based activities and finally toward an environment where students and teacher learn from one another and share authority and responsibility in the learning community.

The sage-on-the-stage/neoclassical square of figure 1 represents the classroom found by Becker and Watts in the United States. In this classroom, the instructor and course text are the authorities, students learn individually, and course content is the neoclassical canon. This classroom, however, is of interest and relevance to fewer and fewer of the increasingly diverse student population in U.S. colleges and universities, and it conflicts with the many culturally determined learning styles that these students bring with them (see, e.g., Adams 1992; Anderson and Adams 1992; Belenky et al. 1986; McIntosh 1983a, b, 1990; Tobias 1990; Treisman 1992). Consequently, remaining in the sage-on-the-stage/neoclassical square perpetuates the status quo—the current neoclassical curriculum taught through lecture—and does not represent the inclusive classroom many feminist economists want to create.

One way that economics teachers can move from the sage-on-the-stage/neoclassical square is to incorporate more inclusive materials. Changes of this nature have already begun, as evidenced by the growing literature on teaching and feminist economics (Shackelford 1992; Bartlett and Feiner 1992; Lewis 1995; Bartlett and Ferber 1998). A second direction for economics instructors to move is from individual learning environments to more group-oriented learning environments. Most of the efforts here are motivated by the development of pedagogical strategies to facilitate student learning as identified by educators in other disciplines, particularly in the humanities and the natural sciences. As the following discussion will suggest, moving in either direction can make the economics classroom more inclusive, but only by moving in both directions will the classroom move toward a feminist pedagogy.

First, it is instructive to examine what does and does not occur when only one facet of the classroom is changed, for this is often how economics educators begin transforming their classes. Suppose, for example, an instructor continues to lecture while modifying course content. Although additional students may be engaged by course materials that more closely reflect their own experiences, retaining hierarchical and passive learning environment may discourage those students who require a more active classroom to learn effectively. Despite more inclusive course material, students may not develop the knowledge, skills, and strategies to become active participants in their communities—a result crucial for a feminist pedagogy.

But suppose, on the other hand, that an instructor recognizes that individual learning environments are ineffective for an increasing number of students and begins incorporating more group and cooperative pedagogical strategies into the classroom, without simultaneously changing course content. Though more students may feel more comfortable in this environment and may learn more of the neoclassical canon, this incomplete picture of economic activity will continue to discourage those students who are seeking to understand their own richly diverse experiences and concerns. Even with a more inclusive learning environment, students still learn only about rational economic man and the dominant public economic institutions—a partial picture of the economy in which they will participate. Again, the resulting classroom does not reflect a feminist pedagogy because it does not account for the activities of all economic actors.

In order to achieve a feminist pedagogy in economics, the authors contend that both course content and the learning environment must become more inclusive. They further believe that as instructors, concerned with improving students' understanding of the world so they can fully participate in it, change either course content or the learning environment, a synergy between the two elements will propel the classroom toward the co-learners/redefined square of figure 1, the classroom most representative of a feminist pedagogy.

The journey from the sage-on-the-stage/neoclassical square and toward co-learners/redefined square may occur through an infinite number of paths. The current discussion will not explore each one in detail; instead, the authors wish to explore one possible scenario for moving toward a feminist pedagogy.

Suppose that an instructor, aware of students' diverse learning styles, begins incorporating group learning activities into class sessions. As students work in cooperative groups or teams that are designed to help them learn traditional material from one another, they also learn that members of different groups are equally capable of doing so, and previously conceived stereotypes are replaced by acquired knowledge about individuals. As students become more knowledgeable about one another's economic lives, the instructor can encourage them to make connections between these lives and what is presented in the text. This may induce students to challenge the course material, and those challenges may in turn prompt the instructor to broaden the course content. She or he may also begin to realize that the diversity among students offers opportunities for fruitful class discussion and for exercises in which students can apply a theory to issues faced by members of diverse groups. Thus, group activities and exercises may motivate the instructor to move from a purely neoclassical course curriculum to one with a broader content that incorporates the special issues facing these groups. With the instructor's guidance, students can learn a great deal from the inconsistencies between the neoclassical models and the real world.

As both instructor and students become increasingly uncomfortable with standard explanations and with "the economic way of thinking," the instructor may begin to include analyses from other perspectives and disciplines. Furthermore, she or he may also allow students to help determine goals and objectives of the course. When this multidisciplinary, multi-pedagogical stage is reached, the instructor, who is often well versed only in economics, is likely to discover, along with her or his students, that other disciplines and other approaches to teaching are also flawed. However, they can now compare the merits and deficiencies of various approaches and can make judgments about their usefulness. At this point the classroom content and environment have reached the final stage. The instructor and the students are co-learners of a redefined course content.

A classroom where redefined and reconstructed economic principles are learned cooperatively reflects the tenets of pedagogy outlined by such feminists as Bernice Sandler, Lisa Silverberg, and Roberta Hall (1996, 40–41): an appreciation for life experiences as a basis for learning; inclusiveness with regard to race, gender and class; and a less hierarchical and more participatory classroom. In such a setting, not only do the needs and interests of the students transform the classroom, but the needs and interests of the community may also be expected to exert an influence on what happens there.

Anderson and Adams (1992, 30) note that "there is an emerging consensus that the repertories of teaching strategies most effective and responsive in socially and culturally diverse college classrooms are the very same strategies that were identified at an earlier time as characteristics of teaching excellence for traditional students." Feminist pedagogy tries to address the multitude of learning styles and to provide a more connected learning environment for students. To learn effectively, many students want and need to be more connected to other students, to the instructor, to the material, and to their communities. Connections to the material and the community are important, as evidenced by the growing interest in environmental studies, international studies, and women's studies. In addition, instructors who use feminist pedagogy also engage in a form of faculty development where they learn from their students. These instructors avail themselves of a broader array of teaching techniques to ensure that each student comprehends the material to the best of her or his abilities through more active "hands-on" experiences. Rather than being taught passively to "think like economists," students are called upon to "be economists" in their communities.

Questions and Challenges

The above discussion of how course content and the learning environment interact to make the classroom more inclusive raises several questions and challenges within which economists can discuss what they do in the classroom, how they do it, and—possibly—how they define economics.

Several practical questions related to the institutional settings of the classroom arise when making these changes:

1. How does the use of more inclusive course content and new learning environments affect the use of traditional student assessment techniques?

2. What role do textbooks and other standard course materials play in the more inclusive classroom?

3. How are feminist teachers evaluated by their students and their colleagues when they make an effort to create more challenging, inclusive classrooms?

4. How do U.S. experiences compare with those of economic educators in other countries?

We leave these questions for the readers to ponder. We do, however, want to address the challenges raised by a feminist pedagogy, in particular whether a more inclusive classroom necessarily leads economists to rethink/redefine their discipline. Some economists, for example, may argue that changing the content of economics courses to include a feminist perspective is sufficient to change the discipline, with new pedagogical strategies evolving on their own. Others may argue that the classroom learning environment needs to change first before the discipline can stop perpetuating itself with myopic views of economics. The implications of a feminist pedagogy for economic theory and research are only beginning to understood in the profession. But as this exploration suggests, given the interplay between teaching and research, changing how economics is taught will surely change economics. As many economists know from their own classrooms, the last three decades provide testimony to how changing economic theory and research can change the classroom and how economics is taught.

Because solving all the existing problems is not easy, one may readily agree with bell hooks, who notes that "the academy is not paradise." Nonetheless, the authors agree with her when she says: "But learning is a place where paradise can be created. The classroom, with all its limitations, remains a location of possibility. In that field of possibility we have the opportunity to labor for freedom, to demand of ourselves and our comrades, an openness of mind and heart that allows us to face reality even as we collectively imagine ways to move beyond boundaries, to transgress. This is education as the practice of freedom" (1994, 207). The authors of this essay believe that economists moving toward a feminist pedagogy have the opportunity to relocate the economics classroom and the economics discipline in a "paradise" of social action and freedom, and they invite other economists to join in this exciting transformation.

NOTES

This essay also appeared in *Feminist Economics* 5(1) (1999): 29–44. Reprinted by permission of Routledge Journals.

1. These were the factors cited by those economics educators who were concerned with the decline in the number of majors.

2. The Voluntary National Content Standards in Economics, which were agreed upon by members of the Economics America network, representatives of the National Council for the Social Sciences, readers of the Advanced Placement Exams in economics, a review committee of the National Association of Business Economists, and a specially convened group of noted U.S. university–based economists, consist of twenty content standards for primary and secondary economics education.

3. Reciprocity here refers to the concept as developed by Karl Polanyi. As J. R. Stanfield explains, "Reciprocity refers to the circulation of goods and services on the basis of familial or political obligation, reinforced by ritualistic or religious principles" (1986, 20). Thus, for Polanyi reciprocity occurs within a different cultural context and serves a different function from market exchange.

4. Although the Socratic method may suggest increased student involvement in the course—since students are now asked to contribute orally—they are not expected to go beyond regurgitating the course text or lecture. Thus, there is still little opportunity for students to apply their knowledge or to question the authority of the instructor or text. In addition, the individualistic learning environment is reinforced as students compete against one another to provide the "correct" answer to the instructor's questions in order to improve—at the expense of other students—their course participation grade.

REFERENCES

Adams, Maurianne. 1992. "Cultural Inclusion in the American College Curriculum." In *Teaching for Diversity*, no. 49, ed. Laura L. B. Border and Nancy Van Note Chism, 5–17. San Francisco: Jossey-Bass.

Anderson, James A., and Maurianne Adams. 1992. "Acknowledging the Learning Styles of Diverse Student Populations: Implications for Instructional Design." In *Teaching for Diversity*, no. 49, ed. Laura L. B. Border and Nancy Van Note Chism, 19–33. San Francisco: Jossey-Bass.

Andersen, Margaret L. 1987. "Changing the Curriculum in Higher Education." *Signs: Journal of Women in Culture and Society* 12(2): 222–54.

Bartlett, Robin L. 1995. "A Flip of the Coin—A Roll of the Die: An Answer to the Free-Rider Problem in Economic instruction." *Journal of Economic Education* 26(2): 131–39.

Bartlett, Robin L., and Susan Feiner. 1992. "Balancing the Curriculum: Content, Method, and Pedagogy." *American Economic Review* 82(2): 559–64.

Bartlett, Robin L., and Marianne A. Ferber. 1998. "Humanizing Content and Pedagogy in Economics Classrooms." In *Teaching Undergraduate Economics: A Handbook for Instructors*, ed. William B. Wallstad and Phillip Saunders, 109–26. New York: McGraw Hill.

Becker, William E. 1997. "Teaching Economics to Undergraduates." *Journal of Economic Literature* 35:1347–73.

Becker, William E., and Michael Watts. 1996. "Chalk and Talk: A National Survey on Teaching Undergraduate Economics." *American Economics Review* 86(2) (May): 448–53.

Belenky, Mary, Blythe Clinchy, Nancy Goldberger, and Jill Tarule. 1986. *Women's Ways of Knowing*. New York: Basic Books.

Brufee, Kenneth A. 1993. *Collaborative Learning.* Baltimore: Johns Hopkins University Press.

Dugger, Karen. 1990. "Notes on Curriculum Transformation in the Social Sciences." MS, Lewisburg, PA.

England, Paula. 1993. "The Separative Self: Androcentric Bias in Neoclassical Assumptions." In *Beyond Economic Man: Feminist Theory and Economics,* ed. Marianne A. Ferber and Julie A. Nelson, 37–53. Chicago: University of Chicago Press.

Feiner, Susan F., and Morgan, B. A. 1987. "Women and Minorities in Introductory Economics Textbooks: 1974–1984." *Journal of Economic Education* 18(4): 376–92.

Ferber, Marianne A. 1997. "Gender and the Study of Economics: A Feminist Critique." In *Introducing Race and Gender into Economics,* ed. Robin L. Bartlett, 147–55. New York: Routledge.

Harding, Sandra. 1991. *Whose Science? Whose Knowledge: Thinking from Women's Lives.* Ithaca, NY: Cornell University Press.

hooks, bell. 1994. *Teaching to Transgress: Education as the Practice of Freedom.* New York: Routledge.

Johnson, David W., Roger T. Johnson, and Karl A. Smith. 1991. *Cooperative Learning: Increasing College Faculty Instructional Productivity.* ASHE-ERIC Higher Education Report no. 4. Washington, DC: George Washington University, School of Education and Human Development.

Lewis, Margaret. 1995. "Breaking Down the Walls, Opening up the Field: Situating the Economics Classroom in the Site of Social Action." *Journal of Economic Issues* 29(2): 555–65.

Maher, Francis A., and Mary Kay Thompson Tetreault. 1994. *The Feminist Classroom.* New York: Basic Books.

McGoldrick, KimMarie. 1998. "Service Learning in Economics: A Detailed Application." *Journal of Economic Education* 24(4): 365–76.

McIntosh, Peggy. 1990. "Interactive Phases of Curricular and Personal Re-Vision with Regard to Race." Center for Research on Women, Working Paper no. 219, Wellesley, MA, Wellesley College.

———. 1983a. "Interactive Phases of the Curricular Re-Vision: A Feminist Perspective." Center for Research on Women, Working Paper no. 124, Wellesley, MA, Wellesley College.

———. 1983b. "The Study of Women: Processes of Personal and Curricular Re-vision." *Forum for Liberal Education* 6(5): 2–4.

Nelson, Julie A. 1996. *Feminism, Objectivity and Economics.* London, Routledge.

Rosser, Sue V. 1990. *Female-Friendly Science: Applying Women's Studies Methods and Theories to Attract Students.* New York: Pergamon Press.

Sandler, Bernice R., Lisa A. Silverberg, and Roberta M. Hall. 1996. *The Chilly Climate: A Guide to Improve the Education of Women.* Washington, DC: National Association for Women in Education.

Schuster, Marilyn R., and Susan R. Van Dyne. 1985. *Women's Place in the Academy: Transforming the Liberal Arts Curriculum.* Totowa, NJ.: Rowman and Allanheld.

Shackelford, Jean. 1992. "Feminist Pedagogy: A Means for Bringing Critical Thinking, and Creativity to the Economics Classroom." *American Economic Review* 82(2): 570–76.

Siegfried, John J., and Charles E. Scott. 1994. "Recent Trends in Undergraduate Economics Degrees." *Journal of Economic Education* 25(3) (summer 1994): 281–86.

Stanfield, J. R. 1986. *The Economic Thought of Karl Polanyi.* New York: St. Martin's Press.

Tobias, Sheila. 1990. *They're Not Dumb, They're Different: Stalking the Second Tier.* Tucson: Research Corporation.

Treisman, Uri. 1992. "Studying Students Studying Calculus: A Look at the Lives of Minority Mathematics Students in College." *College Mathematics Journal* 23(5): 362–72.

U.S. Department of Education, National Council of Educational Statistics. 1997. *Digest of Educational Statistics 1997.* <http://nces.ed.gov/pubs/digest97/d970003.html#enrollmt>.

Veblen, Thorstein. 1993. "Why Is Economics Not an Evolutionary Science?" In *A Veblen Treasury,* ed. Rick Tilman, 129–43. Armonk, NY: M. E. Sharpe.

Wells, Gordon, Gen Ling M. Chang, and Ann Maher. 1990. "Creating Classroom Communities of Literate Thinkers." In *Cooperative Learning: Theory and Research,* ed. Shlomo Sharan, 95–121. New York: Praeger Publishers.

Feminist Pedagogy

A Means for Bringing Critical Thinking and Creativity to the Economics Classroom

Jean Shackelford

The past decade has produced a plethora of reports critical of higher education, and many of these reports suggest that classroom activities focus on more than the transmission or transfer of knowledge from teacher to student (Derek Bok 1986; Ernest L. Boyer 1987; Association of American Colleges 1985). Economic education has not escaped these critiques (John Siegfried et al. 1991). Within the same time span pedagogical approaches that focus on critical thinking and inquiry have emerged. Exposure to innovative curricular-reform programs introduced many instructors to Socratic or dialogic approaches to teaching and to collaborative learning. Programs focusing on transforming courses and curricula to include race, class, and gender acquainted some instructors with methods involved in feminist pedagogy and inquiry.

The term *feminist pedagogy* was coined during the 1980s to incorporate a wide variety of teaching methods and approaches in the classroom that were first adopted by feminists in women's studies programs and later adopted by men and women teaching in various disciplines. This essay introduces economists to feminist pedagogy and its underlying foundations and focuses on how feminist pedagogy fosters elements of critical thinking. Economists will recognize a distinct contrast to the prevailing discourse in the discipline.

Feminist Pedagogy—An Overview

Central to the agenda of feminist pedagogy is empowering students to become critical and creative learners. In fostering critical and creative thinking, it is important that students are encouraged to engage freely in the discourse of the discipline and come to rely less on the authority of the instructor. Feminist pedagogy is often described as student-centered (as opposed to subject- or teacher-centered). It is less hierarchical and emphasizes cooperation and community.

One must recognize at the outset that feminist pedagogy relies, like feminist theory, on ideologies, epistemologies, and methodologies that are negotiated and changing. Mary Bricker-Jenkins and Nancy Hooyman (1987, 36) point out that any discussion of feminist ideology must be one of "an open system . . . criticized from within and open to exchange with other ideologies, it advances through dialogue." Knowledge claims are filtered through one's social position or social location (Helen E. Longino 1990). The philosopher Sandra Harding (1991, 6) notes that "Feminist analyses of science, technology, and knowledge are not monolithic. . . . There is no single set of claims beyond a few generalities that could be called 'feminism' without controversy among feminists. The feminist science discussions are both enriched and constrained by the different political, practical, and conceptual perspectives that they bring to bear on science, its beliefs, practices, and institutions." For these reasons, I cannot argue here that there is some "essential feminist pedagogy." There are, however, characteristics or enduring themes and principles which relate to the ideology and practice of feminism that help describe, rather than define, what employing a feminist pedagogy might entail.

Recurring themes and principles that are consistent throughout feminist analysis and on which feminist pedagogy can be grounded include: an explicit goal of ending patriarchy and oppression and empowering or giving voice and influence to those disempowered by patriarchal structures; validation of forms of knowing other than "objective," "hierarchical," or "authority-laden" models; and a focus on practice, with an emphasis on process over product or content. These three themes provide a different lens through which students may expand their critical repertoire and thereby develop a more multifaceted understanding of economics. Knowledge that students construct rather than memorize becomes more meaningful, because it is about them and therefore important to their lives.

The first of these themes deals with patriarchal structures, examining white male dominance over other groups, including minorities as well as women. Feminist pedagogy seeks to interrupt this patriarchal dominance and give power to *all* students within the classroom. Instead of seeking a reversal of the power structure, feminist analysis seeks to empower, to give voice and influence, to those who have been excluded from traditional power structures. In the sciences, including economics, feminists seek analyses applying to all classes, races, and cultures:

> Feminists (male and female) want to close the gender gap in scientific and technological literacy, to invent modes of thought and learn the existing techniques and skills that will enable women to get more con-

trol over the conditions of their lives. Such sciences can and must benefit men, too—especially those marginalized by racism, imperialism, and class exploitation; the new sciences are not to be *only* for women. (Harding 1991, 5)

In traditional classrooms continued male dominance is reinforced by underlying assumptions supporting theories and beliefs about society, "others," and existing institutions. Among those institutions are the natural and social sciences and traditional forms of education. Harding argues that knowledge in the sciences, like all other knowledge, has been "created through political struggles. . . . They are no less scientific for being driven by particular historical and political projects" (1991, 10). It is important to see these as "truths" that speak to some but are not necessarily universal.

A second theme that underscores feminist pedagogy is based on a feminist analysis of gender, which offers women and minorities a safe place to express their ideas and explore their experiences as legitimate subjects of inquiry. A feminist understanding recognizes that women's historical position has been established under patriarchy. This has determined the experiences, influenced values, shaped perspectives, and hence established women's social location in constructing knowledge. Within feminist analyses "lived" experiences are given a voice that is often denied in a society that values "objectivity, empiricism, and value-free" analysis. So-called feminine values are also given privilege within feminist analysis (Bricker-Jenkins and Hooyman 1987, 36). Feminist pedagogy challenges theories that do not attend to historical underpinnings or to cultural diversity. Feminist pedagogy invites a multiplicity of narratives which avoid overly simplistic reductionist explanations and creates a more inclusive study of economics.

An operative feminist pedagogy allows students, through open dialogue and conversation, to compare, contrast, and connect their views and ideas with those of others toward a goal of achieving a greater understanding of the subject. The result of this process is that students are actively engaged in the production of knowledge, as opposed to being the passive recipients of teacher-imparted "truth."

A third theme found in feminist pedagogy is that knowledge goes hand in hand with process. There is an emphasis on the importance of process relative to solutions or content. Feminists note that many different voices, definitions of problems, positions, and solutions might be operative in a variety of situations. This suggests that how one teaches is as important as what one teaches. Teachers of economics could benefit from such a multiplicity of approaches in the teaching of economics.

Economists may be somewhat uneasy with the "underlying themes" of feminist analysis, as they may appear antithetical to those that underlie mainstream economics. Issues that surround economic method and epistemology influence the rhetoric and the discourse, as well as the content of economic analysis, and thus the conditions and location that enable instructors to teach students to "think like an economist."

Feminist Pedagogy in the Economics Classroom

Course Content and Materials

The content and context of economics derive from the questions asked and the conclusions made by economists concerning teaching traditions. What is and is not important revolves around the goal of teaching students to "think like an economist." "Problem-solving skills that emphasize analytical reasoning using the techniques and principles of economics . . . and creative skills that help determine how to frame questions, what tools and principles apply to particular problems, what data and information are pertinent to those problems, and how to understand or explain surprising or unexpected results," are skills to be addressed by the instructor teaching students how to "think like an economist" (Siegfried et al. 1991, 21).

However, thinking like an economist may exclude analyses of race, class, and gender. In 1974 Carolyn Shaw Bell observed, "One must first inquire how human beings, people themselves and women among them, enter into the economic calculus. It turns out that they don't, for the most part" (615–16). Nearly two decades later, one would be hard pressed to assert that gender issues have attained even threshold entry into the "economic calculus." Susan Feiner and Barbara Morgan's (1987) work confirms that there is little inclusion of race or gender in introductory economics textbooks, and that when there is coverage it is often stereotypical or biased. Such texts may well prepare instructors for teaching students how to "think like an economist" and provide the "content" as defined by the discipline in any particular course. Often, however, these texts generate few opportunities for students to discuss or explore economic ideas.

To employ feminist pedagogy effectively in economics classes one must include material that allows students to analyze as well as synthesize and, just as importantly, to explore ways of discovering. Providing some context for understanding the economic content is important in this process. This includes a history of ideas as well as a history motivating the development of important tools and concepts. Economics texts are notorious for providing little history or context for the discussion of issues or the development of theory, while ideology is assumed away and objectivity is assumed to be ever present, simply as a part of good science. Clearly, readings or materials that are more inclusive and that allow students to question and to ask about models, about the political implications of assumptions and policy, and about who wins and who loses within a given solution are important to establishing dialogue. Depending on the course, newspaper articles, films, data use and data gathering, short stories, and even novels may provide both the content and context to allow students to discuss, describe, analyze, assess, and discover the nature of economic theory and policy. Teachers are, after all, imparting more than a body of knowledge to unsuspecting students; and this needs to be indicated.

Classroom Environment and Attitudes

While the hierarchical organization and structure of traditional institutions of higher education and especially the position of the professor within this scheme are contradictory to feminist notions of power and authority, recall that feminist analysis focuses on process as well as content and product.

Instructors are vested with power over a class from the moment class rosters are received until final grades are handed in. There is no escaping the authority that comes with the roster. However, it is possible to develop an alternative to a pedagogy of domination. While instructors cannot deny or give away power and authority, no matter how egalitarian and democratic they may wish to seem, it is still possible to create a classroom environment that relies on democracy rather than dominance. Teachers of economics can establish a forum for student input into the course, where students can enter into conversations and explore ideas as equals. This forum can include student input into the process, goals, content, course design, and even evaluation.

By centering student experiences as a primary source from which learning proceeds, the resulting dialogue establishes that "even students" understand, are affected by, and have differing opinions about economics. Student-centered, rather than teacher-centered, discussion allows students to understand that the way they explore and construct their views may have to do with their experiences as workers, as students, as members of families, as union members, as women, or as men and women of color, among many other things. Qualitative as well as quantitative information influences our knowledge about economics. Dialogue can begin to inform students about how knowledge is formed, revealing the importance of questioning, supporting, or documenting ideas. Conducting a class in this environment not only enables students to learn the structure and arguments of the discipline but also encourages critical insights and questions, which foster critical thinking and inquiry. Classroom practices, including assignments, examinations, and discussion, need to provide students with a context sensitive to the content and discourse of the discipline.

Assignments

Developing assignments, discussions, and other activities that focus on discovery and encourage students to use their personal experience is the challenge to employing feminist pedagogy. Joanne Gainen Kurfiss (1988) notes that in courses emphasizing critical thinking, "Courses are assignment centered rather than text and lecture centered. Goals, methods, and evaluation emphasize using content rather than simply acquiring it" (88). Personal knowledge as well as digression can be a source of creativity and insight, fostering student awareness and interest in the subject. Dialogue allows students to explore the language, argument, and discourse of economics, and at the same time to create knowledge as part of an emerging community of learners. While class dialogue should focus on content within this framework, if courses continue to require memorization of facts they may well become Alfred North Whitehead's "inert ideas" by the end of the term.

I have found that writing assignments play an essential role in encouraging both student learning and the exploration of ideas. Writing assignments may include essays, abstracts, responses to inquiries, and data collection and analysis, along with journals in which students write to learn rather than to perform or demonstrate knowledge. Collaboration and peer review of this writing encourage students to become responsible not only for themselves but to one another. This fosters a sense of community within the classroom and promotes the pursuit of knowledge.

The lecture, in which it is difficult to inspire dialogue or encourage creative or critical thinking, can also introduce assignments which may serve to motivate critical thinking. In very large lecture sections the instructor may periodically "check in" with the students, pausing to allow short writing tasks: making lists of what they see to be the main points of the lecture, summarizing the lecture in their own words, or "free writing" about issues raised in the lecture.

Projects and assignments which require the use of concepts, tools, goals, and dialogue allow students the opportunity to internalize the process of "thinking like an economist." Games can be used to foster and reinforce the use of tools and concepts as well as the skills required to employ them. Through these kinds of projects and activities, students begin to rely upon themselves and the group for answers. This empowers students to seek answers beyond texts or lectures and to reconstruct questions, thereby fostering lifelong learning attitudes and skills. This active learning process is central to critical thinking and creativity.

Evaluation of Students

Evaluation is always a dicey subject between students and teachers—and even dicier between teachers and teachers. I believe that it is possible and certainly desirable to construct evaluation procedures that are consistent with feminist pedagogy, even if grades are required. Daily participation, group dialogue, journals, abstracts, essays—all of which use and explore economic ideas—combined with constant and consistent feedback are essential to establishing a learning environment. Students should know where they stand at all times. Certainly, exams and grading may be necessary, but instructors should consider the message conveyed in the examination and evaluation process. I can think of no better way to explain this than excerpting a response by Cindy Fowler Clarke, a Bucknell alumna, to an article on academic integrity:

> As the Bucknell academic community searches for an agenda for addressing the "integrity issue," I urge them to consider the entire system of evaluating student knowledge and learning, meeting out punishments and bestowing rewards. I am referring to testing and grading. . . . This means of testing knowledge only reinforces isolation from society and a belief that 100 percent self-reliance is the optimum or only way to get the job done. . . .
>
> Community spirit and cooperation do not exist here. It is the student and the exam. Does the test mirror life? Or, worse yet, does it help to create a distorted view of how life should be lived? What are we teaching students about the system? . . .
>
> I challenge all educators in every teaching and learning context to review the purpose of what they teach as it relates to our world. If testing is necessary, the task is to create a "real-life" environment that will enable students as individuals and as group members to face, analyze, and solve problems in their community with honesty and integrity. Trust, cooperation and collaboration can be encouraged in the classroom. In the right environment, the purpose of learning is not furthered by dishonesty or cheating. Integrity, then, would not be relegated to "Honesty 101" but would form an intrinsic part of problem-solving and decision-making. (Clark 1991, 16–17)

As long as grade-getting and grade-giving are part of our endeavor, instructors may indeed find this the most difficult arena in which to establish a feminist pedagogy in their courses.

Conclusion

Economists, and those studying the educational system and its mission, concur in suggesting that the skills needed for success in the twenty-first century are those of critical and creative thinking and learning (Bok 1986; Boyer 1986; Kurfiss 1988; Solow 1990). By adopting pedagogical strategies that attend to these skills directly, one may more successfully enable and empower students to approach economics and their lives beyond college. Feminist pedagogy helps directly address these analytical, creative and critical skills by promoting less hierarchical, more inclusive techniques and assignments in the economics classroom.

Imparting knowledge is easier than fostering critical strategies and creative thinking skills, however. In his discussion of training Ph.D. students in economics, Solow suggests that economists most often teach what they are taught, particularly theory and econometrics, which develop analytical and mathematical skills. Solow observes: "Life seems to call much less for mathematics and even a bit less for analytics and much more for creativity, critical judgement, and the ability to communicate." He adds:

> If I knew how to teach creativity and critical judgement, I guess I would do it. I know how to recognize them all right, and can even offer examples. But that is far from being able to teach them. Communication skills are much more straightforward, and I think we should emphasize them more. The trouble is that teaching communication skills is not our skill. But I do think I will go home and urge that we force all of our first-year graduate students into a writing course to be taught by the MIT Writing Program. (1990, 449)

While I believe that Solow is largely correct in his assessment of why economists do teach what they do, I would contest his view that economists do not know how to (or do not) teach communication or creative and critical judgement. Instructors show their knowledge of these skills daily and so must begin to teach them actively. Teachers of economics are constantly demonstrating or "modeling" a critical thinking agenda in lectures and in the questions raised in class. Perhaps economists need to recognize, examine, and question their teaching agendas, particularly as they unconsciously relate to critical thinking skills. Feminist pedagogical methods can assist instructors in recognizing what they are doing in their courses, and it offers direction in helping students understand the discourse, conventions, and community of economists.

In addition to providing insights on how one should teach, feminist pedagogy also offers advice about what should be taught, encouraging the incorporation of a more inclusive and contextual set of materials that avoid gender and racial biases. Currently, instructors are likely to employ, as models or assumptions, metaphors that perhaps unconsciously reflect social values. One gendered metaphor that pervades economic models is that of the "economic man." Julie Nelson has written of this arrogant economic actor:

> Economic man, "the agent" of the prototypical economic model, springs up fully formed, with preferences fully developed, and is fully active and self-contained. He has no childhood or old age; no dependence on anyone; no responsibility for anyone but himself. The environment has no effect on him, but rather is merely the passive material, presented as "constraints," over which his rationality has play. He interacts in society without being influenced by society; his mode of interaction is through an ideal market in which prices form the only, and only necessary form of communication. *Homo economicus* is the central character in a romance of individuality without connection to nature or society. (Nelson 1992, 16)

Nancy Folbre and Heidi Hartmann add: "Feminist economic approaches, however diverse, are all suspicious of any rhetoric that describes women as less self-interested than men or automatically places gender interests on a lower level of analysis than family interests or class interests" (1988, 193). A feminist pedagogy employed in the economics classroom would attend to these perspectives, metaphors, and contexts.

Of course, there are costs to this pedagogical strategy. Clearly, dialogue is impossible in very large classes. Developing materials, assignments, and projects that address critical thinking skills, responding frequently to student projects, papers, and journals is extremely time-consuming. Classroom dynamics are never the same, and one must always respond to that. Even with all this investment of time, there is no recipe guaranteeing success, particularly when methods which evaluate these strategies are still emerging (McPeck 1981; Kurfiss 1988). Furthermore, despite growing lip service to the importance of teaching, the reward structure in the economics discipline and in higher education is on research. So long as the payoff is skewed toward the research model of higher education, few will choose to devote the time necessary to dialogic methods of teaching.

While these costs may seem high, what are the costs of the alternative? The studies critical of higher education only address the national and international costs of producing students who have not acquired skills in critical thinking and learning in general terms. Economists might want to assess more explicitly the cost of not changing teaching methods; of not addressing critical learning and thinking skills within the context of disciplinary organization, content, and discourse. In doing so economists might begin developing a curriculum and a pedagogy that is meaningful not only to the students today, but to those increasingly diverse student bodies expected in the next decades. If students are challenged to think critically in the classroom about economics, perhaps they will be engaged as creative theorists and policy makers. To this end I believe that economists can employ feminist pedagogy to encourage students to explore economics actively and critically.

NOTE

This essay originally appeared in *American Economic Review* (May 1992): 570–76. Reprinted by permission of the American Economic Association.

REFERENCES

Association of American Colleges. 1985. *Integrity in the College Curriculum: A Report to the Academic Community.* Washington, DC: Association of American Colleges.
Bell, Carolyn Shaw. 1974. "Economics, Sex, and Gender." *Social Science Quarterly* 55 (December): 615–31.
Bok, Derek. 1986. *Higher Learning.* Cambridge, MA: Harvard University Press.
Boyer, Ernest L. 1987. *College: The Undergraduate Experience in America.* New York: Harper and Row.
Bricker-Jenkins, Mary, and Nancy Hooyman. 1987. "Feminist Pedagogy in Education for Social Change." *Feminist Teacher* 2 (fall): 36–41.
Clark, Cindy Fowler. 1991. "Is Testing Necessary?" *Bucknell World* 19 (July): 16–17.
Feiner, Susan F., and Morgan, Barbara A. 1987. "Women and Minorities in Introductory Economic Textbooks: 1974–1984." *Journal of Economic Education* 18 (fall): 376–92.
Folbre, Nancy, and Hartmann, Heidi. 1988. "The Rhetoric of Self-Interest: Ideology and Gender in Economic Theory." In *The Consequences of Economic Rhetoric,* ed. Arjo Klamer, Donald N. McCloskey, and Robert M. Solow, 184–203. Cambridge: Cambridge University Press.
Harding, Sandra. 1991. *Whose Science? Whose Knowledge? Thinking from Women's Lives.* Ithaca, NY: Cornell University Press.
Kurfiss, Joanne Gainen. 1988. *Critical Thinking: Theory, Research, Practice, and Possibili-*

ties. ASHE-ERIC Higher Education Report no. 2. Washington, DC: Association for the Study of Higher Education.

Longino, Helen E. 1990. *Science as Social Knowledge: Values and Objectivity in Scientific Inquiry.* Princeton, NJ: Princeton University Press.

McPeck, John E. 1981. *Critical Thinking in Education.* New York: St. Martin's Press.

Nelson, Julie A. 1992. "Gender, Metaphor and the Definition of Economics." *Economics and Philosophy* 8 (spring): 103–25.

Siegfried, John, Bartlett, Robin L., Hansen, W. Lee, Kelly, Allen C., McCloskey, Donald N. and Tietenberg, Thomas H. 1991. "The Economics Major: Can and Should We Do Better than a B−?"

American Economic Review (Papers and Proceedings) 81 (May): 20–25.

Solow, Robert M. 1990. "Discussion" (Comments on "Educating and Training New Economics Ph.D.'s: How Good a Job Are We Doing?" by W. Lee Hansen). *American Economic Review (Papers and Proceedings)* 80 (May): 448–50.

Breaking Down the Walls, Opening Up the Field

Situating the Economics Classroom in the Site of Social Action

Margaret Lewis

The curtain rises on a scene: an introductory economics classroom, where students are sitting in neat rows. The professor begins the class by reminding students that "economics is the study of how scarce resources are allocated among unlimited wants" and proceeds to draw on the board a graph examining how the price and quantity of good X are affected by an increase in demand. In order to explain how the market achieves its new equilibrium, the professor then goes through, in a linear, logical fashion, exactly how inventory shortages lead the sellers of good X to raise its price, which causes buyers to purchase fewer units while simultaneously causing the sellers to increase the number of units they offer on the market. Sellers continue to raise prices until they eliminate their shortages, at which point supply equals demand, and the market achieves equilibrium. Enthusiastically, the professor concludes that due to the workings of the market, our scarce resources can be shown to be allocated efficiently and all is right with the world—a point missed by most students who are at best disengaged or at worst asleep—because the professor's explanation neither reflects the complex world in which those students live nor does his or her analysis seem terribly relevant to the contemporary economic issues facing these students.

As a feminist-institutionalist economist, I find this scene disturbing for several reasons: first because of the abstract reductionism of the neoclassical paradigm and its limitations in addressing contemporary social issues, and the lack of connection between the simplistic economics of the classroom and the complex economic activity in the world. In addition, I am disturbed because the scenario captures the flavor of the economics classroom that, until recently, I taught in—a classroom where the professor, as authority, disciplines the students in how economists think by showing them the abstract theoretical models of neoclassical economics, models emphasizing linear, logical, and rational analysis premised on the scarcity definition of economics. In that classroom of the past I quickly learned that my students would not sit with rapt attention, marveling at the elegance of these abstract models, and that they were more than a little disturbed by the model's apparent lack of applicability to contemporary economic issues, as well as by many of the underlying assumptions and limited scope of analysis. In addition, in that classroom of the past, I was increasingly concerned that my students did not fully appreciate how helpful economics could be in understanding today's complex world and that my classes also did little to prepare them to be engaged, critical citizens in the world; that is, I found that my classroom was not serving as a site of social action in which my students learned to use economics to engage the world. These observations and concerns led me to believe that significant changes were needed to break down the four walls enclosing the stereotypical economics classroom and to transform that room into a site of action. Here I wish to identify the four walls that I believe have fostered the scenario and to explore how a feminist-institutionalist economics can be instrumental in making the changes necessary for creating a more effective educational environment. These four walls are, in brief, pedagogy, content, methodology, and definition.

The First Wall: Pedagogy

The first wall that must be tumbled is the pedagogical wall. Active and critical engagement that encourages "doing" is one of the primary goals of both feminist and active learning pedagogical practices, both of which have evolved, in part, from John Dewey's progressive education tradition (Maher and Tetreault 1994, 9; Bonwell and Eisen 1994, 1). Thus, these pedagogical practices are rooted in the same pragmatic philosophical tradition as institutional economics itself, and, as I have argued elsewhere, share the goal of creating environments that foster social action (Lewis 1994, 6–9).

As Jean Shackelford (1992, 570) has noted, a primary goal of feminist pedagogy is to empower students "to become critical and creative thinkers," a goal compatible with the concept of active learning, "that is, increasing students' involvement in the learning process" (Bonwell and Eison 1991, xvii). Empowering and involving students, in turn, requires breaking down the barriers between students and the professor as well as the barriers between the student and what is studied.

Breaking down barriers between students and professor is crucial to engaging students and can be achieved by asking students about their own experiences and viewpoints regarding the issues being discussed and then integrating their contributions into the analysis of the issues (see, e.g., Maher and Tetreault 1994; McIntosh 1983; Shackelford 1992). This barrier can further be removed by sending students into the field to observe and interview participants in economic activities and to collect data and information that they then bring back into the classroom to analyze and integrate into their understanding of the issues. Involving students by incorporating their experiences and by integrating field work into the learning process not only reflects feminist pedagogical practices, but also reflects the institutionalist structural approach to collecting evidence as discussed by Wilber and Harrison (Dugger 1988, 317–19).

The Second Wall: Content

Situating students in the world also requires refocusing the content of economics courses, wall number 2. Instead of beginning with models abstracted from reality—in which the first purpose is to teach students to manipulate graphs or equations that signify an idealized reduction of complex economic life as in the classroom scene depicted here—we need to begin with current economic issues representing paradigmatically significant problems that give rise to economic investigation and explanation. By putting contemporary economic issues in the foreground, we emphasize in our courses the pragmatic belief articulated by Gruchy that economics, as "a functional science, should have the 'social value' of enabling mankind more easily to solve its various economic difficulties" (1967, 325). In addition, we also need to teach our students that economic theories and concepts grow out of the world of human action, rather than teach them that the world of action must conform to laws identified by economic theories and to concepts that exist prior to and outside of that world (Rogin 1971, chap. 1).

Situating the economics course in the real world of contemporary economic issues engages students by appealing to their desire for relevance to the "real" world in which they live. In addition, it reinforces the students' basic understanding of the economy. While we may be amazed at the explanations of economic phenomena our students sometimes provide, I find that many students start their economic education with an intuitive understanding of much economic activity in all its complexity as well as with the interest to learn more. By beginning classroom discussion with economic issues of interest to the students, we can use effectively the students' own experiences and intuitive understanding to help them realize that economic analysis can further enhance and refine their knowledge of complex economic activity. Moreover, starting the classroom discussion with what students know and are interested in exploring, in turn, encourages students to develop their skills in doing economic analysis. As the ancient Greeks noted, "All knowledge begins in wonder"—a necessary condition for educating students that we as educators too often ignore.

Emphasizing contemporary issues also requires that we discuss economic policies. That is, if we wish to fully explore contemporary issues, it is not sufficient to identify a social problem without also examining and analyzing the public policies that typically accompany these problems. Discussing these policies, in turn, not only engages students, who are usually aware of the policy debates surrounding the issue, but it also achieves the teaching objective of "preparing students for intelligent and effective participation in the civic life of their communities" (Trepp 1939, 39).

Thus, if we wish to prepare our students to become engaged citizens situated in the world of human action, we must emphasize contemporary social issues and related policies in our courses. This requires tearing down the content wall of the classroom built from the abstract models that have little applicability to the world and rebuilding it, pragmatically, to focus on issues of concern and relevance to our students' lives. But, as with the pedagogical wall, we have only succeeded in weakening the classroom; liberation requires moving onto the third wall, methodology.

The Third Wall: Methodology

While we do not want to diminish our students' engagement as citizens in the world with abstract content, neither do we want to limit their engagement with inappropriate method. That is, if we teach our students that the world consists of complex economic activity, then we also need to provide them with ways to address and understand that complexity. Thus, methodology, the third wall, must address the complexity of economic activity rather than reduce it to mathematically elegant, but substantively sterile, methods.

As the opening scene demonstrates, the neoclassical method employed in many economics courses reduces the world to a state of static equilibrium, universal across time and place, rather than acknowledging the world as a dynamic and "evolving scheme of . . . cultural processes" (Gruchy 1967, 19) growing out of particular historical moments. Further, this method is premised on individualistic psychology, which emphasizes rational economic behavior devoid of cultural influences (e.g., the profit-maximizing seller of good X) rather than viewing individuals as participants in the economic system whose behavior is governed by cultural norms. In addition, this method of the past employs an atomistic approach centered on parts of the economic system (e.g., the market of good X) rather than utilizing a holistic approach centered on interrelatedness and interaction. Finally, the method's emphasis on mathematical modeling (e.g., the supply and demand graph) indicates more attention to the "shape and form" of the theory than to the theory's content and its relevance to "the real facts of economic life" (Gruchy 1967, 21), thereby creating a formal, rather than a substantive and thus socially useful, economics.

The holistic method needed for examining contemporary economic issues effectively combines empirical evidence, appropriate analytical frameworks that emphasize the interaction of the institutions and values underlying the issues at hand, and evaluations of proposed public policies. This method first requires that we collect reliable empirical evidence from official data sources, as well as from field work observations and interviews, in order to understand why the issue is important for living better lives. In addition, student experiences can be incorporated so they understand the relevance of the issue to their own lives.[1] Next, we must seek appropriate analytical frameworks for understanding economic phenomena in their complexity.[2] Here we must seek frameworks that incorporate not only all the social values and habits of all economic participants, including the values and habits of our students, but also the constantly changing economic, political, and social institutions and technological pressures that influence those participants' economic behaviors. Identifying these factors is necessary not only for assessing our current "economic lot" but also for evaluating public policies proposed for better living. As part of the latter two steps, our method must, as Rogin (1967, 2–3) says, accommodate practical aims and normative perspectives of those involved in the economic analysis, including our students as they analyze and evaluate the appropriateness and adequacy of the theoretical framework and proposed public policies.

The Fourth Wall: Definition

If the reductionist method is not appropriate for understanding complex economic activity, then neither is a reductionist definition of economics. This leads to the final wall—the load-bearing wall, if you will—the definition of economics supporting neoclassical economics and most economics courses. At the heart of neoclassical economics is the belief that economics is the study of how scarce resources are allocated among unlimited wants. As institutional economists are well aware, Karl Polanyi has argued that this scarcity definition reproduces the economistic fallacy of equating "the human economy with its market form" (Polanyi 1977, 20), thereby limiting the study of eco-nomics to the study of economizing or scarcity through market transactions only. Thus, not only are we unable to study nonmarket economic activities in any way other than how these activities would occur within a market environ-ment, we are also unable to analyze institutional frameworks in society and the social goals and values that give rise to all economic activity. This, in turn, reduces economic study to a discussion of choice and efficiency—hardly a complete basis for human action.

In order to completely transform the classroom into a site of social action, it is necessary to use an institutionalist definition of economics such as the following: economics is the study of how people interact within the social and biophysical environments for the purpose of providing material goods and services to people and to society (Larkin 1993, 1). This institu-tional definition is based on Polanyi's definition of substantive economics where livelihood and provisioning, not choice, is the basis for study. And since Polanyi includes as part of this definition the instituted process of interaction by which society provisions itself, this aspect of substantive eco-nomics allows for discussion of the roles of change, technology, social cus-toms, and values in the process of provisioning-elements that students not only find interesting, but also crucial for understanding contemporary eco-nomic issues and policies.

How does all this wall-toppling transform the economics classroom into a site for social action? I will illustrate with a topic from my own class-room: the issue of health care.

My classroom is initially destabilized by placing health care in the foreground as an important social issue worthy of economic analysis; that is, I remove the content wall by focusing on contemporary social issues rather than on theoretical constructs as the course's content. In the classroom of the past the supply-demand model would have taken center stage with health care as an application, an example to illustrate how the market works when agriculture or sports applications have been exhausted. In today's classroom course content moves from the technical to the practical; that is, the content is not the graphical manipulation of supply and demand but, rather, the whole complex of institutions and values that shape the provi-sioning of health care in our culture.

Thus, we begin the health care discussion by highlighting some of the issues in the ongoing health care debate, beginning with a 1972 quote from Senator Ted Kennedy,[3] to demonstrate how long adequate and afford-able health care has been an issue in the United States. We then focus on why health care continues to be a major issue by discussing the rising costs of health care and lack of universal coverage. This provides the first opportunity to examine the societal values underlying the current health care debate, the belief held by most Americans that health care is a basic human right. At this point we also begin to consider the institutions that affect how health care is currently provided; the private health insurance industry, the federal government, the American Medical Association, and health maintenance organizations are among those institutions examined.

This leads us to the second wall: definition. In light of the feminist-institutionalist perspective of the course the definition governing the health care discussion is provisioning, not the allocation of scarce resources among unlimited wants. The absurdity of the scarcity definition quickly becomes apparent to students when they consider, for example, the empty hospital beds in St. Cloud, a major regional health center. And the idea of unlimited wants for health care ceases to be absurd only if students are willing to grant that the entire population consists of hypochondriacs. Finally, the notion that the study of economics can be reduced to individual choices is difficult for my students to accept as they wonder why the parents of fifteen million uninsured children would willingly choose not to acquire health care for their children. Thus, my students recognize that the current health care situation requires moving beyond the economic definition of scarcity governing individual choice to examine how different economic, political, and technological factors interact to provide health care to some members of society but not to others. In conducting their examinations, the students learn to discern and apply different methodological strategies that will identify how health care is currently provided as well as what specific changes might be made to the current system in order to rectify the health care crisis facing so many Americans.

Here then is the third wall: methodology. While my students are very aware that health care is a major issue, they are not always fully aware of the underlying reasons. To help them develop a picture of the "current economic lot of mankind [sic]" fueling the health care debate, our beginning discussion includes examining statistics on health care costs and the number of Americans under- and uninsured. We also discuss the students' own experiences with the current health care system; because someone inevitably has paid fifty dollars for an aspirin in the hospital or is currently not insured, this typically serves to reinforce the factors we have identified. By examining empirical evidence and incorporating the students' experiences, we thus ground the discussion of health care in the world in which these students live and provide a concrete basis for the economic analysis that follows.

The next step is to understand the current situation using economic concepts and theories. I begin this discussion by referring to the course text, which explains why economists are not concerned about the rising costs of health care: these rising costs are the result of the combined effects of changes in supply and demand; if the price rises, it is due to decreases in supply and/or increases in demand. This is the outcome of market forces responding to increasingly scarce resources in an efficient way (Sharp et al. 1994, 237).[4] We first discuss why efficiency is not the only concern Americans have about health care, considering the widely held belief that health care is a basic right; this begins to establish the limitations of the market model and reinforces the limitations of the scarcity definition. Next, we examine the text's claim that rising costs can be fully explained within the supply-demand framework. Focusing on the concepts of a "market" and "pure competition," we explore why the purely competitive market metaphor does not accurately and completely describe the current private health insurance system.[5] This critical analysis of the market model leads us to a more appropriate framework for understanding the current private provision of health care as well as for analyzing proposed reforms to that system.

The framework I have developed for understanding the current private health insurance system addresses four questions: (1) How are health care costs (prices) determined in the system? (2) How is the system financed? (3) What are the incentives in the system to control health care costs? (4) Is universal coverage guaranteed under the system; if so, how, and if not, what factors prevent it? Answering these questions enables us to identify the complex workings of the current private health insurance system, including factors that are not captured in the supply-demand framework such as the fee-for-service and prospective payment schemes and current federal tax deductions for employer-provided health care. These questions also allow us to evaluate the current system in light of the social goals of affordable and adequate health care for all Americans.

The last step in the health care discussion is to explore how we as a society might reform the current provision of health care. Here we examine two proposals: the managed competition plan and the single-payer plan, using the framework described earlier. After we have analyzed the two plans by answering the four questions, the students are then given the assignment to evaluate which of those two plans they believe will be more effective in achieving the social goals of affordable and adequate health care based on their own concerns and values, evidence we have collected, and their economic analysis of the proposal.

This leads to the fourth wall: pedagogy. The final health care assignment is an out-of-class essay intended to move classroom learning into the world of human action with the students doing economic analysis to support their political and ethical positions regarding health care. In preparation for this final project, the students work individually and in small groups to analyze the health care statistics, describe the supply-demand explanation of rising health care costs, and evaluate the two proposed reforms to the current system. In addition, the class as a whole discusses particular issues such as their own experiences with the current health care system, the limitations of the market metaphor, and the analysis of the current private health insurance system; here I use a question-and-answer approach to guide them through the material and to introduce them to the analytical framework. All of these pedagogical techniques—student exercises, small group discussion, and question-and-answer sessions—are intended to enable students to do an economic analysis of the current health care crisis and proposed reforms. Thus, the pedagogies employed are designed to move the classroom into a site of social action.

Transforming the economics classroom into a site of social action not only requires the removal of four walls—pedagogy, content, method, and definition—it also requires rebuilding those walls to create a feminist-institutionalist environment. And as my example illustrates, it is not adequate to tear down and rebuild only one or two of the walls; like both feminist and institutional economics themselves, all four walls must be torn down and rebuilt simultaneously because of the interrelatedness and interaction between them. By rebuilding those four walls, we transform our classrooms into places where students learn practical economic reasoning that leads to critical understanding and judgment of the economic realities they face. And, by opening up the field to embrace a feminist-institutionalist economics, we create a site of social action in which our students learn how to use economics to engage the world as informed, critical citizens and to improve the economic lot of us all.

NOTES

This essay originally appeared in *Journal of Economic Issues* 29(2) (1995): 555–65. Reprinted by permission.

1. I should note that I am not advocating that student experiences should be taken at face value. Students need to be encouraged to be as accurate as possible in their reporting, and they also need to be reminded that experiences may be anecdotal and thus may not reflect systematic problems or outcomes.

2. Because this step typically necessitates moving beyond the reductionism of neoclassical models, it may require a critique of the neoclassical model presented in the course text, which will usually present neoclassical models as the framework for analysis.

3. This quote is especially effective in demonstrating the duration of the health care crisis, since most of my students were not even born in 1972.

4. In fairness to the text's authors, they do acknowledge the following irregularities

in the provision of health care: entry restrictions into the health care industry, supply responses to demand, and the impact of government subsidies on demand. This only begins, however, to identify the relevant factors in the current provisioning of health care.

5. Two notes here: first, we focus on private health care insurance because of time constraints and the students' limited experience with government-provided health care systems such as Medicaid and Medicare; second, we draw on the definition and characteristics of a purely competitive market found in Sharp et al. 1994 and some found in Tilly 1989.

REFERENCES

Bonwell, Charles C., and James A. Eison. 1991. *Active Learning, Creating Excitement in the Classroom.* ASHEERIC Higher Education Report no. 1. Washington, DC: George Washington University, School of Education and Human Development, 1991.

Dugger, William. 1988. "Methodological Differences between Institutional and Neoclassical Economics." In *The Philosophy of Economics: An Anthology,* ed. Daniel M. Hausman, 312–22. Cambridge: Cambridge University Press.

Gruchy, Allan G. 1967. *Modern Economic Thought: The American Contribution.* New York: Augustus M. Kelley.

Maher, Frances A., and Mary Kay Thompson Tetreault. 1994. *The Feminist Classroom.* New York: Basic Books.

Larkin, Andrew. 1993. *An Introduction to Economics.* St. Cloud, MN: Kinko's Copies.

Lewis, Margaret. 1994. "Doing Economics in the Real World: Jean Carol Trepp's Emergent Principles for a Feminist Economics." Paper presented at the Midwest Economics Association meetings, Chicago, March.

McIntosh, Peggy. 1983. "Interactive Phases of Curricular ReVision: A Feminist Perspective." Working Paper, Wellesley College Center for Research on Women.

Polanyi, Karl. 1977. *The Livelihood of Man,* ed. Harry W. Pearson. New York: Academic Press.

Rogin, Leo. 1965. *The Meaning and Validity of Economic Theory: An Historical Approach.* York: Harper and Brothers. Reprint, Freeport, NY: Books for Libraries Press, 1971.

Shackelford, Jean. 1992. "Feminist Pedagogy: A Means for Bringing Critical Thinking and Creativity to the Economics Classroom." *American Economic Review* 82(2) (May): 570–76.

Sharp, Ansel M., Charles A. Register, and Richard H. Leftwich. 1994. *Economics of Social Issues,* 11th ed. Burr Ridge, IL: Irwin.

Tilly, Chris. 1989. "Shaking the Invisible Hand." *Dollars and Sense* 151 (November): 9–11.

Trepp, Jean Carol. 1939. *The Uses of Field Work in Teaching Economics.* Bronxville, NY: Sarah Lawrence College, April.

PART 2

Content

Hidden by the Invisible Hand

Neoclassical Economic Theory and the Textbook Treatment of Race and Gender

Susan F. Feiner and Bruce B. Roberts

The economics textbooks most widely used in the United States have a long tradition of blindness toward questions concerning the economic status of minorities and women, and over the past decade neither the quality nor the quantity of attention paid to these issues has improved. Scant attention is paid to questions of race and gender in introductory economics texts, and many types of racial or gender bias are evident. The most common of these biases reflect the race and gender blindness of mainstream economic theory and the concomitant tendency to define the economic status and experiences of white men as the norm. Minorities and women are most frequently portrayed in stereotypical ways, and their socioeconomic experiences are treated as anomalous or deviant (Feiner and Morgan 1987). This essay links the academic marginalization of the problems of women and minorities in the United States to the internal logic of neoclassical economics.

In the United States economics, more than any other social science, is dominated by a single theoretical paradigm: marginalist or neoclassical theory. This approach explains pricing, allocation, and, indeed, all economic outcomes as the result of the constrained choices of rational, utility-maximizing individuals (Wolff and Resnick 1987). For the majority of economists this paradigm permits analysis of a vast array of situations of human choice, analyses viewed as both systematic and value free (Ferber and Teimani 1981). Both of these perceived virtues of neoclassical economics help explain the minimal nature of the impact made by feminists on the way economists think and teach. The neoclassical commitment to "equilibrium" analysis subtly shapes the form of the questions admitted for consideration, and so this systematic approach becomes a barrier to a more eclectic examination of issues, options, and arguments (cf. Glazer 1987). At the same time, economics seeks to be value free by grounding itself philosophically in the traditional

positivist notion of a strict separation between positive and normative statements, and this separation further reinforces the general reluctance of economists to tread in areas where strong normative interests are at stake.

The textbooks typically used in the introductory economics curriculum
in the United States share these traits of neoclassical theory. It is this common
theoretical paradigm that we see as responsible for the striking lack of discussion of the economic situation of women and minorities in these texts.
According to an analysis of twenty-one major introductory economics texts
(Feiner and Morgan 1987), the number of pages that make even a passing
reference to economic topics of special salience to women and minorities is
remarkably small. Those texts were chosen as representative of the field. Some
are regarded as "high level" introductory texts because of the stress on theoretical analysis; others emphasize the goal of being accessible to the broadest
possible number of students. All have a claim to be significant in at least some
part of the overall textbook market, and, taken together, they account for the
vast majority of economics textbook sales in this country (see table 1).

TABLE 1. Treatment of Women and Minorities in U.S. Economics Textbooks

Author	Date	Edition	Number of Pages Referring to Minorities and/or Women	Total Pages	Percentage of Total
Amacher	1983	1st	5	725	0.69
Atkinson	1982	1st	5	723	0.69
Baumol and Blinder	1982	2d	16	836	1.91
Bronfenbrenner, Sichel, and Gardiner	1984	1st	15	915	1.64
Dolan	1983	2d	4	773	0.52
Fischer and Dombusch	1983	1st	21	955	2.20
Fusfeld	1982	1st	6	718	0.84
Gwartney and Stroup	1982	3d	5	766	0.65
Heilbroner and Thurow	1981	6th	12	670	1.79
Leftwich	1984	2d	0	399	0
Lipsey and Steiner	1981	6th	15	958	1.57
McConnell	1984	9th	16	850	2.05
Mansfield	1983	4th	13	877	1.47
Miller	1982	4th	17	830	2.05
Ruffin and Gregory	1983	1st	6	798	0.75
Samuelson	1980	11th	22	861	2.56
Scott and Nigro	1982	1st	18	909	1.98
Spencer	1983	5th	4	868	0.46
Truett and Truett	1982	1st	7	848	0.83
Waud	1983	2d	2	856	0.23
Wonnacott and Wonnacott	1982	2d	9	858	1.05
All books (average)			10.38	810	1.34
First editions (average)			10.38	823	1.26
Revised editions (average)			10.38	743	1.40

Obviously, it would be possible for authors simply to expand treatment of these issues without any fundamental change in perspective. But the minimal focus on gender and race is linked to the theoretical perspective the texts employ. We argue that two fundamental characteristics of neoclassical economics unavoidably bias its treatment of gender and race: its philosophical premises, including the positive-normative distinction, and the equilibrium structure of its analyses, which are based on deriving economic outcomes from the rational character of constrained individual choice.

These paradigm premises give neoclassical analysis its distinctive tone, characterized by general reverence for "natural" market forces and reluctance to interrogate social factors constitutive of individual behavior. The result is a standard economics curriculum in which it is inherently difficult to treat the problems of women and minorities as worthy of serious or prolonged study. In recent years, however, each of these twin pillars of neoclassical logic has come under attack, and the critiques provide, we think, both the opening and the justification for alternative approaches. Neoclassical economics is frequently powerful and persuasive in its argument, but it is not and should not be the only option worthy of presentation. It is especially important for scholars from disciplines other than economics who study the intersection of race, gender, and class to be aware of both the nakedness of the emperor and the availability of an entirely different wardrobe.

Philosophical and Theoretical Foundations of the Economics Textbook Treatment of Race and Gender

To understand the way gender and race are treated, and not treated, in economics texts requires an appreciation of both the philosophical and analytical premises that shape the brief references to these topics. Most economics textbooks make an immediate and substantial effort to impress upon the student the distinction between positive and normative economics. Positive economics is generally defined as statements about "what is, was or will be" (Lipsey and Steiner 1981, 17). It involves "questions that can be resolved only by reference to the facts" (Samuelson and Nordhaus 1985, 7) and statements that can "be tested by an appeal to the facts" (Mansfield 1983, 15). By assertion, such statements can be rationally discussed, and these statements, substantiated by the facts, can be regarded as being as objective as the facts themselves.

In contrast, normative economics concerns "statements about what ought to be" (Lipsey and Steiner 1981, 17). Normative statements involve "deeply held values or moral judgments. They can be argued about, but they can never be settled by science or by appeal to facts" (Samuelson and

Nordhaus 1985, 7). In normative economics, "the results you get depend on your values or preferences" (Mansfield 1983, 15). While normative statements are relevant to economic policy decisions, they must be "handled with care" lest they infect the positive status of economic science. Economists may make normative statements, but they do so only as individual human beings, not as professional economists: The "advocacy role of the economist as a private, involved, informed citizen should be kept apart from the scientific role of evaluating how the economy works" (Fischer and Dombusch 1983, 17).

The dichotomy between positive and normative science shapes the goals of economics textbooks in important ways. Typical is the text that, announces: "In general the chapters that follow . . . will be concerned with positive economics. However, they will often analyze the positive economic aspects of issues on which strong normative economic opinions are held, such as unionism and poverty" (Truett and Truett 1982, 12). Thus, priority is given to the presentation of the positive core of theoretical statements that present the "objective" and verifiable explanation of "what is." Normative issues are then considered in light of that positive theory, in order to distinguish the effects of different normative prescriptions.

Having distinguished normative from positive statements, the texts set out to present a positive theory of economic outcomes. Here there is nearly total unanimity on the broad outlines of what constitutes a satisfactory theoretical position (Frey et al. 1984; Kearl et al. 1979). The position presented by the texts examined for this study is inextricably bound up with the idea that markets tend systematically to a stable position where the quantity supplied equals the quantity demanded at the equilibrium market price. Not merely will each market individually tend toward such an equilibrium, but all markets together are argued to tend systematically toward a long-run, general equilibrium position. This means that neoclassical economists, when given appropriately specified information on individual tastes and preferences; technology; distribution of initial endowments of land, labor, and capital; and the institutional features of the market, can determine all the prices and quantities toward which all markets (including the markets for land, labor, and capital) tend in the long run.

Although an explicit treatment of general equilibrium is usually regarded as too advanced for introductory students, so that little actual space is given to these issues, the logic of the general equilibrium approach permeates the texts. Whether one examines the microeconomic theory of the perfectly competitive firm, or the macroeconomic presentation of aggregate supply and demand, one finds the students being trained in models that treat short-run adjustments as governed by the necessity of a long-run return to a pre-specifiable position. For example, in microeconomics students are taught that the behavior of firms guarantees that consumers get the goods and services they want at the lowest possible prices because market competition forces each firm to a long-run equilibrium in which "zero economic profits" (e.g., a profit rate equal to the normal rate of return on capital) are earned. Similarly, the macroeconomy is said to reach equilibrium only when the "natural rate of unemployment" prevails (i.e., when only the normal frictions of gathering and acting upon information impede the matching of jobs and job seekers).

In the equilibrium model "real-world conditions" (i.e., the economist's externalities, public goods, and imperfections) are complications regarded as impediments to what is seen as an otherwise perfectly functioning market mechanism that is both efficient and equitable. For the orthodox economist efficiency means that all available resources are used efficiently to produce just those goods and services consumers most value. Equity means that the income earned by each factor of production (land, labor, and capital) is determined by the contribution to total output made by the last unit employed of each productive factor (this latter is termed *marginal productivity*). Thus, the pattern of rewards is said to be equitable when the distribution of income follows the principle of marginal productivity and inequitable when circumstances produce any other result.

Both the positivist philosophical premises and the equilibrium perspective come into play whenever the texts present race and gender issues. All texts recognize the presence of inequality, and all present at least some of the data revealing gender and racial disparities in income or in the frequency or duration of unemployment. Yet, even those texts that pursue the reasons for income inequality do so in a way that is preordained by positive equilibrium theory. For example, variables such as "ability, chance and luck, occupational differences and human capital choices" (Ruffin and Gregory 1983, 667) are singled out to explain the differences in marginal productivity that presumably account for inequalities in the distribution of income. Other texts mention genetics, institutional features, and discrimination as part of their explanation of the economic status of minorities and women. Factors such as luck, human capital, occupational choice, and variances in skill and ability generally receive far greater attention than do factors like discrimination, segregation, or inequality of opportunity.

When textbook authors explicitly address these issues they introduce either the "crowding" model or the statistical discrimination model. The crowding model explains occupational segregation as the result of the "typical" skills of female or minority male and female workers, which crowd them into a limited number of jobs. Authors who use this model (Atkinson

1982, 550–51; Gwartney and Stroup 1987, 556) fail to explain why women and minorities so irrationally continue to acquire only "traditional" skills. Ferber and Birnbaum (1977, 21) point out that "the very concepts of maximization and tradition are, in principle, mutually exclusive," since maximization (of one's chances for earning a high income) involves the conscious weighing of alternative choices, while tradition closes off alternatives. The social context responsible for the power of tradition is left undiscussed, even though its results are transparently necessary for an understanding of the choices that create occupational crowding.

The statistical discrimination model explains biases in the hiring process by suggesting that employers generalize about the behavior of all male and female minorities and all white women based on the behavior of statistically significant segments of these groups; such employers do not see individuals, they see only representatives of the group. Users of these models (Lipsey and Steiner 1981, 380–88; Scott and Nigro 1982, 414) fail to discuss the social conditions that allow employers' rational choices to lead to discriminatory (i.e., socially irrational) outcomes. Nor do they discuss the aggregate economic implications of individual employers' biases.

These brief and fragmentary discussions of race and gender in the "micro" sections of textbooks seem substantial in comparison to the nearly complete silence of macroeconomic sections. Most texts do present data showing racial and gender differences in unemployment rates, for example, but little effort is made to explain these data using macrotheory. That business cycles, economic growth, inflation, and monetary and fiscal policy could have different impacts on minorities and women is a possibility conspicuously absent from introductory economics textbooks. Race and gender, if a problem at all, affect only individual decisions in specific (microeconomic) market settings; the results then show up in macroeconomic data, but no macroeconomic explanation is offered.

In sum, virtually all the economics textbooks widely used in U.S. colleges and universities confront the causes of racial and gender inequality via a more or less complete list of exogenous factors—those individual tastes and preferences, technologies, endowments, and market structures that necessitate equilibrium outcomes in various markets (like labor, housing, health, and so on). If results are unequal, the fault lies with the given circumstances underlying the individually rational choices of the participants in that market. Since neoclassical economics explains all events as the consequences of individuals maximizing behavior on the basis of exogenously given preferences, technologies, endowments, and institutions, racial and gender outcomes are simply a special case of the general theory and do not need further explanation.

As a result, introductory economics textbooks have little to say about so-called normative questions. Although most texts make at least a passing reference to the principle of social equality, noting that greater equity is a goal that many people value, discussion of these value-laden issues is clearly an uncomfortable subject for many textbook authors. In part, the problem seems to be a definitional one: "Equity has no universally agreed-upon meaning . . . a difficulty that did not occur in the case of efficiency. . . . We might wish to establish beyond doubt that a particular meaning of equity is the right one. But to attempt it would take us deep into details of philosophy" (Dolan 1983, 15) or the "completely subjective" (Atkinson 1982, 14) nature of value judgments (Miller 1982, 680).

The most the texts offer are one or two alternative "philosophical" notions of equity that can be contrasted to the outcomes produced by market equilibrium forces. In fact, the only extended discussion of equity issues that most texts present tells the student, in the voice reserved for positive statements of fact, that greater social equity comes about only by deliberately choosing to impose costs injurious to everyone. Typically, authors carefully distinguish the normative and "philosophical" question of "a just distribution of income" from the presumably positive "economic" question of "what specific steps can be taken to alter the distribution of income" (Spencer 1983, 550). But ironically, with the sole exception of Heilbroner and Thurow (1981), no text even discusses such steps, abjuring even those positive statements that could be made about income alteration. Instead of an analysis of the means to greater equity, the texts discuss what the costs would be.

Without exception, the texts stress that steps to increase equity are socially costly due to a "fundamental trade-off between efficiency and equity" (McConnell 1982, 670). Since positive equilibrium theory states that, imperfections and special cases aside, markets gravitate in the long run to a position embodying an efficient allocation of resources, any exogenously imposed change designed to increase equity must result in a deviation from the previously established efficient equilibrium. Students are always informed that "there is often a trade-off between the size of a nation's output and the degree of equality with which that output is distributed" (Baumol and Blinder 1982, 654). By implication, then, "the size of the national pie is reduced if we try to carve it up in a more equitable way" (Wonnacott and Wonnacott 1982, 796). Consequently, "society must decide whether the costs of greater equality are worth the price" (Ruffin and Gregory 1983, 668).

This minimal treatment of race and gender is, in our view, an inevitable effect of the positivist methodology and marginalist equilibrium premises of the texts. In the next two sections we present critiques of the philosophical and analytical foundations of textbooks' treatments of economic outcomes relevant to issues of race and gender and then present an alternative perspective.

The Fallacy of the Normative-Positive Divide

The positive, objective theoretical statements in economics texts are seen as factual because they conform to the bounds of normal inquiry, the realm that most economists find acceptable. Textbook authors regard the dominant paradigm as having a validated and privileged connection to reality. In actuality, the paradigm's acceptance has led to the perception of its validity; its status as validated did not compel its acceptance. This interpretation emerges from a growing literature critical of the philosophical premises common in neoclassical theory. Although these critiques are not discussed in the textbooks, they have a potentially profound message bearing on the typical treatment of issues like gender and race.

All contemporary critiques of orthodox notions of science owe a debt to Kuhn (1970) and his conception of the textbook as an "exemplar" that buttresses the process of "normal" inquiry. In every discipline, textbooks socialize students into accepting the currently dominant theories (Rider 1984). As Kuhn has argued:

> Students ... accept theories on the authority of teacher and text, not because of evidence. ... The applications given in texts are not there as evidence but because learning them is part of learning the paradigm at the base of current practice. Consequently, only information which neatly fits into the dominant paradigm will be selected for inclusion in any given field's textbooks. (1970, 37)

In any field textbooks define the legitimacy of topic areas, distill the current body of knowledge, and mirror the field's research priorities. The paradigm articulated by the texts gives

> criteria for choosing problems that ... can be assumed to have solutions. To a great extent, these are the only problems that the community will admit as scientific or encourage its members to undertake. Other problems ... are rejected as metaphysical, as the concern of another discipline, or sometimes as just too problematical to be worth the time. A paradigm can ... even insulate the community from those socially important problems that are not reducible to the puzzle form,

because they cannot be stated in terms of the conceptual and instrumental tools the paradigm supplies. (Kuhn 1970, 37)

Economists' acceptance of the positivist belief in the separability of "facts" and "values" and of positive and normative statements blurs "the fact that alternative descriptions are possible in addition to those offered by the results of normal inquiries" (Rorty 1979, 63). The decision of textbook authors to present one set of voices, those that speak the language of the dominant paradigm, as the factual set, hides what is in actuality a normative bias. The dominant paradigm is given a privileged position; all other paradigms are pushed across the positivist divide into the netherworld occupied by normative statements. This favoritism is implicitly premised on the existence of a neutral, value-free, transtheoretical language that can be used to evaluate competing theoretical claims. We argue that there is no conceptually neutral language that would allow one, first, to treat as commensurable, and second, to judge, the heterogeneous sets of theoretical statements possible about economic phenomena. The so-called theory-choice problem is insoluble, except on normative—that is, political and ideological—grounds.

The presentation of market-equilibrium economics as the only worthy subject matter in the introductory curriculum has far-reaching consequences. As Rorty (1979, 359) puts it, "From the educational . . . point of view, the ways things are said is more important than the possession of truths." The way things are said in the economics texts devalues comparative critical thinking. The texts would have students divide themselves in two, with the positive and rational knower of true statements held rigorously separate from the subjective chooser of individual and social values, a stance that fosters fatalism about the status quo and discourages criticism and imaginative thinking about alternative ways of producing goods and distributing economic rewards. "If one cannot reason about values, and if most of what matters is placed in the value half of the fact-value split, then it follows that one will embrace unreason when talking about things that matter" (McCloskey 1983, 514).

The way things are *not* said is important, too. The texts' use of the language of positive and objective economics masks an implicit political agenda. The almost total silence of the texts on the economic status of minorities and women speaks louder than words: The student cannot help but absorb the message that these are matters of relative unimportance. Unavoidably, all textbooks have a "political" viewpoint, and "it is better to admit that metaphors in economics can contain such a political message than to use the jargon innocent of its potential" (McCloskey 1983, 508).

The Analytical Shortcomings of the Equilibrium Model

The positive economic theory that receives the overwhelming share of attention in the texts is, of course, neoclassical to the core. There is, however, another body of recent critical literature that seeks to problematize that positive theory itself, by disputing the ability of neoclassical logic to produce a consistent and meaningful solution for the economy's long-run equilibrium position.

The orthodox neoclassical model of economic behavior sees all economic outcomes as the result of individual rational choices registered in impersonal market exchanges. Individuals' rational choices, under various constraints, are represented by the economists' familiar supply-and-demand schedules. Together, individual choices in competitive markets determine all prices, all quantities, and the distribution of income. The highly refined version of neoclassical economics found in the introductory textbooks melds the dual logics of market competition and individual choice in a manner that shows them to be the ultimate determinants of economic events. This model tells students that "the consumer is king." The questions of what is produced, how much it costs, and who gets it are all answered by appeal to individual—choice that is, the production, distribution, and allocation of goods and services are what they are because people, acting in markets, choose these outcomes.

To be compelling, the analysis of one market in isolation from others (the "partial equilibrium" approach) must have foundations in a more general model with characteristics that support and justify the premises of single-market models. It is not saying much to note that supply and demand determine the price and quantity of apples if the model does not simultaneously explain, on the same logical basis, the forces determining those supply-and-demand schedules as well as all other supply-and-demand schedules, because both the supply of and the demand for apples are influenced by the supplies and demands registered in all other markets. In other words, the partial equilibrium approach that receives the most attention in the texts is compelling only to the extent that its typical assumption ("all other variables held constant") can be relaxed in a more general model. Because textbook authors believe that general equilibrium models actually do confirm the tendency toward competitive equilibrium in all markets simultaneously, texts typically proceed by means of the partial approach, viewing that approach as merely a simplification of the more complex interactions modeled in general equilibrium theory.

As noted earlier, textbooks insist that there is an inevitable trade-off between the goals of equity and efficiency. General equilibrium models conclude that competitive markets produce the maximum outputs of the goods and services most desired by the population and at the lowest possible cost. With no wasted resources and the "right" goods being produced, there is, by definition, efficiency. Moreover, such an efficient outcome carries within it, as a necessary component, a particular pattern of income distribution. Logically then, policy decisions that alter that distribution of income must interfere with efficiency. To further describe this trade-off, texts typically invoke the "leaky bucket" analogy: Dollars directed toward improving equity lead to disproportionate decreases in efficiency. And since an efficiency loss is a cost born by all, while equity is assumed to benefit only those receiving income transfers, economics textbooks characterize the call for greater economic equity as at best a costly sort of moral claim.

But if the claims of general equilibrium do not hold, that is, if it cannot be shown that competitive behavior will enforce an automatic and necessary solution for prices, quantities, and income distribution, then the usual arguments against the implementation of economic policies designed to alter the income distribution (or prices or quantities) are no longer so compelling. The literature, pro and con, on general equilibrium theory is highly abstract and mathematical and thus is usually viewed as a province only for specialists. But the consequences of the theory are everywhere in neoclassical economics, and its implications for gender and race issues merit a summary of the theory as groundwork for explaining the critique.

General equilibrium theory provides a system of mathematical relations used to solve for the outcomes of all markets simultaneously. Traditionally, economists have viewed as the appropriate solution the specification of a long-run equilibrium position, one in which prices have adjusted to the point that two criteria are satisfied. First, quantities supplied and demanded must be equal in all markets, including both markets for produced goods and for the services of produced and nonproduced factors of production. Since imbalance of supply and demand would produce ongoing market adjustments, absence of such imbalance is required for equilibrium. Second, homogeneous factors of production must receive uniform rewards, including a competitively equalized uniform rate of return on capital deployed in each alternative use. If a person deploying resources in one fashion can gain increased income by shifting those resources to some other use, then the situation can hardly be considered a sustainable equilibrium. A position fulfilling both criteria can be compellingly argued to represent a "center of gravity" for the short-run adjustments of prices and quantities; thus a theory that can move from initially given data to a solution for such a position can convincingly claim to have specified "where the economy will go."

As Eatwell (1977) has argued, the neoclassical derivation of such an equilibrium takes as data: (a) preferences (utility functions), (b) technology, (c) the size of the initial resource endowments, and (d) the initial distribution of those endowments. The universal principle of behavior in this approach is that, in all markets and at all times, individuals act rationally to maximize their utility subject to these ultimate constraints. All the various supply-and-demand curves employed in neoclassical analysis are derived as aggregate summations of individual choices made in this universal fashion. When these supplies and demands are combined into a general equilibrium model, neoclassical theory claims to derive a simultaneous solution for all the variables of interest: prices, quantities, and a particular pattern of the distribution of labor and capital incomes. Ultimately, all the components of the equilibrium solution are regarded as jointly necessary implications of the given preferences, endowments, and technology that define the situation. What happens in competitive markets is desirable because it is chosen by the aggregate of individual actors.

The problem with all this is that even if neoclassical economics is granted all of the assumptions and restrictions ordinarily imposed, no long-run solution will exist in general, a result that problematizes the claim that market outcomes can be explained as the result of rational individual choice. The specification of resource endowments is at the root of the difficulties that emerge: However one specifies the "capital factor"—as a scalar (a fund of finance) or a vector (a list of heterogeneous capital goods)—unsatisfactory results of one sort or another follow.

If capital is treated as a scalar for purposes of specifying initial endowments (the "production function" approach taken by Samuelson [1962] and virtually every textbook model of production), then, with appropriate assumptions concerning the form of the various functions, a determinate solution emerges that embodies the usual neoclassical propositions. But the result is not general: A scalar magnitude of "capital" (the economists' traditional K) in the same units as "output" means that the economy is effectively a "one-commodity world." More important, the result is not generalizable: The simplification made possible by the production function fails, in that none of the conclusions about distribution or efficiency expressed by means-of-production functions hold, in general, in a world with more than one produced means of production. It is obviously unsatisfactory if the logical consistency of basic economics depends on a degree of abstraction such that the millions of different consumer and capital goods produced become indistinguishable parts of some homogeneous, all-purpose "stuff." And yet these models must assume just that, since, as Garegnani (1972, 271) has shown, there is *no* production function in labor and "capital" outside of a one-commodity world, and consequently, "no definition of 'capital' allows us to say that its marginal product is equal to the rate of interest."

The alternative to production function exercises is the full-scale "Walrasian" treatment of the capital endowment as a vector of heterogeneous capital goods used in production, such as the Nobel Prize–winning "intertemporal equilibrium" model of Debreu (1959). Again, with appropriate assumptions, a solution exists that is, on its own terms, perfectly valid, in that individual decisions produce market-clearing outcomes that are efficient and socially optimal. Problems remain, however, since that solution does not generally fulfill both of the characteristics of long-run equilibrium already mentioned. The system can be solved for meaningful (nonnegative) values for market-clearing quantities and prices only if it is expressed in terms of inequalities, which means that in general, the rate of interest earned on capital within a single time period will not be uniform. Whatever the virtues of such a model, the solution does not represent a position toward which the economy will gravitate, since inconsistent rates of return on alternative uses of capital would provoke changes leading the economy away from the outcomes the model specifies (Eatwell 1982, 223; 1983, 211). To demonstrate the efficiency of free-market outcomes, neoclassical theory has, in effect, assumed away capitalism, since the heart of capitalist production is the profit-maximizing, response to opportunities for a higher rate of return. Eatwell states the strong conclusion: "It is not logically possible to solve a neoclassical system for the determination of long run equilibrium" (1983, 210).

Despite these analytical shortcomings, textbook explanations of the data on minorities and women rely on the neoclassical claim to have a consistent and general solution for the perfectly competitive long-run equilibrium center of gravity for all markets, including labor and capital markets. The power of the neoclassical position is based in large part on the simplicity of that claim: The premise of individual maximizing behavior, combined with the requirement for market clearing, enables one to specify a necessary equilibrium outcome, one toward which a competitive capitalist system will gravitate. Since one part of that equilibrium solution is the particular pattern of income distribution viewed as necessary given the exogenous factors taken as data, the theory of distribution within which race and gender issues are treated is explicitly a part of the broader equilibrium theory. But the inability of mathematical microeconomics to back up its claim, even when granted a host of extreme simplifying assumptions, implies weakness precisely where the theory needs to be strong. If neoclassicism is unable to demonstrate the existence of an equilibrium position toward which income, employment and all other prices and quantities are moving, then it is unable to assert the necessity of any overall distributional pattern. And in that case those, like minorities and women, who occupy the least-desirable places in the existing distribution would seem entitled to ask: If preferences, technology, and the endowment structure are not sufficient to explain the long-run distributional pattern in capitalism, how is that pattern determined and what further, presumably social (political and ideological), factors are involved?

While the theoretical critique of neoclassical equilibrium analysis presented earlier has implications for propositions made in a number of economic fields, it is especially relevant to the one proposition that all texts invariably put forward when considering the possibilities for distributional change: the presence of an inevitable trade-off between efficiency and equity. The inevitability of such a trade-off is defensible only on the basis of a general equilibrium theory asserting the automatic efficiency of competitive markets, at least in the absence of a well-known list of complicating factors. But the necessity of the conclusion depends upon the premise, and if the critique outlined earlier is correct, then the theoretical basis for any generalized trade-off between efficiency and equity is undercut. There may well still be grounds for the economist's intuition that there must be a price tag attached to efforts to increase equity, but in the absence of a consistent theory of long-run gravitational equilibrium, that intuition cannot be defended in the traditional way.

An Alternative Treatment of Gender and Race

We have argued that textbook discussions of race and gender are shaped by the philosophical and analytical premises of the orthodox paradigm in economics. The form of the discussion is limited by allegiance to the positivist conception of a fact-value distinction; the content of the discussion is then almost exclusively defined by marginalist equilibrium analysis. The neoclassical approach makes a tactical distinction between the underlying abstract theory, in which the sum of individual choices is decisive and factors like gender and race are inherently irrelevant, and the various applications of that theory. In the applications, the phenomena of concern to minorities and women, such as unemployment or earnings differentials, emerge as effects of tastes and preferences or endowments or market imperfections. This distinction has the value-laden effect of devaluing these concerns by treating them as secondary to the "real" tasks of positive economic theory. Discrimination, for example, becomes simply a source of deviations from an otherwise automatic and desirable equilibrium, rather than a historically intrinsic part of the economic system.

The economic effects of race and gender can be handled differently, by using the different philosophical and analytic approach of radical economics. Two texts exemplify the possibilities inherent in this alternative (Bowles and Edwards 1985; Wolff and Resnick 1987).

The premise of radical economics is that every human society produces a surplus (an excess of output over that amount required to reproduce the performers of labor and the consumed means of production) that is then distributed to different groups or classes through the social organization of the society in question. This surplus product is necessarily associated with the performance of surplus labor: If, from the total product of a society, we subtract the goods necessary to replace consumed means of production, then the remainder, the social net product, must be associated with the total labor performed in producing it (since the "contribution" of nonlabor inputs has already been accounted for through the goods set aside for replacement). The total net product can be divided into two portions, one representing the customary claims of the workers engaged in its production (the product of necessary labor) and the remainder representing the surplus product (produced by surplus labor). This distinction between necessary and surplus labor then can be applied to the labor of individual workers as well.

These basic categories permit the specification of two types of class arrangements. First is the set of social arrangements within which surplus is produced and appropriated. The poles of this relationship are the class of direct producers (those who perform necessary and surplus labor) and the class of direct extractors (those who directly control the product of surplus labor). The performance of surplus labor by direct producers and its appropriation by direct extractors is, however, only the beginning of the story, for once a surplus has been successfully produced, it is distributed in a variety of complex ways to groups that may have no direct involvement in the generation of the surplus. The second sort of class arrangement refers to those groups whose incomes represent claims on the already produced surplus. These groups can be called indirect extractors (since they receive what are effectively redistributed shares of previously extracted surplus labor). Thus, in a capitalist economy, the surplus labor of productive workers is initially appropriated by the capitalist firms that employ them, but it is then redistributed via competition, negotiation, monopoly extraction, debt, taxation, and so on.

Gender and race have no a priori bearing on an individual's economic position or behavior, but in particular historical circumstances, race and gender distinctions may become significant variables in the processes through which surplus labor is performed, appropriated, and redistributed. A radical analysis does not use information on preferences, endowments, and similar factors to specify the results of individual rational choices. No distribution has the status of an equilibrium made necessary by exogenous forces. Rather, the object is to understand the flows of surplus, including the patterns of its distribution, that result from current political and economic struggles and the balance of power among groups with contradictory interests. Every distribution is a contingent result that is continually called into question by class conflicts, group interests, and individual choices. Not only is the destination of the surplus an issue of conflict, but so is the form of the process. Participation in the decisions governing the production and distribution of the surplus is as open to contest as are the rewards themselves. Lack of participation is central to what the radical tradition means by "exploitation," which is quite different from the neoclassical notion of inequity or quantitative disparity in rewards. Radical analyses are much more concerned with the form of the social processes through which rewards are determined. Consequently, groups that are excluded from participation in decision making are subject to economic inequity, irrespective of the size of the incomes they receive (Feiner and Roberts 1986, 1990).

The issue of discrimination starkly illustrates the contrast between radical and neoclassical analyses. Neoclassicals view market competition as the means by which equilibrium prices and quantities are established. The orthodox texts argue that competition should undercut discriminatory pay differentials:

> If an employer could really hire women who were willing and able to do the same work as men for 35 percent less, the profit motive would provide the employer with a strong incentive to do so. . . . Of course, as more and more employers substituted women for men workers, the earnings ratio of women to men would move toward parity. (Gwartney and Stroup 1987, 564–65)

But since "this is not what is observed in the real world" (564), the cause of pay differentials must be located in gender-based differences in preferences and the choices that result:

> Married men and women have different areas of traditional specialization within the family. Married men typically pursue paid employment aggressively because they are expected to be the family's primary breadwinner. . . . In contrast, married women have generally had the primary responsibility for operating the household and caring for children. . . . Thus, women seek different sorts of jobs than men, jobs with less travel time, flexible hours, and those that are complementary with household

responsibilities.... Viewed in this light, it is not particularly surprising that women find nursing, teaching, secretarial, and other jobs with easily transportable skills highly attractive. (564–66)

In this view, since the possible range of such child care–compatible occupations is restricted relative to the occupational range open to men, crowding and low pay are inevitable results of women's job preferences.

In the radical approach competition is not a means to any particular outcome, but is instead an economic dimension of a much broader and inherent set of class and nonclass struggles. This different view of competition makes visible further dimensions of discrimination. A radical text states:

Conventional economics argues that discrimination is costly and hence competition for profits will eliminate discrimination. But ... when employers discriminate, it may be precisely because discrimination is profitable and indeed competition may drive (non-prejudiced) employers to discriminate.... [Thus] capitalism affects discrimination in two ways—one way weakens it and the other strengthens it. Discrimination is weakened when firms compete with one another by attempting to minimize costs through hiring the best person at the lowest wage.... On the other hand, discrimination is perpetuated when capitalists try to use discrimination in their conflict with workers over wages and the pace of work.... Capitalists did not invent racism or sexism, but they have used pre-existing prejudices or biases among workers to divide and weaken workers. (Bowles and Edwards 1985, 190–91)

As for job preferences, while it is not false to point out that some women do choose traditionally female jobs, the radical approach socially locates that choice, since "the gender system—the way our culture determines what is 'male' and what is 'female'—heavily influences these choices" (Bowles and Edwards 1985, 229).

Radical economists' awareness of the social and cultural context for economic activity emerges from a historical perspective absent from neoclassical theory. For example, while most orthodox texts briefly mention occupational segregation and the theories of dual or segmented labor markets that seek to explain it, the radical text explicitly discusses the way the occupational structure emerges from the historical evolution of concentrated hierarchical firms, unionism, and the expanded scope of governmental policies (Bowles and Edwards 1985, chaps. 10 and 14). The neoclassical inclination to treat current inequities as the effects of millions of constrained maximizing choices effectively obliterates history by admitting it only in the form of exogenously given preferences, endowments, and institutional imperfections. In a curious way, history comes to look like destiny, since equilibrium concepts obscure the open-ended historical process that has enmeshed gender and race in a wider pattern of class and nonclass alliances and conflicts (Acker 1988; Hartmann 1976; Williams 1987). In a similar vein those few orthodox texts that discuss the economic structure of the household do so through the Becker model of gender specialization based on individual choice and "comparative advantage." It is only in another radical text that a student will find a full-fledged alternative, an extended discussion of the class dimension of historically traditional household gender roles (Wolff and Resnick 1987, 218–22).

These analytical differences affect the importance granted to race and gender discrimination in the United States economy. Neoclassical economists admit the reality of such discrimination, but question its significance by stressing the many factors other than discrimination that can generate inequality (preferences, abilities, luck, and so on). Radical economists, in contrast, treat discrimination as an unambiguous part of the contemporary economic system.

The contrast is perhaps most apparent in what the texts consider appropriate reactions to inequality. Every neoclassical text cautions the student to be aware of the allegedly unavoidable trade-off between equity and efficiency. The trade-off is presented as a positive statement of fact; on that basis the student is left to determine, on the basis of personal normative values, whether greater equity is worth its inevitable price. Little is said about what values one might use as criteria for judgment or what practical options might be open to someone with, say, feminist values. The radical alternative confronts the neoclassical textbook logic:

> Many economists have come to see the amount of inequality in a capitalist society as simply a choice based on a trade-off between more equality and more output. Their reasoning is as follows: if the government is democratic, then the voters can simply decide how much equality they want. But if the capitalist economy is efficient, voters will have to "pay" for more equality, [and] . . . the more equality they vote for, the less output or economic growth they will get. (Bowles and Edwards 1985, 382)

The *ifs* make it clear that the trade-off is a theoretical conclusion and not a statement of fact. Indeed, "there are many reasons to believe that the capitalist economy is not efficient," and there are "serious limits to the democratic choices that the voters may make, because in a capitalist system capitalists are free to invest elsewhere (or not at all) if they do not like what the voters do" (Bowles and Edwards 1985, 382–83). Radical economists buttress their argument that the United States faces no such inevitable trade-off with international data on growth and distributional possibilities of a sort absent from neoclassical texts. Moreover, Bowles and Edwards offer an explicit statement of the values that underlie their analysis (equity, fairness, and democracy) and apply those values in suggesting prescriptions to implement in pursuing the goals on both sides of the neoclassical trade-off.

The differences between the two approaches are partly, though not simply, a result of radical economists expressing a commitment to social change and neoclassical economists deliberately avoiding or suppressing discussion in the interest of maintaining the intellectual and social status quo. More important are the underlying differences between the theoretical perspectives themselves. Gender and race take on a new economic significance when approached in the radical way, based on the rejection of positivist philosophy and the use of historical class categories in place of individual utility and equilibrium. Like the practitioners of every other discipline, economists of every stripe can only "see" what their chosen theoretical categories permit to be seen. Unfortunately, only one theoretical vocabulary, together with its implicit and explicit values, is offered to most economics students in the United States.

Conclusion

Perhaps one of the most far-reaching contributions of the recent scholarship on the intersection of race, gender, and class is the repeated demonstration that theory and methodology are never neutral. Indeed, "feminist challenges reveal that the questions asked—and even more significantly, those that are not asked—are at least as determining of the adequacy of our total picture" (Harding 1987, 7). We have focused on the "picture" presented by economics textbooks to U.S. students initially coming to terms with economics. But the theory and methodology of orthodox economics has implications that are important for feminists in other disciplines, especially those in which an "economic" perspective is often invoked.

One of the common tasks of much feminist scholarship is the delineation of differences, distinctions, or asymmetries that have been painted out of the picture visible to the "normal science" of different disciplines. The neoclassical approach is no exception; it too enforces a particular and deliberate homogenization of human experience: Different individuals may make different choices or undertake dissimilar actions, but we all supposedly choose and respond in the same way, through the same calculus of maximization. The "economic problem" is always the same; technology may vary, endowments and institutions may evolve historically, and preferences may be unique to the individual, but the form of the question is constant. It is: What choices express rational utility maximization (subject to constrained resources and a particular institutional setting), and what equilibrium is established by the aggregated choices of individual agents? All the interactions and the particulars of a social situation that may give rise to "different realities," including gender, are swept from a constitutive place and viewed instead as information exogenous to a uniform reality of choice. The seductive simplicity and universality of this approach have contributed to the inroads made by economics into fields across the disciplinary spectrum, including not only the social sciences but also areas as disparate as biology and law. Feminists in any of these fields who are interested in expanding the diversity of insights into the causes and effects of gendered identity have good reason to be wary of economists bearing the gift of rational choice models.

Not only does orthodox economics deliberately homogenize human behavior, it does so through conceptual metaphors that have a masculine content: the isolated individual rationally using free will, without emotional constraint. Ever since Adam Smith's celebration of the "invisible hand" of the marketplace, orthodox economics has touted the virtues of the competitive market as the institutional solution to the dilemma posed by separate individuals, all seeking maximal opportunities to exercise their rights to self-interested behavior. Faced with social problems, the neoclassical instinct is to create markets where none exist in order to harness the benefits of competition, where competition is viewed as an automatic effect of the autonomous individual's freedom to buy or sell at will. This vision of the separateness of individuals as agents in the marketplace has made exchange the universal metaphor for interpreting all human behavior: If one either "supplies" or "demands," alienates or acquires, then every aspect of human activity can be interpreted as, in essence, a species of supply or demand behavior. The very activity of production itself becomes little more than a market transaction in which "inputs" are exchanged at a price for final "output" In contrast, radical economics sees the process of production as a fundamentally social interaction structured by social roles, relations, and attachments among human beings. This focus on relations and attachments, power and responsibilities, is closer to feminist analysis in recognizing that what happens in the economy is partially the result of conflicts among people with different interests and different values.

Ultimately, any evaluation of textbooks presupposes some vision of what education ought to be, and in our view, an economics education should not be merely instruction in the tools and results of normal inquiry. While more attention to gender and race issues is needed, the problem is not simply one of quantity. Progress will be made when the texts present alternatives and become open to the arguments that will inevitably follow. Only where the possibility of disagreement is acknowledged is it possible for students to be challenged to critical thinking. At present that is not the case, and for one interested in race and gender issues the obstacle is an orthodox approach that, in effect, if not intent, is closed to the dialogue of conflicting values. The sad result is that at present race and gender are hidden by the invisible hand.

NOTES

We are indebted to many, inside as well as outside mainstream economics, whose comments and suggestions strengthened this work. In 1985 a substantially different version of this essay was presented at the American Economic Association meetings, and we thank then AEA President Alice Rivlin for inviting our participation. An earlier version of the essay was also presented at the Southern Economic Association meetings in 1988, and we thank Marjorie McElroy for including us on the program. Numerous others have contributed, but special thanks are due to Donald McCloskey, Lester Thurow, Barbara Bergmann, Robert Clower, Richard Wolff, Robin Bartlett, and Marianne Ferber. Of course, the views expressed here are entirely our own. Research support from the College of William and Mary is gratefully acknowledged. We hope that this essay will help broaden the perspective of academic economists.

This essay also appeared in *Gender and Society* 4(2) (1990): 159–81. Copyright © 1990 by Sage Publications, Inc. Reprinted by permission of Sage Publications, Inc.

REFERENCES

Acker, Joan. 1988. Class, gender, and the relations of distribution. *Signs* 13:473–97.

Amacher, R. C. 1983. *Principles of economics.* Cincinnati: Southwestern.

Atkinson, L 1982. *Economics.* Homewood, IL: Irwin.

Baumol, W., and A. Blinder. 1982. *Economics.* New York: Harcourt Brace Jovanovich.

Bowles S., and R. Edwards. 1985. *Understanding capitalism: Competition, command and change in the U.S. economy.* New York: Harper and Row.

Bronfenbrenner M., W. Becher, and W. Gardiner. 1984. *Macro and micro economics.* Boston: Houghton Mifflin.

Debreu, G. 1959. *Theory of value.* New Haven, CT: Yale University Press.

Dolan, E. 1983. *Basic economics.* Chicago: Dryden.

Eatwell, J. 1977. The irrelevance of returns to scale in Sraffa's analysis. *Journal of Economic Literature* 15:61–68.

———. 1982. Competition. In *Classical and Marxian political economy,* ed. L. Bradley and M. Howard. New York: St. Martin's.

————. 1983. The analytical foundations of monetarism. In *Keynes's economics and the theory of value and distribution,* ed. J. Eatwell and M. Milgate. New York: Oxford University Press.

Feiner, S., and B. Morgan. 1987. Women and minorities in introductory economics textbooks: 1974 to 1984. *Journal of Economic Education* 10:376–92.

Feiner, S., and D. Roberts. 1986. Marx and Keynes and Kalecki. *Journal of Economic Issues* 20:1135–36.

————. 1990. Slave exploitation in neoclassical economics: Criticism and an alternative direction. In *Race, restitution and public policy,* ed. R. America. Westport, CT: Greenwood.

Ferber, M., and B. Birnbaum. 1977. The "new home economics": Retrospects and prospects. *Journal of Consumer Research* 4:19–28.

Ferber, M., and N. Teimani. 1981. The oldest, the most established, the most quantitative of the social sciences . . . and the most dominated by men: The impact of feminism on economics. In *Men's studies modified,* ed. D. Spender. New York: Pergamon.

Fischer, S., and R. Dornbusch. 1983. *Economics.* New York: McGraw-Hill.

Frey, B., W. Pomerehne, F. Schneider, and G. Gilbert. 1984. Consensus and dissension among economists: An empirical inquiry. *American Economic Review* 74:986–94.

Fusfeld, D. 1982. *Principles of political economy.* Glenview, IL: Scott, Foresman.

Garegnani, P. 1972. Heterogeneous capital, the production function and the theory of distribution. In *A critique of economic theory,* ed. E. K. Hunt and J. Schwartz. Harmondsworth: Penguin.

Glazer, N. 1987. Questioning eclectic practice in curriculum change: A Marxist perspective. *Signs* 12:293–304.

Gwartney, J., and R. Stroup. 1982. *Economics.* New York: Academic Press.

Harding, S., ed. 1987. *Feminism and methodology: Social science issues.* Bloomington: Indiana University Press.

Hartmann, H. 1976. Capitalism, patriarchy and job segregation by sex. *Signs* 1:137–69.

Heilbroner, R., and L. Thurow. 1981. *The economic problem.* Englewood Cliffs, NJ: Prentice-Hall.

Kearl, J., C. Pope, G. Whitting, and L. Wimmer. 1979. A confusion of economists? *American Economic Review* 69:28–37.

Kuhn, T. 1970. *The structure of scientific revolutions.* Chicago: University of Chicago Press.

Leftwich, R. 1984. *A basic framework for economics.* Dallas: Business Publications.

Lipsey, R., and P. Steiner. 1981. *Economics.* New York: Harper and Row.

Mansfield, E. 1983. *Economics: Principles, problems, decisions.* New York: Norton.

McCloskey, D. 1983. The rhetoric of economics. *Journal of Economic Literature* 21:481–517.

McConnell, C. 1982. *Economics: Principles, problems and policies.* New York: McGraw-Hill.

————. 1984. *Economics: Principles, problems and policies.* New York: McGraw-Hill.

Miller, R. 1982. *Economics today.* New York: Harper and Row.

Rider, C. 1984. Reevaluating economic education: Principles of economics, texts. *Review of Radical Political Economy* 16:167–79.

Rorty, R. 1979. *Philosophy and the mirror of nature.* Princeton, NJ: Princeton University Press.

Ruffin, R., and P. Gregory. 1983. *Principles of economics*. Glenview, IL: Scott, Foresman.

Samuelson, P. 1962. Parable and realism in capital theory: The surrogate production function. *Review of Economic Studies* 39:193–206.

———. 1980. *Economics*. New York: McGraw-Hill.

Samuelson, P., and W. Nordhaus. 1985. *Economics*. New York: McGraw-Hill.

Scott, R., and N. Nigro. 1982. *Principles of economics*. New York: Macmillan.

Spencer, M. 1983. *Contemporary economics*. New York: Worth.

Truett, D., and L. Truett. 1982. *Economics*. St. Paul, MN: West.

Waud, R. 1983. *Economics*. New York: Harper and Row.

Williams, R. 1987. Capital, competition, and discrimination: A reconsideration of racial earnings inequality. *Review of Radical Political Economy* 19:1–15.

Wolff, R., and S. Resnick. 1987. *Economics: Marxian versus neoclassical*. Baltimore: Johns Hopkins University Press.

Wonnacott P., and R. Wonnacott. 1982. *Economics*. New York: McGraw-Hill.

Adding Feminist Re-Visions to the Economics Curriculum

The Case of the Labor Supply Decision

Margaret Lewis

Feminism's influence on the discipline of economics is finally being recognized, and one area that has been particularly affected is how we teach economics. This essay explores how a feminist perspective can transform the economics curriculum into a more inclusive, more realistic site where students gain an active and critical understanding of their worlds. By applying the curricular phase model outlined in the first essay in this book and using the example of an individual's decision to participate in the paid labor force, the following discussion will demonstrate how a feminist pedagogy can help us revise the economics classroom to move beyond the often restrictive and unrealistic neoclassical paradigm and toward an economics that includes all economic actors and activities.

The specific example of an individual's decision to participate in the labor force is interesting for several reasons. First, the tremendous influx of women, especially married white women, into the United States paid labor market during the twentieth century is a socioeconomic event that has significantly affected not only individual women but also the American family, the workplace, and the United States economy as a whole. Thus, discussing the theoretical explanations for these changes would resonate with most students, whose own experiences could be drawn upon to enhance their understanding of economic models and, perhaps, to challenge these explanations. In addition, a variety of theoretical models have been developed by economists to explain the labor supply decision. This then offers the opportunity for comparing alternative explanations and for seeing the connections between theory, method, and empirical observation. Consequently, examining the labor supply decision offers the possibility for creating a Phase 4 classroom since this example can be used to incorporate student experiences, present alternative theories and methods, and examine the complexity of economic life.

In order to understand how this Phase 4 course might result, it is helpful to begin by looking at how the labor supply decision might be examined in a Phase 1 course, which is descriptive of most United States classrooms today. Since the standard textbook shares co-authority with the instructor in these courses, it is possible to use a sample of these texts to surmise how this topic might be taught or is not taught, which is more likely to be the case. An examination of an unscientific but typical sample of introductory and principles texts[1] indicates that in most, the decision to participate in the paid labor force is not even included, and in the few where this topic does appear, it is relegated to the end of the micro section, meaning the instructor will probably never get to the material.

Omitting a discussion of labor supply in most introductory course texts is what we might predict for a Phase 1 course, since such courses discuss only those individuals who have the most public power. In today's climate of downsizing, waning labor union power, and the view of workers as nothing more than a cost of production, the decisions of individual workers are not terribly important to those with economic power. At the same time, it is not surprising that, given the disproportionate economic power currently commanded by "the firm" in today's workplace, all texts do devote considerable attention to examining how the individual corporate firm makes its decisions. Like the model of consumer behavior typically preceding it, the analysis of the firm is based on neoclassical economic principles that emphasize an autonomous rational maximizer who makes decisions that are acultural and ahistorical. Thus the economic activities of the firm and the consumer, the two key players in a capitalist economic system, are privileged while the activities of workers are ignored.

In those textbooks that do present a model for labor supply, albeit at the end of the book, the discussion is typically confined to the labor-leisure model developed by neoclassical economists. According to this model, a utility-maximizing (and genderless) individual is faced with a choice of allocating the scarce resource of time between labor (work in the paid competitive labor force) and leisure. Because time is scarce, the individual must weigh the (private) benefits and costs of each activity to find the optimal (utility-maximizing) combination of labor and leisure. This trade-off between labor and leisure includes a substitution effect and an income effect, the latter of which may lead to the individual facing a backward-bending labor supply curve, and this result ends the discussion. Thus, these texts typically do not mention the numerous criticisms of the labor-leisure model and its attendant neoclassical assumptions of rational, self-interested, autonomous behavior, nor do they note that the empirical evidence indicates the backward-bending supply curve is found only for (some) men but not women, nor do these texts examine alternative models. So even when discussed, the labor supply decision is presented as a decision made by a genderless individual in the universal neoclassical world. This, in turn, perpetuates the exclusionary and simplistic Phase 1 classroom.

Instructors concerned with discussing the labor supply decision more fully, thereby moving the classroom into Phase 2, may correct for one or more of the limitations of Phase 1 scholarship. For example, one popular change appearing in Phase 2 is to present empirical evidence as it relates to women, which in the labor supply example, strongly suggests that women's labor supply decisions, even within the neoclassical framework, are quite different from men's. Thus, instructors concerned with "finding and adding women" may turn to labor or gender texts[2] to find some discussion of the empirical results for women's labor supply decisions. Unfortunately, if these results are discussed only within the context of the labor-leisure model, it will likely simply reinforce the idea that women are aberrant because their experiences cannot be explained by the model.[3]

Another, more progressive step into Phase 2 would occur if instructors added a more in-depth discussion of women's individual labor supply decisions. Here again instructors would need to utilize materials from labor or gender courses since these materials often go beyond noting the empirical evidence for women by suggesting that another factor—work in the home—be added to the basic labor-leisure model. But, as the following excerpt suggests, the neoclassical model, with its assumptions of rationality, autonomy, and universality, is still the basis for the discussion, so the subsequent discussion provides little concrete information for understanding gender differences:

> "male labor supply is much less sensitive to wage changes than is female labor supply" . . . Apparently for men the income effect slightly dominates the substitution effect when wage rates rise. For women the substitution effect seems to dominate substantially the income effect. . . . [The differences hinge on] existing differences in the allocation of time. (McConnell and Brue 1989, 28–29)

After briefly elaborating that women actually make time choices between market work, leisure, *and* work in the home, the text's discussion ends, leaving instructors and students with a nonilluminating explanation of women's labor supply decisions. While instructors can use this situation to generate questions about the universality of the model and its attendant assumptions, a characteristic often observed as course development moves toward Phase 3, more is needed to propel the classroom into the next stage of "challenging and proposing."

For those instructors interested in moving to a Phase 3 classroom, one possible avenue is to examine other neoclassical models that account more completely for factors affecting women's labor supply decisions, which is a second characteristic of Phase 3 scholarship. One such model is presented by Francine Blau, Marianne Ferber, and Anne Winkler in *The Economics of Women, Men, and Work* (1998), in which they modify the basic neoclassical model to examine the relative values of market time and nonmarket time, rather than of labor and leisure.

As Blau, Ferber and Winkler acknowledge, their model is essentially a neoclassical model, where an individual, facing the scarce resource of time, rationally evaluates competing values—the value of time spent in the market (or paid labor force) and the value of time devoted to nonmarket activities—with the goal of maximizing utility. If the value of market time exceeds that of nonmarket time, then the individual will decide to enter the paid labor force, a decision that may change over time if such underlying factors as the acquisition of human capital or labor market demand conditions alter the value of market time and/or if demographic factors, spousal income, or tastes and preferences affect the value of nonmarket time. While this model shares many features of the Phase 2 labor-leisure model, it does consider economic activities previously neglected by including the value of nonmarket time as an element for analysis. Thus, it could be argued that by explicitly valuing economic activities experienced by most women—unpaid work performed in the home—the Blau-Ferber-Winkler text presents a model exemplifying characteristics of Phase 3 scholarship.

Using the Blau-Ferber-Winkler text also provides students the opportunity to examine explicitly women's actual experiences within an historical context, another characteristic of Phase 3 scholarship. By applying their model to the empirical trends in labor force participation, the authors provide a persuasive explanation of several twentieth century labor force participation trends in the United States. In addition, they acknowledge that the model does not fully identify all factors for understanding others.[4] The authors, unlike most others, also provide some critique of the more standard neoclassical models, and they do discuss the effects of women's labor supply decisions on the family.

Because of these features, using the labor supply material presented in Blau, Ferber, and Winkler can move the classroom into Phase 3. Here existing neoclassical theories are modified to describe more effectively women's labor supply decisions, labor force participation and other relevant data are included and analyzed in the context of the modified model, some discussion of the models' limitations is included, and the connections between an individual's labor supply decision and the family, workplace and economy are explored. But if the classroom is to reach Phase 4, several additional steps still need to be taken.

Up to now the discussion has focused entirely on neoclassical models. But as feminists both in and out of economics are increasingly realizing, this paradigm has severe limitations when describing women's economic activities and may, in fact, even be inappropriate more often than not (see, e.g., England 1993; Nelson 1996). One way instructors might explore this possibility with their students is to introduce alternative economic explanations for women's labor force participation, thus taking the final step in Phase 3 and setting the stage for moving into Phase 4.

One non-neoclassical model for explaining the increasing labor force participation of women is that developed by institutional economist Clair Brown.[5] Like Blau, Ferber and Winkler's discussion, Brown's article mostly exemplifies Phase 3 scholarship but when her model is combined with the neoclassical model, the two provide a potential springboard into the Phase 4 classroom envisioned by feminist economists, where competing economic explanations are presented and evaluated. Before examining that issue, however, a brief description of Brown's work will be provided for those readers unfamiliar with institutional political economy.

In "Consumption Norms, Work Roles, and Economic Growth, 1918–80" Brown offers an explanation of changes in women's and men's work roles during the twentieth century using an institutional framework. Brown first identifies the family as an institution, which places the focus of analysis on those "social rules and customs that provide the framework by which people order their everyday lives and resolve conflicts." Brown next "assumes that a family's activities are primarily determined by the societal norms that govern its class" and that "maintaining class position . . . is the family's primary goal" since "improving class position is seldom a realistic goal" (Brown 1987, 14). Thus the institutional emphasis on individuals interacting as members of families influenced by cultural norms with the goal of maintaining class status differs considerably from the neoclassical emphasis on the family as an autonomous individual unit making rational decisions with the goal of maximizing utility.

Brown's institutionalist approach differs from the neoclassical approach in several other ways. First is the emphasis on the provisioning definition of economics—material goods and services that define socioeconomic class[6]—rather than on the scarcity definition underlying neoclassical economics. Consequently, women's and men's labor supply decisions "are not based on efficiency principles. Rather, such decisions are governed by social norms within a historical process" (Brown 1987, 15). In addition, Brown's analysis emphasizes the interactions between social norms, economic growth, and demographic changes rather than on isolated, discrete, and "purely static" economic factors, and it acknowledges racial and class distinctions rather than assuming a universal family unaffected by that family's place in the social hierarchy.

Brown's methodological approach further exemplifies differences between neoclassical and institutional economics. In neoclassical analysis, it is typically assumed that the rational economic man model applies across time and cultures, and empirical data are examined within that specific context. When the data do not "fit" the model, rarely is the model reconsidered; rather, it is the individuals themselves who are viewed as atypical. In institutional analysis, however, there is no a priori model of human behavior imposed on a specific situation; instead, "the productive and reproductive modes of a society are [seen to be] interrelated and interact dynamically over time" (Brown 1987, 15). This leads Brown to hypothesize that the "well-being, comfort, and status [that] together compose the standard of living" (Brown 1987, 13) in the twentieth century consumer economy of the United States can be identified by examining the consumption norms of particular social classes. She turns to data from the Bureau of Labor Statistics' Consumer Expenditure Survey in order to identify changing consumption patterns for different socioeconomic groups. These empirical patterns, along with changes in economic growth patterns which affect "the differential access families have to paid work" (Brown 1987, 14), are then used to explain observed changes in women's and men's work roles. Thus, an institutional approach, which incorporates the complexity of interacting institutions and changing social norms with empirical evidence as to how families actually have acted, presents a rather different understanding of women's changing work roles from the neoclassical explanation of the autonomous individual rationally evaluating relative values of time.

The question now is how might incorporating Brown's model, in addition to examining the Blau-Ferber-Winkler neoclassical model, help propel the economics classroom toward Phase 4. First, by presenting two, notably different explanations of women's labor supply decisions, with their distinctive focuses of analysis and methodologies, students will not only recognize that alternative economic theories and methodologies exist, they will also gain a broader and more complex understanding of this important topic. In addition, students can begin to understand how economists *do* economics since both models, as presented by the authors, demonstrate the interaction between economic theory and empirical observation. Finally, because the discussions both in Blau, Ferber and Winkler and in Brown explore the policy implications of women's increasing participation in the paid labor force, students will recognize that economics can be used not only to better understand their world but also to provide information for engaging in social action.

Examining both these models move the classroom closer to a Phase 4 classroom, but some unresolved issues remain. For example, while both models provide relatively complete explanations of white women's labor supply decisions, they are less effective in explaining the experiences of white men and women and men in other race-ethnic groups.[7] Thus, in a Phase 4 course, further discussion of race and gender differentials would need to be included. Another issue is that the neoclassical model in particular was developed to explain women's movement into the paid labor force, thereby emphasizing women's public sphere activity only. In a Phase 4 course this point would need to be acknowledged, and some discussion of women (and men) engaged in provisioning activities in the private, or nonpaid, economic sphere would need to be added. One additional change would be to incorporate theoretical insights, empirical findings, and methodological approaches from outside the economics discipline for the purpose of fully understanding the provisioning activities of all economic participants. Only then would the classroom exemplify the environment imagined for Phase 4.

At this point it is obvious that moving toward a Phase 4 classroom will change considerably the way economics is typically taught. Among the challenges facing instructors who contemplate this move are learning about alternative economic and noneconomic approaches (since most instructors are likely to be trained only in neoclassical economics), discovering appropriate course materials (since the standard text is not likely to be of use in this case), developing inclusive pedagogical strategies to complement the content changes (since lecturing will defeat the goals in a Phase 4 classroom), and addressing the concerns of colleagues who may not see the value of these changes. While these concerns may discourage some, for those of us interested in educating our students to be informed citizens who can engage in social action and who also see the classroom as a site for transforming both economics education as well as the discipline itself, the need to create a more inclusive and complete experience for our students is our paramount concern.

NOTES

1. The texts examined were McConnell and Brue; Wonnacott and Wonnacott; Mansfield; Levi; Riddell, Shackelford, and Stamos; Hunt and Sherman; Edgmond,

Moomaw, and Olson; Sharp, Leftwich, and Register; Schiller (*The Economy Today*); and Samuelson's 1980 edition. It should be mentioned that in a recent advertisement for McConnell and Brue (1999) "new to this edition" is "expanded content on women, racial and ethnic minorities, and discrimination." From the brief description provided, however, it is not clear that the labor supply decision is discussed, and, while the increase in women's labor force participation is discussed, as "a new Last Word," it is done so in the context of the production possibilities curve, a neoclassical concept premised on scarcity.

2. It is also possible that an instructor might have students read relevant journal articles. It is very unlikely, however, that introductory students have the ability to read and understand such materials.

3. Another change that could move the course into Phase 2 to acknowledge women who have made it in the world of the firm as a CEO or in another visible salaried position. Unfortunately, it is not likely that a text noting such women will also include a discussion of how she (or any other worker) moved into this position. Thus, it remains for the instructor to supplement the text discussion. While this could be done through additional materials, student reports, or guest lecturers, it is not clear that these strategies would be as effective as finding this information in the authoritative text, particularly if this were the only time in the course that outside materials were used.

4. "A number of studies suggest that the increase in married women's participation [in the 1990s] cannot be fully explained by changes in such measurable factors" (Blau, Ferber, Winkler 1998, 114), and "it seems the participation trends for the poorly educated have been even more unfavorable for blacks than whites. The reasons for this have not been identified" (117–18). It is interesting that the language presented suggests that the problem is with the trends rather than the underlying model.

5. While I have used both the Blau-Ferber-Winkler and Brown materials in my Political Economy of Gender and Race course, I have not yet incorporated the labor supply discussion into my Introductory classes. The reasons for those are typical: the topic of labor supply is not covered in my course text, and it is not considered a "must cover" topic in my department. Despite these limitations, I am attempting to include this topic in subsequent semesters as part of our discussion of the various roles played by economic actors.

6. For institutionalists *class* is defined not in Marxist terms but, rather, in terms of social stratification and economic distance.

7. Assignment number 3 in Lewis and Peterson 1997 provides, in the case of the neoclassical model, one exercise for students to discover the limitations of the model when it comes to explaining the labor force participation rates for nonwhite women.

REFERENCES

Aerni, April L., Robin L. Bartlett, Margaret Lewis, KimMarie McGoldrick, and Jean Shackelford. 1999. "Toward Feminist Pedagogy in Economics." *Feminist Economics* 5(1): 29–44.

Bartlett, Robin L., and Susan F. Feiner. 1992. "Balancing the Economics Curriculum: Content, Method, and Pedagogy." *American Economic Review* 82 (May): 559–69.

Blau, Francine D., Marianne A. Ferber, and Anne E. Winkler. 1998. *The Economics of Women, Men, and Work*. 3d ed. Englewood Cliffs, NJ: Prentice-Hall.

Brown, Clair. 1987. "Consumption Norms, Work Roles, and Economic Growth, 1918–80." In *Gender in the Workplace,* ed. by Clair Brown and Joseph Pechman, 13–49. Washington, DC: Brookings Institution.

England, Paula. 1993. "The Separative Self: Androcentric Bias in Neoclassical Assumptions." In *Beyond Economic Man: Feminist Theory and Economics,* ed. by Marianne A. Ferber and Julie A. Nelson, 37–53. Chicago: University of Chicago Press.

Larkin, Andrew. 1996. *An Introduction to Economics.* St. Cloud, MN: Kinko's Copies.

Lewis, Margaret. 1994. "Doing Economics in the Real World: Jean Carol Trepp's Emergent Principles for a Feminist Economics." Paper presented at the Midwest Economics Association Meetings, March, Chicago.

———. 1995. "Breaking Down the Walls, Opening up the Field: Situating the Economics Classroom in the Site of Social Action." *Journal of Economic Issues* 29 (June): 555–65.

Lewis, Margaret, and Janice L. Peterson. 1997. "The Labor Supply Decision—Differences between Genders and Races." In *Introductory Economics from a Race and Gender Perspective,* ed. Robin L. Bartlett, 67–88. London: Routledge.

McConnell, Campbell R., and Stanley L. Bruce. 1989. *Contemporary Labor Economics.* New York: McGraw-Hill.

McIntosh, Peggy. 1983. "Interactive Phases of Curricular Re-Vision: A Feminist Perspective." Center for Research on Women, Working Papers no. 124. Wellesley, MA: Wellesley College.

Nelson, Julie A. 1996. *Feminism, Objectivty and Economics.* London: Routledge.

Shackelford, Jean. 1992. "Feminist Pedagogy: A Means for Bringing Critical Thinking and Creativity to the Economics Classroom." *American Economic Review* 82 (May): 570–76.

Tetreault, Mary Kay Thompson. 1985. "Feminist Phase Theory: An Experience-Derived Evaluation Model." *Journal of Higher Education* 56 (July–August): 363–84.

Trepp, Jean Carol. 1939. *The Uses of Field Work in Teaching Economics.* Bronxville, NY: Sarah Lawrence College.

Addressing U.S. Poverty in Introductory Economics Courses

Insights from Feminist Economics

Janice Peterson

Over the past decade concerns about declining numbers of economics majors and the lack of race and gender diversity among professional economists have focused increasing attention on the state of undergraduate education in economics (Ferber 1995; Bartlett 1995). Increasingly, members of the economics profession have questioned the relevance of what is taught in undergraduate economics programs and have called for the curricular reforms necessary to prepare students to use the economics they learn in college to deal with the challenges they face in the real world (Bartlett 1995; Colander 1995).

Feminist economists have made important contributions to the discussion of the relevance of undergraduate economics education, arguing that the necessary curricular changes will require a rethinking of the method, content and pedagogy employed in economics courses (Bartlett and Feiner 1992). To date feminist economic work in this area has focused on the introductory economics courses which introduce future economists to the discipline and provide many students with their only exposure to formal economic theories and concepts.[1] This work has emphasized the need to integrate issues of race and gender into the introductory curriculum and to focus introductory courses on current issues of importance to an increasingly diverse student body (see Feiner 1994; Bartlett 1997).

An examination of introductory economics textbooks, however, reveals that they offer little assistance to instructors attempting to revise their introductory courses to address many of the economic and social issues that our students are confronted with in the real world. Welfare reform, for example, has been one of the most significant and highly publicized policy issues of the 1990s. The ongoing debate surrounding this policy change contains many contentious assertions about the nature of poverty in the United States and raises important questions concerning the importance of gender, race and class in the U.S. economy.[2] Yet the content of most introductory economics texts suggests that poverty is largely a nonissue for economists and students of the U.S. economy. Poverty is typically mentioned only very briefly in a special topics chapter at the end of the book, and the gender, race, and class issues raised by contemporary poverty and welfare policies are generally ignored.

The purpose of this essay is to provide suggestions for instructors who wish to incorporate a richer treatment of poverty into their introductory economics courses. In particular, it seeks to illustrate how structuring the introductory course around an institutionalist, feminist vision of economics can provide a framework within which topics such as poverty receive more attention and are covered in a more inclusive way than they are in many traditional economics courses.[3]

The curricular phase theory presented in the first essay of this volume provides a useful framework for examining the process of curricular transformation necessary to achieve this goal. Introductory economics courses are typically taught at the level of Phase 1 ("The Received Neoclassical Canon") and characterized by a focus on individual choices, competition, and market exchange. The emphasis on market outcomes, and their interpretation as socially optimal, constrains the discussion of poverty, casting it as the outcome of inappropriate individual choices and the failure of individuals to compete adequately in the market economy. Gender and race occasionally enter into such discussions of poverty through the presentation of poverty statistics that have been disaggregated by race, gender, or type of household. This moves the discussion to Phase 2 ("Finding and Adding Heretofore Members of Underrepresented Groups"), providing an examination of poverty where women and people of color are "viewed simply as problems, anomalies or members of a disadvantaged or subordinate group." While gender and race differences in poverty rates may be noted, the economic significance of gender and race in the operation of the economy is not discussed, leading to explanations of these differences that are incomplete and obscure many key issues and questions.

A discussion of poverty that will provide students with the understanding they need to address current policy issues such as welfare reform must move beyond this narrow Phase 2 treatment of the topic. This essay argues that bringing insights from feminist economics into the introductory course can begin the transformation of course content to Phase 3 ("Challenging Core Concepts and Proposing Alternatives") and Phase 4 ("Economics Redefined and Reconstructed to Include Us All") where an inclusive, multifaceted discussion of poverty provides the basis for assessing complex policy debates.

Most introductory texts begin with a discussion of several "core concepts" which define the conceptual framework and goals of the course, determining what questions will be asked and how they will be addressed. Thus, the process of transforming introductory course content must begin with the questioning and redefinition of these core concepts in order to establish a framework where poverty is treated as an issue of central importance, not merely a marginalized special topic. Four core concepts that are particularly important in shaping the discussion of poverty in introductory economics courses are the definition of economics, the performance criteria chosen to evaluate economic outcomes, the role of values in economic inquiry, and the role of government in the economy.[4] The next section examines the definition of these four core concepts in traditional introductory economic courses and the treatment of poverty that emerges in this framework. This is followed by a discussion of how insights from feminist economics can be used to reframe the discussion of poverty in a more inclusive way.

Traditional Course Content

Most introductory economics texts and courses begin with the neoclassical definition of economics, which defines the discipline in terms of the study of rational individual choices made under conditions of scarcity. Competitive markets are presented as the primary economic institution and market efficiency is defined as the primary success indicator. Efficiency is established as the most important goal of an economy and students learn that societies are faced with a fundamental trade-off between efficiency and equity. Questions concerning the role of values in economics are generally dismissed by invoking the positive-normative dichotomy, where students learn that economics, practiced correctly, is value-free and objective. The economic role of the government is generally modeled in terms of "interference," where government involvement in the economy is seen to distort market values and reduce efficiency. While government policies may occasionally be justified to correct efficiency-reducing market failure, "laissez faire" is seen to be the most desirable philosophy.

In this context poverty becomes a "microeconomic issue" to be examined in terms of individual productivity and individual choices in resource markets. In introductory economics texts poverty is typically included as part of a chapter on income distribution and linked with "redistributional" policies such taxes and income transfers. Such discussions stress that issues concerning the redistribution of income are different than other economic issues and polices, reflecting normative concerns about equity issues. Discussions of the costs and benefits of redistribution are often framed in the context of the efficiency-equity trade-off, with a focus on the difficulties involved in defining "fairness" and the potential costs of redistributive policies.

Introductory economics texts that offer more specific coverage of the topic of U.S. poverty typically begin with a discussion of the official definition of poverty used by the U.S. government. Students learn that the government establishes a "poverty line" (or "poverty thresholds") based on an estimate of "minimum needs," which is adjusted for family size and inflation. The discussion of the history and critiques of the official poverty measure tends to be limited. When critiques are presented, they are generally those focused on what is not included in the income measure used to calculate poverty statistics (such as the value of various noncash income transfers) and suggest that the official poverty statistics overestimate the amount of poverty.

Questions concerning the extent and nature of poverty are generally addressed through the presentation of statistics on the "incidence of poverty" (the "poverty rate"), which is defined as the number of poor persons, families or households as a percent of all persons, families or households.[5] Poverty rate statistics are often presented over time for the nation as a whole and, increasingly, for different demographic groups (usually race, gender, and/or family structure). Typically, other measures of poverty are not presented.

Although the fact that the incidence of poverty varies significantly across different groups in society is illustrated by the statistics presented in many introductory texts, issues of gender, race, and class are typically not addressed in discussions of the causes of poverty. These discussions tend to focus on the participation of individuals in resource markets, where the "willingness and ability" of individuals to participate in such markets is presented as the key determinant of their income, and, thus, poverty status. The complex interactions of gender, race and class in resource markets, and the importance of nonmarket issues in the determination of income, are typically not addressed.

The emphasis on resource markets is reflected in the discussion of government policies that conclude most introductory presentations of poverty. Typically, a variety of "income transfer" or "low income programs" are mentioned, with very little discussion of their history, institutional structure or the characteristics of their recipients. Students learn that the primary concerns that economists have with such programs are their costs to the taxpayers and their potentially negative impacts on "work incentives." Welfare reform is often presented as a response to such concerns.

Although the discussions of poverty found in many traditional introductory texts raise important issues and questions that instructors may wish to address, the presentation of official poverty statistics with little discussion of their construction and limitations, the reliance on neoclassical theories of resource markets to explain poverty, and the lack of attention to gender, race, and class issues limits them to a Phase 2 treatment of the topic. Insights drawn from feminist economic thought, and resources drawn from the feminist economics literature, offer a great deal to instructors wishing to expand and broaden the discussion of poverty in their introductory economics courses.[6]

Feminist Insights

Feminist economics is grounded in a very different definition of economics, which establishes a much broader context for the discussion of poverty than is found in most introductory economics texts. Like institutional political economy, feminist economics defines its task as the study of social provisioning. Thus, the focus of economic inquiry shifts from individual choices made in response to scarcity to the processes through which societies secure the material goods necessary to maintain and reproduce themselves. This expands the boundaries of "economics" to include the provisioning activities of nonmarket institutions (such as the government and the family) and allows for a richer consideration of the role of social customs and values in economic processes.

In this context poverty is not an outcome that can be narrowly explained in terms of inappropriate individual choices and scarcity. The choices made by individuals are shaped and constrained by the social and economic institutions (such as families, labor markets, and governments) involved in the provisioning process and, therefore, must be studied in this context. Poverty is viewed in terms of the failure of the social and economic institutions responsible for social provisioning, not simply the failure of individuals to compete effectively.

Thus, when social provisioning is the focus of economic analysis, poverty becomes an important indicator of the success of the economic system and equity becomes an important social and economic goal. Feminist economics, therefore, questions the neoclassical notion of a fundamental trade-off between efficiency and equity and rejects the privileging of market efficiency over other goals. This broader emphasis also leads feminist economists to call for the use of a wider range of indicators and methodologies in the evaluation of economic outcomes and the assessment of economic well-being.

In addition, feminist economics challenges the neoclassical positive-normative dichotomy, arguing that all knowledge is socially constructed and reflects the values and biases of the individual researchers and cultures that produce it. Feminist economists argue that economic analyses that explicitly recognize the values they embody are more honest and objective than analyses that make claims of value-free neutrality. Consequently, issues such as poverty that are often seen to be too value-laden by traditional economists are viewed as legitimate areas of inquiry by feminist economists who accept that economic questions involve values and value judgments.

Like many other political economists, feminist economists also reject the neoclassical view that the government can and should exist outside of the economy. The government is viewed as an inherent part of the social provisioning process, defining and legitimizing the institutions and power relationships that shape economic outcomes. The relationship between the government and the rest of the economy is seen to be a complex and often contradictory one, with government policies acting to ameliorate social and economic problems at the same time that they support status quo power relationships. Feminists argue that the contradictory nature of government policy is particularly important in analyses of poverty and social welfare polices (see Abramovitz 1988; Gordon 1990).

Bringing feminist economic insights to the definition of the core concepts allows the topic of poverty to be introduced as a key issue much earlier in the introductory economics course, integrating it into the discussion of what the study of economics is all about. Establishing early in the course that poverty is an important and legitimate concern for economists provides a context for a much more detailed discussion of the topic. And, while the same types of questions concerning the measurement, extent, and causes of poverty can be addressed, a feminist economic perspective emphasizes different issues than traditional discussions of these questions.

The question of how poverty is defined and measured, for example, becomes a much more important topic when poverty is examined from a feminist economic perspective. Feminists have contributed a great deal to the critique of the official definition of poverty, focusing attention on the adequacy of the poverty thresholds themselves, rather than the income measures typically highlighted in traditional discussions of poverty. Feminist economists stress that the estimates of "minimum basic needs" that underlie the official poverty thresholds are inadequate for a variety of reasons, including the fact that the child care expenses required by many families to earn income are ignored (see Ruggles 1990; Renwick and Bergmann 1993; Folbre 1995; and Albelda and Folbre 1996). Thus, contrary to the critiques typically presented in introductory economics courses, feminist economic critiques raise the concern that the official poverty statistics actually underestimate U.S. poverty.

Providing a broader discussion of the critiques of the official definition of poverty not only provides students with more context for interpreting the official statistics, but also reinforces the notion that knowledge is socially constructed and that economic statistics are not "neutral facts." This discussion also provides a context for instructors to raise issues concerning the ways in which economists conduct their research, indicating, for example, the problems associated with an over reliance on official published data and the benefits of expanding our knowledge through other methods such as field work and case studies. In addition, students can be introduced to the other types of "social indicators" that are used by scholars in other disciplines to assess well-being and deprivation (see, e.g., Bronfenbrenner et al. 1996).

Even when the official definition and published data are used as the primary measures of poverty, it is possible to provide a much richer discussion of the nature and extent of poverty in the United States than is often offered in introductory courses.[7] In addition to the poverty rates for different groups, it may also be useful to consider the distribution of poverty (the share of the poverty population held by different groups), comparing the composition of the poverty population to the general population and examining how it has changed over time. The intensity of poverty, which can be measured by the "poverty gap" (the difference between a poverty threshold and the mean income of the population below that threshold) is another important indicator of poverty status.

From a feminist economic perspective it is particularly important for students to realize that the aggregate poverty statistics that are so often reported in newspapers, magazines, and textbooks hide a great deal of variation in the incidence, distribution, and intensity of poverty. The fact that poverty is borne disproportionately by different groups in society is critically important to understanding the nature of U.S. poverty and the relevance of recent policy changes. Feminist economists emphasize this point through the presentation of poverty statistics that are disaggregated in ways that reflect, as much as possible, gender, race and class differences (see Folbre 1995; Albelda and Folbre 1996; and Albelda and Tilly 1997).

Introducing students to a more complex and diverse set of poverty statistics provides them with a more realistic and honest picture of U.S. poverty. From the perspective of curricular transformation, however, the critical contribution of feminist economics is the insights it offers for ways to incorporate these differences into the discussion of the causes of poverty in a meaningful way. Instead of being noted and then ignored, as they typically are in introductory economics courses, gender, race and class differences need to become key elements in the discussion of the economic forces that result in poverty.

To date a great deal of feminist research on poverty has focused on the disproportionately high share of poor persons living in families maintained by women.[8] In the late 1970s and early 1980s feminist scholars sought to explain the rapid increase in the percentage of poor persons living in such families, a trend referred to as the "feminization of poverty." This new research on poverty argued that women were uniquely vulnerable to poverty and highlighted causes of poverty particularly related to gender (see Pearce 1978; Pearce 1983; Ehrenreich and Piven 1984; and Stallard, Ehrenreich, and Sklar 1983).

This research made important contributions to the literature on poverty, shifting the focus from the general operation of resource markets to issues concerning the economic status of women, such as changes in family structure, labor market discrimination and occupational segregation, and the structure and adequacy of welfare programs. This research was also criticized, however, for its primary focus on gender and its hypothesis that women are uniquely vulnerable to poverty. Critics argued that such a focus obscured the importance of race and class divisions, and thus, misrepresented the nature of poverty in many communities (see Burnham 1985; Malveaux 1985; and Sparr 1984).

Thus, introducing the concept of the "feminization of poverty" into introductory economics courses provides the opportunity to take an important step toward Phase 3. By recognizing that women constitute a substantial share of the poverty population in the United States and acknowledging that this requires rethinking our analyses of poverty to specifically address gender, course content moves beyond Phase 2, where women are simply added to the discussion, and begins to challenge the approaches typically used to examine poverty. Recognizing, and explicitly addressing, the importance of race and class as well as gender in the impoverishment of women is essential, however, in moving the discussion further toward Phase 4.

Recent work on poverty and welfare reform by feminist economists has a great deal to offer instructors working to achieve this goal. In *Glass Ceilings and Bottomless Pits* (1997), for example, Randy Albelda and Chris Tilly examine women's poverty in the context of the changing status of women more generally, paying close attention to gender, race and class relations.[9] They examine a variety of social and economic trends, as well as societal values and myths, that shape the economic reality of women. While the labor market is an important part of this discussion, the emphasis is on "glass ceilings" and "sticky floors," not individual choices and competitive outcomes. The recent welfare reform is examined in its historical context, illustrating the contentious and contradictory history of welfare programs in the United States. Albelda and Tilly also present an alternative vision of "real" welfare reform, emphasizing the need to "resolve the contradictions many women currently face" through reforms in child care, wages and jobs as well as income transfers. This illustrates very clearly how different understandings of the nature and causes of poverty lead to very different policy prescriptions.

Thus, introducing insights from feminist economics into the introductory economics course creates a context for a discussion of poverty that presents students with alternative theories and policies, and is multidisciplinary and multicultural in content. This represents a movement toward Phase 4, where course content reflects the increasing complexity of real world economies and policy debates. Such changes in content may also enhance efforts to broaden the pedagogical methods used in the introductory economics course by creating classroom environments more open to active and cooperative learning methods. For example, asking students to construct their own "minimum needs" budgets allows them to think about definitions of poverty in terms of their own economic realities and to explore the meanings of these realities with their peers. Assignments involving the collection, interpretation and presentation of various poverty statistics provide students with some experience "doing economics" and exploring the type of work many economists engage in. Obtaining more local information on poverty can be achieved through fieldwork assignments in the students' own communities, and community social service organizations may provide good environments for service learning projects. Encouraging students to engage these issues in conversations with their peers and in the context of their own communities is a crucial step in transforming economics courses into experiences that will be interesting and benefit students in their "real world" lives.

NOTES

1. Currently, over nine hundred universities and colleges offer introductory economics courses (Bartlett 1997, xii).

2. In August 1996 Bill Clinton fulfilled his 1992 campaign promise to "end welfare as we know it" by signing the Personal Responsibility and Work Opportunity Act, thus eliminating Aid to Families with Dependent Children (AFDC), the program designed primarily to aid poor, single-mother families, and replacing it the Temporary Assistance for Needy Families (TANF) block grant.

3. There is diversity among feminist economists whose different perspectives reflect a variety of different theoretical backgrounds in economics. The feminist economic perspective presented in this essay is grounded in the principles of institutional political economy (see Lewis 1995).

4. The discussion of core concepts presented here draws on earlier work (see Peterson 1995) focused more specifically on institutional economics.

5. Poverty data are reported for a variety of units of measurement, including persons, families, and households (see Folbre 1995, T5). This chapter uses the units of measurement reported in the sources cited.

6. Ferber and Nelson (1993) and Nelson (1996) provide very useful discussions of the principles of feminist economics.

7. A number of U.S. Census Bureau publications contain a variety of income and poverty statistics. The *State of Working America* book series is also a good source for poverty and income data (see Mishel, Bernstein, and Schmitt 1997). Good sources for information focused more specifically on women are *The American Woman* book series (see Costello and Krimgold 1996) and the various editions of Harrell Rodgers' books on poverty and single-mother families (see Rodgers 1996).

8. The U.S. Census refers to families headed by a single females as "female-headed families" or "families with female householders, no husband present" in its poverty and income data (see Folbre 1995, T5).

9. Folbre (1995), Albelda and Folbre (1996), Albelda and Tilly (1996), and Albelda (1996) also provide accessible discussions of poverty and/or welfare reform that would be very useful to instructors of introductory economics courses.

REFERENCES

Abramovitz, Mimi. 1988. *Regulating the Lives of Women*. Boston: South End Press.

Aerni, April L., Robin L. Bartlett, Margaret Lewis, KimMarie McGoldrick, and Jean Shackelford. 1999. "Toward Feminist Pedagogy in Economics." *Feminist Economics* 5(1): 29–44.

Albelda, Randy. 1996. "Farewell to Welfare: But Not to Poverty." *Dollars and Sense* (November–December): 16–29.

Albelda, Randy, and Chris Tilly. 1996. "Once upon a Time: A Brief History of Welfare." *Dollars and Sense* (November–December): 20–21.

———. 1997. *Glass Ceilings and Bottomless Pits*. Boston: South End Press.

Albelda, Randy, and Nancy Folbre. 1996. *The War on the Poor: A Defense Manual*. New York: New Press.

Bartlett, Robin. 1995. "Attracting 'Otherwise Bright Students' to Economics 101." *American Economic Review* 85 (May): 362–66.

———. 1997. *Introducing Race and Gender into Economics*. London: Routledge.

Bartlett, Robin, and Susan Feiner. 1992. "Balancing the Economics Curriculum: Content, Method, and Pedagogy." *American Economic Review* 82 (May): 559–64.

Bronfenbrenner, Urie, Peter McClelland, Elaine Wethington, Phyllis Moen, and Stephen Ceci. 1996. *The State of Americans*. New York: Free Press.

Burnham, Linda. 1985. "Has Poverty Been Feminized in Black America?" *Black Scholar* 16 (March–April): 14–24.

Colander, David. 1995. "Reform of Undergraduate Economics Education." In *Educating Economists*, ed. David Colander and Rueven Brenner, 231–41. Ann Arbor: University of Michigan Press.

Costello, Cynthia, and Barbara Kivimae Krimgold. 1996. *The American Women: 1996–1997*. New York: W. W. Norton.

Ehrenreich, Barbara, and Frances Fox Piven. 1984. "The Feminization of Poverty." *Dissent* 31 (spring): 162–70.

Feiner, Susan. 1994. *Race and Gender in the American Economy: Views from across the Spectrum.* Englewood Cliffs, NJ: Prentice-Hall.

Ferber, Marianne. 1995. "The Study of Economics: A Feminist Critique." *American Economic Review* 85 (May): 357–61.

Ferber, Marianne, and Julie Nelson, eds. 1993. *Beyond Economic Man: Feminist Theory and Economics.* Chicago: University of Chicago Press.

Folbre, Nancy. 1995. *The New Field Guide to the U.S. Economy: A Compact and Irreverent Guide to Economic Life in America.* New York: Free Press.

Gordon, Linda, ed. 1990. *Women, the State and Welfare.* Madison: University of Wisconsin Press.

Lewis, Margaret. 1995. "Breaking Down the Walls, Opening Up the Field: Situating the Economics Classroom as a Site for Social Action." *Journal of Economic Issues* 29 (June): 555–65.

Malveaux, Julianne. 1985. "The Economic Interests of Black and White Women: Are They Similar?" *Review of Black Political Economy* 14 (summer) : 5–27.

Mishel, Lawrence, Jared Bernstein, and John Schmitt. 1997. *The State of Working America: 1996–1997* Armonk, NY: M. E. Sharpe.

Nelson, Julie. 1996. *Feminism, Objectivity and Economics.* London: Routledge.

Pearce, Diana. 1978. "The Feminization of Poverty: Women, Work, and Welfare." *Urban and Social Change Review* 2(1–2): 28–36.

———. 1983. "The Feminization of Ghetto Poverty" *Society* 21 (November–December): 70–74.

Peterson, Janice. 1995. "For Whom? Institutional Economics and Distributional Issues in the Economics Classroom." *Journal of Economic Issues* 29 (June): 567–74.

Renwick, Trudi, and Barbara Bergmann. 1993. "A Budget-Based Definition of Poverty." *Journal of Human Resources* 28 (winter): 1–24.

Rodgers, Harrell. 1996. *Poor Women, Poor Families: American Poverty in the 1990s,* 3d ed. Armonk, NK: M. E. Sharpe.

Ruggles, Patricia. 1990. *Drawing the Line: Alternative Poverty Measures and Their Implications for Public Policy.* Washington DC: Urban Institute Press.

Sparr, Pamela. 1984. "Re-Evaluating Feminist Economics: 'Feminization of Poverty' Ignores Key Issues." *Dollars and Sense* (September): 12–14.

Stallard, Karin, Barabara Ehrenreich, and Holly Sklar. 1983. *Poverty in the American Dream: Women and Children First.* Boston: South End Press.

What Do My Students Need to Know?

Experiences with Developing a More Feminist "Principles of Macroeconomics" Course

April Laskey Aerni

I began teaching principles of macroeconomics fifteen years ago by lecturing on the standard list of macroeconomic topics that I had been exposed to during graduate studies. In addition to teaching principles, my department chair requested that I teach women in the economy. My experiences with this latter course and feminist theory informed my desire to change the principles of macroeconomics course. As I gained more knowledge in the field of feminist theory and more experience in the classroom I sought to integrate feminist pedagogy or a more inclusive curriculum into courses beyond women's studies. In this essay I discuss the changes I have made to the content of my principles of macroeconomics course after a decade of attempting to integrate more feminist/inclusive pedagogy.

Although my feminist studies had led me to desire a change in curriculum, I had trouble ascertaining what content to change; after all, what I had been taught must be all there was to macroeconomics. At first, although I did make some revisions to course content, they were of the "add women and stir" variety. More important, I began to revise the methodology and processes of teaching in my classroom. Indeed, as has been argued elsewhere in this book, this is a fundamental part of feminist or inclusive curriculum. In table 1 I provide an overview of the differences as I see them between feminist and economic methodology and pedagogy. For example, neoclassical economists have considered their models to be objective and value-free, while no feminist theorist would accept that as possible in any field. Since knowledge is constructed feminists recognize that it must be partly subjective and value laden. A researcher is always influenced by her or his frames of reference and experiences in setting agendas for what and how to study.

One might describe the process I began in changing my principles of macroeconomics class in terms of the Phase Theory presented in the first essay in this volume. The development of this course began in Phase 1 (The

Received Neoclassical Canon / Individual Learning) and moved toward more inclusive learning environments. In Phase 2 I experimented with many types of active learning techniques, incorporated numerous techniques for facilitating student discussion, and lectured less often. Further, I developed exercises that organized students into small groups and encouraged cooperation and taught the class as "writing intensive." Finally, I experimented with textbooks, non-textbooks, and videos.

This experimentation with different pedagogical strategies and learning environments included exercises developed to encourage students to apply economic concepts and models to the economy as well as to their lives. As I developed a list of reading assignments that would reinforce the application of economic concepts, I introduced related and overlapping issues from other disciplines such as history, sociology, and women's studies. A standard question at the end of each reading became "How does this economic concept affect your life?" My teaching became focused on showing the interconnections across disciplines and on critically evaluating existing economic models based on our individual and collective life experiences. Consistent with one of the processes of transforming the classroom discussed in the first essay in this book, my changes in teaching methodology developed into changes in content. Thus, what occurred in my classroom was a certain synergy between changes in the learning environment and course content.

TABLE 1.   Comparing Feminist Economics and Traditional Economics Methodology and Pedagogy

Feminist	Traditional
Methodology	
All knowledge is value laden, or subjective	Economic models are ethically neutral, or value free
Emphasis is on lived experience	Emphasis is on analytical reasoning
The personal is political	Math is particularly useful
Behavior is partly socially, culturally determined; behavior variables must be analyzed in context	Assume autonomous human behavior; ceteris paribus conditions hold
Emphasis is on cooperation, empowerment, and production for use	Emphasis is on competition, control, and production for exchange
Commitment to social/political change	Politically neutral
Pedagogy	
Focus on practice and process	Focus on product or content
Metaphor-teaching as midwifery	Metaphor-teaching as banking
Students are knowers and creators of knowledge	Knowledge is quantifiable; students are passive
Teachers expand the limits of discourse	Teachers dispense knowledge
Discussion	Lecture

I found myself paying more and more attention to the needs of my students and their experiences and asking myself questions such as: What did they need to know? What tools could they use to analyze their experiences and make more informed decisions about their lives and work? What would help them read and understand business and economic news and recognize its importance in their lives? How could they become better citizens and voters? How could/should they interpret proposed economic policies? What knowledge would empower them? As I searched for answers to these questions, a natural shift in my course content continued to occur.

My Students

Nazareth College is a small residential liberal arts college in Rochester, New York, with both bachelor's and master's programs. I teach primarily undergraduates. All undergraduates are required to take a social science course as part of their general education requirements, and principles of macroeconomics (ECO 101) is one course that satisfies this requirement. Additionally, each student is required to take three "writing-intensive" courses, and thus I periodically teach ECO 101 in a way to satisfy this requirement. Students in some majors, including social work and business, are required to take ECO 101 as part of their major.

About 70 percent of the undergraduate student body (fourteen hundred full-time equivalent) at Nazareth is female. A slightly lower percentage, about 60 percent, of my principles students are female. The majority of students are Catholic and grew up within a two-hour drive of the school. Less than 10 percent of students are minority, either African, African-American, or Native American.

I teach small classes of between twenty to forty students. Approximately a third of the students in a typical principles of macroeconomics class will never take another economics course. Most of the rest, primarily business students, will take three or four more economics classes. About ten to sixteen students at any time are majoring in economics. About every other year we have one economics major who chooses to go to graduate school in economics. Our other graduating economics majors will work or pursue graduate study in other areas such as business or law. Although the typical content of a principles of macroeconomics course may benefit some students (especially those who want a Ph.D. degree in economics), it is likely not to be as useful to students who take only a few economics classes. This motivated me to develop the class as suggested earlier.

Students have responded well to changes in my classes at least as judged by uniformly good teaching evaluations by students, by the criteria of full classrooms, and by comments made to me. One of my favorites has always been from those students who tell me long after they have taken my course that now they read the business and economics section of their newspaper. In addition, some of my colleagues steer their advisees who are taking only one economics class into my sections.

Choice of Text

One of the first content-related changes that I made was the choice of text. Since my graduate school days, I had been aware that economics texts are heavily gendered. One such example is found in Heilbroner's history of economic thought text, *The Worldly Philosophers*, which begins as follows:

> This is a book about a handful of men with a curious claim to fame. By all the rules of schoolboy history books, they were nonentities: they commanded no armies, sent no men to their deaths, ruled no empires, took little part in history-making decisions. . . . Yet . . . they shaped and swayed men's minds. And because he who enlists a man's mind yields a power greater than the sword or the scepter, these men shaped and swayed the world. . . . Who are these men? We know them as the Great Economists. (Heilbroner 1986, 13)

Further reinforcing my decision to not adopt a traditional principles text was the comment from a professor in my graduate program: "If you know everything in Samuelson, you'll do fine on your comps." Clearly, if Samuelson was a good text to use as a study guide for Ph.D. comprehensive exams, then it was not a good choice to introduce my students to the field of economics. Although switching from the Samuelson text was fairly simple, switching away from the standard topical material for a principles of macroeconomics course was not. In fact, most texts were modeled on the Samuelson text.

Upon further investigation into the nature of principles texts, I discovered that this bias was prevalent in the discipline. Feiner and Morgan analyzed twenty-one introductory economics texts and found that "the number of pages that have even a passing reference to economic topics of salience to women and minorities is remarkably small" (Feiner and Morgan 1987, 160). The twenty-one texts had an average of 10.38 pages out of 810 average total number of pages or 1.34 percent referring to women and/ or minorities. Coverage of these issues in the twenty-one texts ranged from two to twenty-two pages. Clearly, the issues of relevance to women and minorities were minimized.

Over the years I have tried various texts and more recently often use texts not formally written for students, such as *The Age of Diminishing Expectations* by Paul Krugman and *The New Field Guide to the U.S. Economy* by Nancy Folbre and the Center for Popular Economics. These books are oriented to readers other than professional economists and are therefore less theoretical, mathematical, and graphical than a standard principles text. In addition, the content of these books fits with my desire to present more material on issues of class, gender, and race. Finally, the two books have gotten high marks from my students as readable and useful to them.

Objectives and Topics

In order to illustrate how my course objectives and content might differ as a result of this more inclusive approach, I compared my syllabus with that of a colleague's who teaches at Nazareth College. My colleague is also a Ph.D. economist but one who uses a more traditional approach to teaching principles of macroeconomics. The course objective on his syllabus for this course is as follows.

> Students will be expected to master the ability to use the analysis of macroeconomics as a method of inquiry. Students should be able to analyze situations and predict economic outcomes. Students should be able to recognize underlying economic relations between such groups as households, businesses, governments, and foreign sectors on the topics of inflation, unemployment, taxes, government spending, and money. Students should be able to accomplish the above verbally, algebraically, and graphically.

The course objective on my syllabus is a little different.

> This course will help you to learn economic terms and to read and interpret economic and business news in newspapers, magazines, and on TV. As we discuss unemployment, inflation, GDP, the role of money, taxes, government spending, and fiscal and monetary policies, you will learn to understand and evaluate economic policies of our government as well as proposed policies of politicians, thus allowing

you to participate more effectively in voting, public, and civic life. In addition, you may apply many of these basic economic ideas in your own life to analyze your personal and work experiences.

Clearly, even though we cover many of the same topics, we have different approaches. I stress personal experiences while he stresses analysis and math. Thus, it would follow that the detailed course content would also differ. Table 2 provides a listing of the detailed topics covered for each of these different approaches to the principles of macroeconomics course.

To describe these content changes in greater detail, I have placed them into four categories: content with changed emphasis; new content; content

TABLE 2.   Comparing Course Outlines

My Feminist Outline	His Outline

1. Introduction
    Definitions of *economics, macro, macroeconomic goals, business cycles, recession,* and *expansion,* plus a simplified explanation of business cycles, that is, total spending, production, employment, income, and prices
	1. Introduction
	    Economics: the science of scarcity; basic economic concepts and analysis. Includes society's need to make decisions concerning scarce resources, the production possibilities of society, efficiency in production and allocation, markets, nonprice factors on supply and demand, distribution and the private sector

2. Productivity, GDP, savings, and investment	

3. Income distribution
    Issues, trends, poverty
	2. Macroeconomy: basics
	    Role of public sector, measuring economies, productivity and growth, unemployment and inflation, short-run models, aggregate supply and demand

4. Employment and unemployment Measurement, types, consequences	
5. Supply and demand (basic micro)	3. Macroeconomy: models continued Stability, instability, and fiscal policy; relationships, aggregate expenditure, income, and prices, AD and AS, criticisms; self-correcting economy
6. Inflation, money, and monetary policy Measurement CPI, money, etc. consequences of inflation, Federal Reserve System, role of banks	

7. U.S. government fiscal policy
    Taxes, government spending, budget deficits
	4. Macroeconomic policy
	    Fiscal and monetary policy, money and banking, and the deficit

8. United States in the world economy (if time in the semester permits)	

left out or subtracted; and content that remains basically unchanged. These changes are not necessarily unique to me or to feminist economists, as others throughout the discipline have identified some of the same critiques that these changes were based on. In addition, those outside the discipline (e.g., environmentalists) have also contributed to changes I have made, as described later. Thus, although I do not claim all of these changes as solely feminist, the feminist approach greatly informed my application of these changes to my principles of macroeconomics course.

Content with Changed Emphasis

One of the more critical changes I have made relies on the definition of economics. For example, a related professional debate focuses on the difference between choice and provisioning. I provide my students with the standard definition, "Economics is the study of choices made by people who are faced with scarcity" (O'Sullivan and Sheffrin 1998, 2). I also give students Alfred Marshall's definition, "Economics is a study of mankind [sic] in the ordinary business of life; it examines that part of individual and social action which is most closely connected with the attainment and with the use of the material requisites of wellbeing" (Marshall 1910, 1). Finally, I provide Julie Nelson's feminist definition, that economics is "centrally concerned with the study of how humans, in interaction with each other and the environment, provide for their own survival and health" (Nelson 1993, 34). Nelson suggests defining economics as the study of *provisioning* rather than the study of *choice.* After providing these three definitions, the class participates in a discussion of what these very different definitions imply for economics.

Other topics in which I have changed my emphasis include gross domestic product (GDP), inflation, and unemployment. In presenting the concept of GDP, I discuss feminist and environmentalist critiques of the tools used to measure the economy's output. Students read a variety of perspectives, and I focus on the implications of these critiques as opposed to the measurement process itself. Inflation is another topic on which I spend more time discussing the impacts than calculations measuring inflation. I emphasize that financial asset values are affected by inflation, that those holding these assets are impacted in many ways, and we discuss how specific policies are influenced by financial markets and institutions. As a final example of the emphasis change on typical course content, we spend time in class discussing the differences in employment and unemployment by race, gender, ethnicity, and age.

New Content

One subject that is often relegated to limited coverage in the traditional principles of macroeconomics course is income distribution. Since this topic provides an excellent venue for incorporating feminist discussion, I include two to three weeks of discussion on this topic. Although my motive for expanding the coverage of this topic originated in feminist theory, it can also be traced back to the early principles text. For example, Alfred Marshall started his lengthy discussion of income distribution in the third chapter of his text published in 1910. Thus, it appears that this topic has only been neglected in the latter twentieth century.

Another area of additional coverage is a discussion detailing the use of data to measure economic variables. I address who collects the data, how is it collected, why it is collected, and what questions the agency asks when gathering data via a survey. I then require students to read different perspectives on interpreting data and test their own abilities at analyzing data.

Currently, I allocate more time in class to the topic of productivity than I used to, following Krugman's contention that productivity in an economy determines the long-run standard of living of its citizens. I discuss some of the theories about productivity growth and its slowdown starting in the 1970s in the United States. This is a typical example of my focus on the longer-term economy as well as the shorter term.

Content Left Out or Subtracted

The primary topic I no longer cover is the presentation of a formal model of the equilibrium level of national income, such as that via an aggregate supply and demand or IS/LM models. And, while I do not present the Keynesian neoclassical, supply-side, monetarist, or rational expectations models as such, I do make it clear to students that there are different approaches to analyzing an economy and present conclusions of different approaches. I have also left out production possibility frontier, marginal propensities to save and consume, and the multiplier (derived from a formal model).

In general, formal models, graphs, and math seem to hinder rather than aid in my students' understanding of economics. For example, graphs are usually presented as a shorthand version of the more complicated models used by Ph.D. economists. Thus, since most of my students do not intend to continue in economics beyond college, a graphical presentation is not necessary. In addition, since most of my students are not accustomed to graphs, their use in the classroom takes a great deal of time mastering the technique as opposed to comprehending the underlying economic concept. I have found this to be true for formal models and mathematical models as well.

Content That Is Basically Unchanged

Despite all these changes I have made in the curriculum, there are many topics that remain unchanged, including a discussion of money, monetary policy, government revenues, taxes, and fiscal policy as well as supply and demand. After all, I am a traditionally trained Ph.D. economist as well as a feminist and find much that is useful in that tradition.

Conclusion

My overall goal in teaching is to produce more thoughtful students using the notion of *thoughtfulness* as developed by the philosopher, Hannah Arendt. For Arendt the word thoughtful connoted two things: (1) careful, reasoned thinking, that is, the analytic mode of knowing; and (2) consideration or mindfulness of others, that is, the empathic mode of knowing. Arendt used the word first in reporting on the trial of Nazi Adolf Eichmann. She observed he was an ordinary man who was reasonably intelligent; his complicity in an evil activity was a function of his thoughtlessness. In this definition, he had no empathic mode of knowing (Arendt 1963).

Instructing in careful, reasoned, analytically thinking mode has always been a part of formal education. Teaching consideration or mindfulness of others is less common. In changing my course I have tried to add this component to the traditional macroeconomics presentation. For example, in discussing unemployment, I try to go beyond the theories and the list of types to stories, usually from students, about their own or familial experiences with unemployment. Lacking an understanding of the realities of being unemployed makes it all too easy for students and policymakers to consider the unemployed as voluntarily out of a job and to pursue actions that may actually lead to more unemployment in the short run. Mindfulness, or empathic knowing, really means knowing penetrated with concern. To the extent I can, I emphasize empathic knowing of economies and consider inclusive (feminist) pedagogy to be supportive of this.

For me feminist pedagogy and inclusive curriculum is integrally bound up with my attempts to teach mindfulness of others. The following list is a summary of what I attempt to do in my classes following a feminist or more inclusive curriculum.

Teach knowledge of one's own and of other cultures and worldviews ("other" points of view).

Help students "construct" knowledge that includes alternative points of view.

Study race, gender, ethnicity, and so on as structures or institutions of human relationships (power and oppression).

Analyze troublesome or contentious issues of public discourse, aiming toward clarity in careful reasoned thinking and in mindfulness of others (or at least tolerance and civility).

Examine and revise the standards of one's own discipline, recognizing that standards have been set in most disciplines and across disciplines predominately by white, European, wealthy men; that this is systematic and not necessarily due to any individual; and that these standards have functioned, whether deliberately or not, partly to exclude women, blacks, and other groups and to exclude certain ideas.

Integrate the way we teach with the nature or content of what we teach, recognizing that different people and groups are likely to have different learning styles and approaches to knowledge.

Demonstrate and practice mindfulness and consideration of others in the classroom, using the classroom itself and the experiences of students and teacher as a basis for learning.

REFERENCES

Arendt, Hannah. 1994 [1963]. *Eichmann in Jerusalem: A Report on the Banality of Evil.* New York: Penguin Books.

———. 1958. *The Human Condition.* Chicago: University of Chicago Press.

———. 1951. *The Origins of Totalitarianism.* New York: Harvest/HBJ Books.

Bartlett, Robin, and Susan Feiner. 1992. "Balancing the Economics Curriculum: Content, Method, and Pedagogy." *American Economic Review* 82(5): 559–64.

Bergmann, Barbara. 1987. "The Task of a Feminist Economics: A More Equitable Future." In *The Impact of Feminist Research in the Academy,* ed. Christie Farnham. Bloomington: Indiana University Press.

———. 1986. *The Economic Emergence of Women.* New York: Basic Books.

Blau, Francine, and Marianne Ferber. 1986. *The Economics of Women, Men, and Work.* Englewood Cliffs, NJ: Prentice-Hall.

Feiner, Susan, and B. Morgan. 1987. "Women and Minorities in Introductory Economics Textbooks: 1974 to 1984." *Journal of Economic Education* 10 (fall): 376–92.

Feiner, Susan, and Bruce Roberts. 1990. "Hidden by the Invisible Hand: Neoclassical Economic Theory and the Textbook Treatment of Race and Gender." *Gender and Society* 4 (June): 159–81.

Ferber, Marianne. 1990. "Gender and the Study of Economics." In *The Principles of Economics Course: A Handbook for Instructors,* ed. Phillip Saunders and William Walstad, chap. 6. New York: McGraw-Hill.

Folbre, Nancy, and the Center for Popular Economics. 1995. *The New Field Guide to the U.S. Economy.* Boston: New Press.

Heilbroner, Robert. 1986. *The Worldly Philosophers: The Lives, Times and Ideas of the Great Economic Thinkers.* 6th ed. New York: Simon and Schuster.

Krugman, Paul. 1997. *The Age of Diminished Expectations.* 3d ed. Cambridge: MIT Press.

Marshall, Alfred. 1910. *Principles of Economics.* 6th ed. London: Macmillan.

Nelson, Julie. 1996. *Feminism, Objectivity, and Economics.* New York: Routledge.

Nelson, Julie, and Marianne Ferber, eds. 1993. *Beyond Economic Man: Feminist Theory and Economics.* Chicago: University of Chicago Press.

O'Sullivan, Arthur, and Steven Sheffrin. 1998. *Economics: Principles and Tools.* Englewood Cliffs, NJ: Prentice-Hall.

Samuelson, Paul. 1973. *Economics.* 9th ed. New York: McGraw-Hill.

Sandler, Bernice, and Roberta Hall. 1982. "The Classroom Climate: A Chilly One for Women?" Washington, DC: Project for the Status and Education of Women, Association of American Colleges.

Saunders, Phillip, and William Walstad. 1990. *The Principles of Economics Course: A Handbook for Instructors.* New York: McGraw-Hill.

Shackelford, Jean. 1992. "Feminist Pedagogy: A Means for Bringing Critical Thinking and Creativity to the Economics Classroom." *American Economic Review* 82(2): 570–76.

Waring, Marilyn. 1988. *If Women Counted: A New Feminist Economics.* San Francisco: Harper and Row.

Weiler, Kathleen. 1988. *Women Teaching for Change: Gender, Class, and Power.* Boston: Bergin and Harvey.

The Economics
of Stereotyping

Emily P. Hoffman

This essay offers an example of how the economics of stereotyping can be presented in a way that can broaden course
content and use some of the teaching methods advocated by feminist pedagogy. The stereotyping of occupations as male or female is a root cause of a
major problem: women consistently receiving lower pay than men. While any
stereotyping is invidious, the following material will generally refer to stereotyping by gender; racial (or other) stereotyping has similar reasoning.

While all possible solutions to the problem of pay disparity are obviously of great interest to feminist economists, two possible policies stand
out: encouraging and enabling women to enter better-paying male occupations; and/or supporting the effective implementation of comparable worth.
The discussion that follows shows how a more feminist approach can
broaden the usual neoclassical analysis of labor market discrimination.

Most of the material about pay differentials in "introductory" level
courses starts with a discussion of discrimination. There is very little, if any,
discussion about the *source* of this discrimination. Expanding the usual
presentation to include stereotyping as a cause of discrimination allows the
discussion to move beyond the standard neoclassical canon of Phase 1
content (as described in the first essay of this volume), which ignores
women and minorities. By moving on to Phase 2, in which women and
minorities are included in the discussion, stereotyping can be developed as a
principal cause of discrimination, and the link to affirmative action policies
can be presented. In developing the analysis to be consistent with a Phase 3
classroom, demand and supply models, as well as production possibilities
frontiers, can be challenged and reformulated to take account of the impact
of stereotyping.

As a method of moving the classroom discussion beyond the Phase 1
learning environment, a class survey could be conducted to discover the
stereotypes that are held by many students. Nontraditional, older, and activist students are more likely to have personal experiences that have molded
(or, hopefully, vitiated) their stereotypes. One goal of this exercise would
include identifying and challenging student held stereotypes, clearly moving
beyond a Phase 1 learning environment. Other projects could be designed to

find out whether the students' majors, part-time or summer jobs, and planned future occupations are gender (and/or race) segregated. Such a survey could also include questions considering why students have chosen their majors and their planned jobs and/or careers.

This exercise could then be extended beyond the students' immediate experiences by breaking the class into groups and having each group locate evidence pertaining to one of the following topics: whether their college majors are gender segregated, using either your college's data or national data; and whether their desired occupations are similarly segregated by using alumni data or national data. Students could then link these segregation data to reported mean or median wages, and a discussion regarding the implications of this could begin. Such a discussion should focus on examples, theories, and implications of the economic issues related to stereotyping. Examples of some of the points that this discussion could elucidate follow.

Stereotyping is the assumption that every member of some group has characteristics generally attributed to that group. A common stereotype is, for instance, "All women will get pregnant and quit their jobs." Prejudice, which is the precursor of discrimination, is having a negative *opinion* about a group of people because of a dislike of one or more of these perceived stereotypical characteristics. Discrimination is *action* directed by such prejudice; it represents disparate treatment of a person based solely on their real or imagined membership in a group of people considered to be "different," such as women, African Americans, Hispanics, Jews, Catholics, disabled people, lesbians, gays, old people, short people, fat people, and so forth. The classic neoclassical references on stereotyping as a motivation for discrimination are Kenneth Arrow's essays (1972) on statistical discrimination.

Treating people differently because it is *assumed* that they will have the stereotypical characteristics that a group is *believed* to have is both ethically repugnant and economically inefficient. The basic cause of the economic inefficiency that results from discrimination is that a valuable resource—that person's contribution to the production of goods and/or services—is underutilized, therefore limiting output. By arbitrarily excluding groups from the labor pool, the employer's potential labor force is unnecessarily limited, resulting in higher labor costs and lower productivity.

The seeds of stereotyping can be planted very early in an individual's life. Giving train sets to boys and tea sets to girls is an example of this. This gender stereotyping is reinforced when teachers treat males and females differently in the classroom, such as calling more frequently on male students, providing different types and extent of feedback to male and female students, and acknowledging male but not female accomplishments. Bernice

Sandler and others (1996) has characterized this condition as a "chilly classroom climate" for female students.

Stereotyping can limit an individual's choice of field and amount of education, which then limits their career choice possibilities. An example is societal stereotyping based on the belief that some jobs are more "appropriate" for certain groups; for example, nurses should be females, while carpenters should be males. Also, stereotyping by employers limits entry into particular careers and causes disparate on-the-job treatment and training opportunities, thereby affecting ultimate career success.

Such stereotyping is a major cause of occupational segregation, with males and females concentrated in different occupations. Occupational segregation by gender should be suspected if the proportion of women in a particular occupation differed greatly from the proportion women constitute of the entire U.S. labor force (currently about 46 percent). As can be seen in table 1, this is frequently the case. Women workers are concentrated in "pink-collar" service and support jobs, while they are almost absent from "blue-collar" mechanical trades jobs. Note, however, that personal preferences and/or talents may explain many individual cases of occupational segregation.

As an example of stereotyping leading to occupational segregation at the job entry level, assume that equally qualified males and females apply for jobs at a bank, but the women are hired as tellers, and the men are hired as management trainees. They are steered into different jobs because of the stereotype that females will have shorter job tenure (leaving for "family" reasons), and are thus not worth much investment in on-the-job training by the firm. Even if male and female tellers receive identical wages and male and female management trainees receive identical salaries, occupational discrimination is present because females and males are "steered" to different job classifications.

Stereotyping can also lead to occupational segregation at top management levels if it leads to arbitrary limitation of the candidate pool for promotion. A possible cause of this would be if the typical middle-aged, WASP (White Anglo-Saxon Protestant), male top executives of large corporations believe that people unlike themselves are less qualified for high positions. Many women and minorities believe they are faced with this unvoiced bias, which creates a "glass ceiling" that prevents them from reaching the upper levels of the business world.

The fact that stereotyping, which leads to discrimination, causes economic inefficiency can be illustrated in the neoclassical framework via a production possibilities frontier diagram. Students can identify the opportunity cost of discrimination as the potential output lost from national output

TABLE 1. Rank Percentages of Women in Highly Segregated Occupations in 1997

Detailed Occupation	Total	White	Black	Hispanic
Correspondence clerks	100.0	66.7	16.7	0.0
Secretaries	98.5	87.6	8.4	6.3
Family child care providers	98.2	85.2	10.9	11.1
Dental hygienists	98.1	96.3	1.9	1.9
Teachers, prekindergarten and kindergarten	97.7	83.4	13.1	9.2
Receptionists	96.5	85.7	8.3	9.3
Dental assistants	96.5	87.0	6.1	10.4
Early childhood teacher's assistants	95.6	76.9	16.4	10.2
Stenographers	95.2	88.5	5.8	3.8
Health record technologists and technicians	94.4	83.3	11.1	0.0
Typists	94.4	73.3	16.2	9.0
Licensed practical nurses	94.1	77.5	14.0	5.1
Billing clerks	93.8	77.6	11.8	5.0
Registered nurses	93.5	79.8	7.9	2.5
Teachers' aides	93.1	77.4	13.6	11.6
Payroll and timekeeping clerks	92.9	80.6	9.7	10.3
Bookkeepers, accounting, and auditing clerks	92.3	84.1	5.2	5.0
Billing, posting, and calculating machine operators	91.8	80.6	8.2	9.2
Dressmakers	91.0	71.9	9.0	9.0
Hairdressers and cosmetologists	90.4	75.0	9.2	8.2
Bank tellers	90.1	77.1	9.0	7.4
Supervisors, farmworkers	2.9	2.9	0.0	0.0
Water and sewage treatment plant operators	2.9	2.9	0.0	0.0
Power plant operators	2.6	2.6	2.6	0.0
Cabinet makers and bench carpenters	2.5	2.5	0.0	0.0
Crane and tower operators	2.4	1.2	0.0	0.0
Supervisors, n.e.c.	2.3	2.3	0.0	0.3
Glaziers	2.3	2.3	0.0	0.0
Concrete and terrazzo finishers	2.2	2.2	0.0	1.1
Construction trades, n.e.c.	2.2	1.7	0.0	0.0
Plasterers	2.1	2.1	0.0	0.0
Pest control	2.0	0.0	2.0	0.0
Drywall installers	1.9	1.9	0.0	0.0
Electricians	1.9	1.4	0.4	0.0
Carpet installers	1.7	1.7	0.0	0.0
Carpenters	1.6	1.4	0.1	0.1
Plumbers, pipefitters, and steamfitters	1.5	1.5	0.0	0.0
Grader, dozer, and scraper operators	1.5	1.5	0.0	0.0
Operating engineers	1.3	1.3	0.0	0.0
Excavating and loading machine operators	1.0	1.0	0.0	0.0
Roofers	1.0	0.5	0.0	0.0
Electrical power installers and repairers	0.9	0.9	0.0	0.0
Tool and die makers	0.8	0.8	0.0	0.0
Airplane pilots and navigators	0.8	0.8	0.0	0.0
Brickmasons and stonemasons	0.5	0.5	0.0	0.0

Note: n.e.c. = not elsewhere classified

(gross domestic product) because all groups in the labor market were not utilized to their full potential.

Another example of the implications of stereotyping that expands the use of the neoclassical tools of supply and demand is Barbara Bergmann's (1971) "crowding" theory, which posits that women (and/or blacks) are discouraged by "social custom" or outright discrimination, from entering male (and/or white) dominated "prestige" occupations, and thus are forced into female (and/or black) dominated "menial" occupations. A pair of demand-supply diagrams can be used to illustrate this crowding (excessive supply) effect in the labor market. In the prestige labor market the decreased supply of workers is shown as a leftward shift of the labor supply curve, resulting in fewer workers being hired but at a higher wage. In the menial labor market the increased supply (crowding) of workers causes the labor supply curve to be shifted to the right, resulting in more workers being hired but at a lower wage. Therefore, wages are depressed in the crowded (female or black) labor market relative to the uncrowded (male or white) labor market.

This essay provides an example of the use of stereotyping as a cause of economic discrimination and therefore has the potential to help move toward feminist pedagogy in the economics classroom. The use of student experiences and group work also moves the classroom toward a Phase 2 learning environment. Additionally, the very nature of the discussion of stereotyping encourages expansion beyond the standard neoclassical course content into Phase 2. This essay thus provides a glimpse into what might occur if we move our discussions of discrimination beyond what is typically covered in a principles course. In order to move further toward a feminist pedagogy, much more needs to be accomplished. Examples of this might include: having students research specific discrimination lawsuits, interviewing employers and employees, and developing lists of what is left out of the simplified neoclassical presentation of discrimination.

REFERENCES

Aerni, April L., Robin Bartlett, Meg Lewis, KimMarie McGoldrick, and Jean Shackelford. 1999. "Toward Feminist Pedagogy in Economics." *Feminist Economics*, 5(1): 29–44.

Arrow, Kenneth. 1972. "Models of Job Discrimination." and "Some Mathematical Models of Race in the Labor Market." In *Racial Discrimination in Economic Life*, ed. A. H. Pascal, 83–102, 187–204. Lexington, MA: Lexington Books.

Bergmann, Barbara. 1974. "Occupational Segregation, Wages and Profits When Employers Discriminate by Race or Sex." *Eastern Economic Journal* 1 (April–July): 103–10.

Sandler, Bernice, Lisa Silverberg, and Roberta Hall. 1996. *The Chilly Classroom Climate: A Guide to Improve the Education of Women.* Washington, DC: National Association for Women in Education.

U. S. Department of Labor. 1998. *Employment and Earnings. Household Data Annual Averages,* table 11, "Employed persons by detailed occupation, sex, race, and Hispanic origin." January. <http://stats.bls.gov>.

The Scope of Microeconomics

Implications for Economic Education

Myra H. Strober

In the wake of a multitude of national and state reports on the sorry state of American education, numerous state legislatures have enacted laws toughening the high school curriculum. They have been persuaded by the human capital argument that improved education will enhance American productivity and our international competitive position. One popular reform has been to introduce a mandatory secondary school course in economics.

It is ironic that at the same time that legislators and state departments of education are becoming enthusiastic about teaching economics to high school students, economists are becoming more critical of their discipline. The combination of legislative zeal and professional soul-searching sets up an interesting question: What is it that should be taught in secondary school economics courses?

The answer to this question is, unfortunately (or perhaps fortunately) not solely in the hands of economists. Decker Walker (1999) contends that curriculum policy making, particularly in the American context, is fundamentally political, not technical. It is useful for economists to recall this admonition as we, the technicians, suggest modifications to the economics course content, especially because political, or nontechnical, interest in the economics curriculum is perhaps even greater than in other subjects. Businesses, unions, and government all have an unusually high stake in what students are taught about our economy.

Walker argues that to be effective in curriculum policy-making, one must build what he calls a policy-shaping community, with leaders, public support, political will, and long-term sustained efforts. He points to the Joint Council on Economic Education as an innovative and instructive example of such a policy-shaping community.

If Walker is right, despite the highly politicized context of curriculum policy-making in economics, economists may in fact have an opportunity, through the offices of the Joint Council, to influence curriculum content. This essay represents one economist's views on how several aspects of the microeconomics curriculum should be changed to better reflect new thinking and new uncertainties in economics. I also discuss my views on the goals of teaching economics to precollege students. The paper does not have political "palatability" as one of its objectives. On the other hand, like all economics, it is inevitably political. I tell it as I see it, assuming that others, including other economists, will bring in their own political considerations soon enough.

The microeconomics section of the Joint Council's *Framework* deals with six topics: markets and prices, supply and demand, competition and market structure, income distribution, market failures, and the role of government. My comments here are certainly not a complete catalogue of criticisms on theses topics. For more exhaustive critiques the reader is referred to Ward 1972, Thurow 1983, and McCloskey 1985. Rather, my analysis is confined to three themes.

My criticism of the *Framework* is, in the first instance, a criticism of several of the assumptions underlying microeconomic theory: that human beings are rational and maximizing; that efficiency is "good" because it produces greater welfare; that consumers and workers are hedonistic; that welfare is equivalent to, or at least approximated by, income; and that consumers and workers are atomistic and exhibit constant tastes. Despite the conviction by some that economics is a "value-free" science, these assumptions reflect a very particular set of values that, as we shall see, strongly color and limit economic analysis. To be fair to students and to maintain their credibility, the authors of the *Framework* and its offspring curricula need to address squarely these assumptions and their consequences.

The second line of reproof has to do with the inclusion of additional topics in the *Framework*. I would like to see incorporated into the curriculum a discussion of the nonmarket sector, particularly households and families, more on labor markets and the processes of occupational choices and attainments, and more on income distribution.

Finally, I would like to change the tone of the *Framework* (and, by implication, the tone of the discipline itself). I deal with this issue in the final section of the essay, on the goals I would like to achieve in teaching microeconomics to precollege students. In formulating the *Framework* and in teaching economics, I would like us to convey a sense of modesty about the accomplishments and abilities of economic theory and analysis, portraying the economics not as a "showpiece," marveling at its own cleverness, but as an unfinished social science, struggling to find answers and inviting the participation of students in that effort. I would also like us to put a sense of caring into the *Framework*. I want students who study economics to come away not simply with an ability to analyze but with an ability to care, to feel deeply the excitement and pathos of trying to meet human wants with scarce resources.

Challenges to the Assumptions Underlying Microeconomics Concepts

Rationality, Maximization, and Efficiency

Although the *Framework* has no specific discussion of how consumer demand curves or labor supply curves are generated, the underlying neoclassical assumptions about these matters are implicit. A simplified exposition of these assumptions should be presented and critiqued in the *Framework* so that students understand both the strengths and the weaknesses of economic analysis.

Human rationality in decision making (if not in all endeavors) is a fundamental maxim of economic theory. So is the assumption that, in making choices, the goal of human beings is to maximize their welfare, that is, their well-being or happiness. The value of efficiency, producing the greatest output with the least costly inputs, follows directly from the assumptions of rationality and maximization. If, indeed, people are rational in their decision making and if they seek to maximize their happiness through rational decision making, then they will place great value on efficiency—in their own households, at their workplaces, and at the places that provide their goods and services.

Many of the criticisms of the rationality assumption are too well-known, though generally disregarded, to review here (see, e.g., Ward 1972; and Thurow 1983), yet some recent, extremely interesting work by psychologists Amos Tversky and Daniel Kahneman (1981) has been less well popularized among economists. Tversky and Kahneman's findings call into question two of the fundamental requirements of rationality: consistency and coherence. Consider one of their experiments. Two groups of students are asked to state their preferences between two possible programs to prepare for an outbreak of disease. The first group of students is told that, if Program A is adopted, two hundred people will be saved; if Program B is adopted, there is a one-third probability that six hundred people will be saved and a two-thirds probability that no people will be saved. The second group is given precisely the same choice but framed in different language. They are told that, if Program C is adopted, four hundred people will die; if Program D is adopted, there is a one-third probability that nobody will die and a two-thirds probability that six hundred people will die.

In the first group (the choice between A and B), where the problem was framed as a choice about the number of lives saved, the majority (72 percent) was risk averse, choosing A. In the second group, where the emphasis was on the number of likely deaths, the certain death of four hundred was less acceptable than the two-thirds chance of six hundred deaths. The majority (78 percent) chose Program D.

Not only students shift from risk aversion to risk taking when the framing of a problem is changed. Tversky and Kahneman have noticed the same kind of behavior among several groups of respondents, including university faculty and physicians (1981, 453). Their findings have important implications for the rationality assumption. If a mere change in the wording of a choice set so drastically changes the decisions made, how can we continue with equanimity to postulate that consumers know their own minds?

The assumption of rationality is brought into further question when it is combined with the assumption of welfare maximization. Is it the goal of most people, most of the time, to maximize their welfare? Economists have answered these questions by insisting that they don't need to be answered. The theory of revealed preference argues that the economist need not know the underlying elements of a consumer's preference function: that by watching the consumer in the market and by assuming consumer rationality and market competition the consumer's preferences are "revealed" to the observer, who then may conclude that the consumer has maximized his or her "welfare."

In his theory of the family Gary Becker (1981) similarly fails to specify the arguments of the household utility function, arguing that it doesn't matter what the specific arguments are. Whatever they are, the family will proceed to maximize its welfare. And to do so it will seek efficiency. The problem arises when the consumer or the family has as part of its utility function objectives that are antithetical to the entire maximization process. Suppose a family has as one of its goals that family members regularly prepare meals together. The family is not trying to maximize the "quality" of its meals nor any family member's cooking ability, nor is it particularly interested in the most efficient division of labor for putting food on the table. The parents simply believe that the process of frequently cooking together will add to their experience of family life.

If this goal is one argument in the family utility function, all of the usual behavior postulates made by the "new home economics" are likely to be wrong. For instance, if the economist, knowing nothing about the family's utility function, observed the father in this family efficiently cooking gourmet meals every evening for a month and concluded that the family was maximizing its welfare, the economist would be wrong. To draw conclusions about welfare, it matters what is in the family utility function.

But how could it be, the economist might ask, that the family continued to behave in a way inconsistent with one of its important goals? Easy. People do it all the time. Maybe the kids were particularly uncooperative this month and the mother extremely busy at work. Maybe the father just found it easier to cook than to "motivate" his kids. Well, doesn't that prove that at least the father maximized his welfare? Maybe. But maybe, rather than feeling surges of well-being, he in fact felt frustration. Maybe he was displeased with his behavior, wishing he hadn't taken the easy way out (cooking) and instead had persevered toward the family goal (cooking together). Detachedly observing his behavior (cooking), being sure to avoid studiously his emotional demeanor, would surely fail to tell us much about his welfare.

Similarly, suppose a consumer has been converted to Maslow's (1954) philosophy or to the "take the time to smell the flowers" philosophy popularized in the 1960s. Consumers who espouse these philosophies are not maximizers nor worshipers of efficiency. Like the family that wishes to share cooking, they, too, are particularly interested in the process of living as well as in the outcomes of living. Theirs is a philosophy of taking life as it comes, enjoying every day for what it brings. Many of them will tell you that even the aspects of life that maximizers might try to minimize (sadness, loss of income) contribute to their life experiences and growth, and hence to their satisfaction. They would tell you that concentrating single-mindedly on efficiency causes one to miss many of life's delights.

Are such philosophies of major consequence? Or has the author been too long in California? No, nonmaximizing philosophies are not simply the province of flower children. Nonmaximizing behavior increases in importance whenever, in Maslow's (1954) terms, basic needs are met, whenever an individual or society becomes affluent. Maximizing behavior is used to meet the needs for food, clothing, and shelter; it is not used to improve the quality of one's life. John Stuart Mill recognized this long before the hippies or their gurus or even before modern psychologists were born. In 1857 Mill wrote: "I confess I am not charmed with the ideal of life held out by those who think that the normal state of human beings is that of struggling to get on. . . . There would be . . . as much room for improving the Art of Living and much more likelihood of its being improved, when minds cease to be engrossed by the art of getting on" (1857, 321, 326).

Unfortunately for the power of neoclassical theory, interest in nonmaximizing behavior has grown in the last twenty years as people have met their basic needs and have begun to concentrate more on the quality of their lives. More and more people, like the family interested in sharing cooking, are concerned not simply with outcomes (how many goods and services they own, how much money they earn) or with efficiency but with the process of their lives—the quality of their relationships with people and their interactions with the environment. The way they live their lives is as important in determining their welfare as is the size of their income or their stock of consumer durables.

Many have learned, some through expensive psychotherapy, others through reading or informal group sessions at work or in the community, to "make peace with life," not to try to dominate it or maximize it but simply to take it as it comes. This is not to say that all psychotherapy or popular psychology preaches a "laid-back" approach to life. But many who have met their basic economic needs now aspire to become like Maslow's self-actualizing person, accepting of themselves, others, and nature (1954).

Some of the sense of the importance of process in people's utility functions is captured by the concept of psychic income. Ah, psychic income. Generally, when economists find a phenomenon they can label psychic income, they feel comfortable, for the customary assumption is that psychic income is sufficiently similar to money income to fit right into the usual theories. But, in fact, much of the salience of the concept of process is not captured by the concept of psychic income, which is, after all, an outcome rather than a process variable. Moreover, as Thurow (1983) has argued, resorting to psychic income to explain consumer or worker behavior is severely detrimental to the explanatory power of economic theory. If the welfare of the worker or consumer depends solely on maximizing money income, then economic theory can predict that an increase in the wage rate or a decrease in price will result in an increase in labor supplied or an increase in quantity demanded. Knowing only wage-rate or price changes, what can it predict if welfare depends on maximizing both money and psychic income? Worse, what can it predict if satisfaction doesn't depend on maximizing behavior at all?

Hedonism

In economic theory the assumption of hedonism is close cousin to the principles of rationality, maximization, and efficiency. Thus, the rational worker, trying to maximize utility, will be induced to work only if the wage rate is high enough, and the supply of additional hours requires an increase in the wage rate. Economists' wholehearted endorsement of the concept of hedonism (not necessarily for themselves but for their theories) causes them to look at leisure as a "good" and work as a "bad."

Acceptance of the concept of hedonism leads most economists toward a Theory X view of managerial psychology: most workers have to be induced to work; their inherent disposition is toward leisure (MacGregor 1960; Thurow 1983). But the notion that people prefer leisure to work has recently been challenged by some economists who have actually asked people about their preferences. (This practice is usually frowned upon by economists, who point out that people may lie; only revealed preference can be relied upon to tell the truth.)

In 1975–76 respondents to the University of Michigan Time Use Survey were asked to rate the intrinsic enjoyability of about twenty-two activities, including their job, housework tasks, and various forms of leisure. Comparing preferences among seven activities by gender across five broad occupational groups, F. Thomas Juster (1985, 342) reported that in almost all occupational categories both men and women ranked the intrinsic enjoyability of their job above that of most leisure activities. The only leisure activity consistently preferred to the job was talking with friends. Most respondents found their job intrinsically more enjoyable than home entertainment, watching TV, playing sports, or going to movies and plays. Interestingly, the least favorite activity for all groups was cleaning house.

These findings are certainly not the last word on hedonism. Indeed, the authors view their study as very much a "first pass" at the subject. But the findings do constitute a warning flag that our usual assumptions may be in error. It is a warning flag that ought to be heeded given the centrality of the notion of hedonism in our thinking about such critical issues as worker motivation and management, Aid to Families with Dependent Children, and the workability of a negative income tax.

Welfare

Nowhere in the *Framework* is there mention of welfare economics. Yet the underlying purpose of economic activity and all of its accouterments—markets, prices, supply, demand, competition, and so forth—is to produce welfare. The *Framework* should include at least some examination of this topic. Like the matter of taste change, to be discussed later, this theoretical issue has significant policy implications.

For example, in a recent article, Victor Fuchs (1986) asked what effect the "structural, legal and behavioral changes" of the 1960s and 1970s had on the well-being of women as compared to men. This is an important question. Have changes for both men and women in the distribution of time spent on paid work, housework, and leisure produced changes in relative well-being? Have policies designed to increase equity between men and women succeeded? Do we need additional policies or larger doses of existing policies in order to continue to strive for equity? Or perhaps we've gone too far. Maybe men are now worse off than women.

Fuchs concludes that over the last twenty-five years women's economic well-being did not improve relative to men's. He bases his conclusion on a very narrow definition of welfare. First, he limits his answer solely to economic well-being. Any psychosocial benefits or woes resulting from changes in the distribution of labor force participation, housework, or leisure are omitted from the analysis. Second, he uses average hourly earnings to value the time that an individual spends doing both market work and housework. For those not holding a paid job he sets the value of one hour of housework equal to the average hourly earnings of market workers of the same gender, race, age, and educational attainment. These procedures reflect a critical assumption about the nature of welfare: namely, that the well-being received by an individual from an hour of work at home or in the market is equal to that individual's average hourly wage rate.

The methodology leads to some queer results. Because men earn on average about 50 percent more than women, their housework is valued at 50 percent more than women's housework. Does a man (or his family) really receive 50 percent more well-being from an hour of his housework than does a woman (or her family) from an hour of her housework?

But even apart from the peculiarities that arise from the difficulties in measuring the values of nonmarket work, do we think that the notion of economic welfare is adequately captured by a wage rate? One alternative methodology is to use Juster's (1985) measures of the satisfaction that people get from different types of work.

If we multiply Juster's 1975 satisfaction scores for child care, market work, and housework by Fuch's estimates of the number of hours women and men spent in these activities in 1959 and 1983, we obtain another kind of measure of aggregate satisfaction for men and women. Interestingly, if one performs these calculations and then divides the women's aggregate satisfaction scores by those of the men, one finds that in 1959 women were 90 percent as satisfied as men; by 1983 they were 96 percent as satisfied. Making different assumptions about the amount of different types of housework done changes the values of the female/male satisfaction ratio (the values range from .79 to .91 for 1959 and from .86 to .96 for 1983), but in all instances the ratio increases from 1959 to 1983.

Yet this method of measuring well-being is still problematic. Like the Fuchs methodology, it is too static. For example, in an era of high divorce rates most married women find it too risky to be out of the labor market. They know that in case of divorce, without recent work experience, it is difficult to find employment that pays enough to support oneself, let alone one's children. (Even with recent work experience it is often difficult.) Having a job gives married women a modest amount of divorce insurance. The value of this insurance needs to be included in an accounting of the economic well-being women derive from market work.

The questions just discussed are writ large when we attempt to measure the welfare of one society or nation relative to another or when we attempt to measure changes in the welfare of a society or nation over time. The equivalent of using average hourly wage rates to measure welfare is using GNP; the equivalent of using measures such as Juster's is using a quality of life measure (UNESCO 1983). The *Framework* should have in it some discussion of the pros and cons of each of these approaches.

Atomism and the Constancy of Tastes

Microeconomic theory divides the process of consumption (or employment) into three parts: the formation of the demand curve of the potential consumer (or the labor supply curve of the potential worker), the formation of the supply curve of the potential producer (or demand for labor curve of the potential employer), and, finally, the meeting of the parties, with their respective curves, in the marketplace.

After reading enough economic theory, one envisions potential consumers or workers as supremely hermetic. They come to know their utility functions and then their demand curves through extensive internal contemplation (although they do obtain, in advance of their contemplative sessions, just the right amount of information, given its costs and their own predilections). If one pictures them at their homes, one envisions them removed from all external stimuli—drapes drawn, television silent—as they weigh various alternatives, one against the other, and come to understand their inherent tastes and preferences.

Neoclassical economic descriptions about how married women decide whether or not to enter the work force are particularly evocative of this picture of decision making. Do we really believe that the marked increase in married women's labor force participation in the postwar period came about because millions of women atomistically consulted their independent tastes and preferences and in the face of wage increases decided to go to work? I don't. In my view decision makers are highly social beings, greatly influenced by their friends, neighbors, family, community, nation, and world and greatly influenced by the media's portrayal of all of these influences.

The first group of married women who went to work after the war were influenced by the war itself, by the growth of occupations specifically demanding female employees, by technological and structural changes in the economy that consistently diminished the productivity and importance of household production, and by a change in societal norms about what a good mother and wife could and should do. The subsequent waves of married women who entered the workforce were able to do so in part because of the changes in community attitudes engendered by the labor force participation of the married women who had preceded them. The disregard for this snowball effect in tastes is one of the major contributors to the continual underestimation of increases in women's labor force participation.

The notion that tastes matter, that consumers and workers have different tastes in different places and at different times, and that there are important social influences on their tastes, is very much opposed by some of today's leading microeconomic theorists. For example, George Stigler and Gary Becker (1977, 76) wrote: "Tastes neither change capriciously nor differ importantly between people. . . . one does not argue over tastes for the same reason that one does not argue over the Rocky Mountains—both are there, will be there next year, too, and are the same to all men [*sic*]."

The question of whether tastes are susceptible to change is not simply a theoretical nicety. For example, several years ago I was preparing an article outlining the economic case for the subsidization of child care. When presenting the ideas for the paper at seminars, I found that neoclassical colleagues argued that a subsidization of child care was tantamount to a decrease in the price of raising children and was therefore pronatal. I argued that subsidization of child care would increase women's labor force participation and that women actively participating in the labor force generally had fewer children than other women.

In other words, I contended that labor force participation would lead to a taste change for women that would work in the opposite direction from the price effect. Only if the price effect swamped the taste change would the subsidization of child care be a pronatal policy. In fact, if the taste change were larger than the price effect, child care subsidization could turn out to be antinatal (Strober 1974). The point is that whether tastes are or are not susceptible to change makes a difference in policy discussions.

Adding Material on the Household, Labor Markets, and Income Distribution

A discussion of the economics of the household is not included at all in the *Framework,* and the discussions of labor markets and income distribution are too brief. These three topics are not only some of the most interesting (if controversial) in current economic work but are also particularly relevant for adolescents questioning their role in their parents' household(s) and anticipating adult family and work roles. For both young men and young women figuring out how to combine family and work roles in an era of rapid and relatively uncharted social change represents one of their most important developmental tasks. Economics has a great deal of information to impart to them on this subject.

An economics course in secondary school should include several topics on the household. The primary message should be that, despite the absence of a market with its attendant wages and prices, the household is involved in economic activity and produces valuable goods and services. The organization of work and the distribution of output resulting from that activity should be studied and alternatives to the present system critically evaluated. The curriculum could include discussions about the time spent by various family members on particular tasks, the ways in which information about time use is gathered, and possible methods for placing monetary values on household time.

Examination of household structures would also be useful. What are the motivations, economic and otherwise, for marriage and divorce? What are the motivations, economic and otherwise, for having children? What are the economic effects of marriage and divorce? Why does divorce so often cause poverty for a woman and her children?

Much of the recent economic theory on these subjects is controversial (see Ferber and Birnbaum 1977; Sawhill 1977; and Folbre and Hartmann 1986), difficult to present, and, in my experience, difficult for students to accept. (Is a child really a durable good? Is love really irrelevant to the motivation for marriage? Can one really subsume all of the family members' preferences under those of the father?) Nor in this case, unlike the case of consumer demand theory, is the theory central to the information I would wish to impart or the alternative arrangements I would like students to consider. I would teach these topics with a minimum of theory; whenever I did bring in theory, however, I would bring it in not as irrefutable but as a topic for exploration.

Examination of the household or family leads directly to discussions about the labor market. Numerous questions suggest themselves as exceedingly timely for students about to make decisions about their own education and occupation. How do various members of the household or family decide when and how many hours to work for pay? What factors, including the preferences and needs of other family members, affect their decisions? How do family members decide how much education to obtain? What is the relationship between education and earnings? How do these answers differ for women? For minorities? Why do they differ for these groups?

The current version of the *Framework* has only one sentence on discrimination. I suggest that this is a topic that deserves considerable attention. More than half of the students taking economics (all of the women and the minority men) have a personal interest in understanding why they are unlikely, even if they obtain the same education as their white male counterparts, to enter the same occupations or achieve the same earnings. They may have an equal interest in learning why, on average, women and minority men are not likely to obtain the same education as white men.

Labor market theory, including discrimination theory, is in great turmoil at the moment. But, unlike the theory of the household or family, it is relatively easy to understand the various points of view. When I teach these topics to youngsters, I include a discussion of the various theoretical positions. Students particularly like to learn about internal labor markets; the material seems to give them a sense that they are beginning to understand what really happens in those unknown and mysterious offices and factories they will soon be entering.

The topic of discrimination provides an excellent entree into issues of government regulation. To what extent should the government try to remedy discrimination? What alternative policies are open to a government wishing to remedy it? Which policies are likely (or unlikely) to work? Why? Students quickly see that economic analysis is very useful in trying to answer these questions. But they also see that economic analysis needs to be supplemented with an understanding of politics, and sociology—both useful messages.

Goals of Teaching Economics in Secondary Schools

From "Reasoned Judgment" to "Critical Evaluation"

The first page of the *Framework* states clearly the Joint Council on Economic Education's goal for teaching economics at the precollege level:

> enabling students, by the time they graduate from high school, to understand enough economics to make reasoned judgments about economic questions. These include personal economic questions as well as broader matters of economic policy that students will face as members of a democratic society. (Saunders et al. 1984, 1)

The ensuing sentences clarify the concept of "reasoned judgment." It is "the replacement of emotional judgment by objective, reasoned analysis."

My understanding of economics and education leads me to propose a broader goal: to understand enough economics to make critical evaluations of personal, familial, occupational, and societal economic alternatives.

Why the term *critical?* As *Webster's* (1958) points out, *critical* has two different meanings: "In precise use, 'critical' implies an effort to see a thing clearly and truly in order to judge it fairly; in less precise but acceptable use, 'critical' implies harshness in judging" (197). I use the term *critical* in the first sense. Economics should improve the student's ability to see clearly and truly in order to evaluate fairly. My use of the term in no way implies a desire to engender hypercritical behavior.

Why the term *evaluation?* I use the word *evaluation* rather than *judgment* in defining the goal of economic education because it has more of a democratic and optimistic connotation. As they evaluate alternatives, students need not take on the role of judge, a powerful figure outside and above the fray, issuing edicts and initiating punishments. The term *evaluation* implies that the student is an active participant in the assessment process and that, if a particular route proves unsatisfactory, he or she can design a new tack.

Why the emphasis on alternatives? The notion of alternatives is at the heart of economics; it is the central notion behind the concept of opportunity cost. Evaluation of alternatives is what economic actors do, and it is what economists do. The concept of alternatives should receive greater emphasis in the *Framework*. Students should be invited more frequently to consider alternatives.

For example, regarding competition: What are some alternatives to competition? Which kinds of activities are likely to be fostered best by competition? Which are likely to be fostered best by cooperation? What are the advantages and disadvantages of competition? The *Framework* presents competition as always desirable; but students should be urged to explore alternatives to competition for certain kinds of tasks.

Regarding the role of the state: What are some alternatives to a liberal government whose role is limited to providing necessary services not otherwise forthcoming? When is it useful for the state to facilitate industrial activity? What are the advantages and disadvantages of various forms of state intervention? The role of the state is an important variable in economic policy. Alternative roles should be widely, rather than narrowly, presented.

Generally, in today's economics texts students are taught that there are three types of economies: traditional, command, and market. The U.S. economy is then studied as the prototypical market economy. Little, if anything, is taught about other types of market economies—for example, those of Japan, Sweden, France, or Germany. This practice should be changed. Students should be encouraged to look at the role of the state in these economies as potential models for actions by our own government. Students should learn how the role of the state in these other economies contributes to their success. They should learn to evaluate the extent to which government policies in other market economies can and cannot be transplanted to our own political and cultural setting.

Values and Emotions

The dictionary definition of the term *critical* urges us to link judgment or evaluation with fairness; a critical person is one who knows how to judge or evaluate fairly. What does *fairly* mean in this context? One answer suggests that to evaluate fairly one must be impartial—have all of the evidence, look at all sides of the question, and take a variety of viewpoints into account before coming to a decision. Certainly, one might argue, an economics curriculum should instill this type of behavior; indeed, such behavior would seem to be precisely what the JCEE authors had in mind when they put forth the notion of reasoned judgement. This sense of the word *fairness* fits well with the usual tenor of positive economic analysis: one does economics with one's brain and leaves one's values and emotions outside the library, computer room, or lecture hall.

Should students be taught that it is possible to disassociate one's powers of analysis from one's values and emotions? Or should they be taught that human beings can only approximate impartiality in their evaluations, that two people with different values and experiences will inevitably see different possible alternatives, ask different questions about them, and marshal evidence from different sources? And, equally important, that sometimes two people faced with the same evidence about the same alternatives will make different value judgments about which course of action to take?

The question of whether knowledge is absolute or relative is one that is raging in philosophic circles today (Siegel 1986). As a relativist, I believe it is both impossible and unrealistic to ask students to leave their values and experiences outside the economics classroom door or to pretend that these values and experiences won't affect their economic evaluations. Instead, in teaching economic analysis (and in doing it), I propose that we place the question of how values and experiences affect analyses (and how analyses affect values and experiences) squarely within the curriculum. Students should be encouraged to examine these relationships on a regular basis.

For the most part formal education today, especially at the high school level and beyond, sees its role as educating students' minds. In my view this goal is impossibly narrow. Just as one cannot separate one's values and experiences from one's analyses, one cannot educate only a student's mind.

Emotional affect and moral standards are unavoidably transmitted with information. If one tries to transmit no affect, the emotional messages students receive are those of coldness and dispassion. If one tries to transmit no moral standard, students learn that to be uncaring is acceptable. I would like economics classes not to transmit such messages. I would like economics classes to be places in which students examine their emotional and moral reactions to cognitive material. In my experience most students enter economics passionate and caring; I would like them to come away from economics even more so.

There are those who will argue that trying to educate students about emotions and moral questions in an economics class will kill the discipline, transforming it into a "soft" subject, bereft of its hard-won rigor. Perhaps so. But, as Walter Adams (1982) has argued, the current rigor in economics resembles rigor mortis. From the point of view of precollege education, putting values, emotions, and moral questions back into economics can only make it more exciting to students. Far from killing economics, it should revitalize it.

Moreover, as Nell Noddings notes, allowing emotions and moral questions into one's analysis "must not be used as a cloak for sloppy thinking" (1984, 2). The challenge of teaching the "whole person"— head, heart, left brain, right brain—is not a simple one. Economists will need once again to borrow analytical techniques—this time, not from mathematics and statistics but from such disciplines as linguistics, law, and philosophy, disciplines with long histories of sophisticated, reasoned analysis.

As a part of encouraging students to examine their own emotions and values, I wish to embolden students to discover and critically assess the underlying values of economics. Generally, when economics is taught, even at the graduate level, these underlying values are not made explicit. Indeed, sometimes economists claim that their analyses are "value free," with laws like those of physics applicable everywhere and through all time. But in fact, as we have seen, the assumptions made about such matters as rationality, maximization, welfare, and the constancy of tastes reflect particular worldviews. If these assumptions are modified, the ensuring analyses and the conclusions derived from them are changed.

Realistically Assessing the Power of Economic Analysis and Challenging the Disdain for Other Social Sciences

In addition to elucidating the underlying values of economics, teachers and texts should be frank about the limited power of economic analyses. In general, the abilities of the discipline have been oversold, as is embarrassingly clear every time one of the national media runs an article or a broadcast contrasting recent economic predictions with actual performance. It is sometimes feared that pointing to the warts as well as to the triumphs of economic theory and analysis will make student contemptuous of the discipline's intellectual prowess. In fact, the opposite is true; students, especially the better ones, as they diligently work through difficult problems, quickly see the holes and rough edges of theory and method. If these are not acknowledged, the student begins to lose interest in working through difficult problems; the hard work seems to lead to nonsense, and respect for the discipline is soon lost.

Acknowledging the shortcomings of economics has additional salutary effects. It permits students to take a more open-minded approach to the evaluation of alternatives, be they alternative explanations from other disciplines or alternative methodologies.

Economists are generally singularly disdainful about "resorting" to noneconomic explanations for "economic" phenomena. Recently, I met an economist looking for an explanation for the fact that, even after holding constant a number of control variables, women, on average, use medical services more frequently than men. The explanation offered was that women have a lower price of time than men. Surprised, I asked whether the study had considered any other explanations. "Oh yes," replied the economist, "but all of them were sociological."

Hobnobbing with One's Data

I once served with academicians from several disciplines on a national committee to plan a conference assessing the impact of the women's movement. A committee member from the humanities suggested that one session include a panel combining academics with such leaders of the women's movement as Betty Friedan, Bella Abzug, and Gloria Steinem. A sociologist on the committee responded to the suggestion in horror: "Oh no," he said, "I study the women's movement. I don't hobnob with my data."

I would like to see economists do a bit more "hobnobbing" with their data. And I would like us to teach students that talking to people to find out what they think and why they think they behave as they do is an acceptable, indeed a desirable, method of obtaining evidence. Certainly, that evidence, along with an assessment of possible incentives for lying, needs to be evaluated. But eliminating qualitative data gathering entirely as an acceptable methodology in economics is both unwise and immodest. We need all the help we can get.

Permitting qualitative methodology should also move us away from studying only that which is quantifiable. If we admit that economic issues are more complex than can be modeled in a set of equations, we may learn a great deal. Maybe some of what we learn can ultimately be fed back into the equations. But in the meantime, if we keep our minds open to the insights of other social sciences, look at qualitative as well as quantitative data, and permit ourselves to talk to our subjects, we may find we have a lot more to teach our students than we thought.

NOTE

This essay originally appeared in the *Journal of Economic Education* (spring 1987): 135–49. Reprinted with permission of the Helen Dwight Reid Educational Foundation. Published by Heldref Publications, 1319 Eighteenth St., NW, Washington, DC 20036-1802. Copyright © 1987.

REFERENCES

Adams, W. 1982. Economic theory and economic policy. *Review of Social Economy* 40 (April): 1–12.

Becker, G. S. 1981. *A treatise on the family.* Cambridge: Harvard University Press.

Ferber, M. A., and B. G. Birnbaum. 1977. The new home economics: Retrospects and prospects. *Journal of Consumer Research* 4 (June): 19–28.

Folbre, N., and H. Hartmann. 1986. The rhetoric of self-interest and the ideology of gender. Paper presented at the Conference on the Rhetoric of Economics. Wellesley College, April 17–19.

Fuchs, V. R. 1986. Sex differences in economic well-being. *Science* 232 (April 25): 459–64.

Juster, F. T. 1985. Preferences for work and leisure. In *Time, goods and well-being,* ed. F. T. Juster and F. P. Stafford. Ann Arbor: Institute for Social Research, University of Michigan.

McCloskey, D. M. 1986. *The rhetoric of economics.* Madison: University of Wisconsin Press.

MacGregor, D. M. 1960. *The human side of enterprise.* New York: McGraw-Hill.

Maslow, A. H. 1954. *Motivation and personality.* New York: Harper and Row.

Mill, J. S. 1857. *Principles of political economy II.* London: John W. Parker and Son.

Noddings, N. 1984. *Caring: A feminine approach to ethics and moral education.* Berkeley: University of California Press.

Saunders, P., G. L. Bach, J. D. Calderwood, and W. L. Hansen. 1984. *A framework for teaching the basic concepts.* New York: Joint Council on Economic Education.

Sawhill, I. V. 1977. Economic perspectives on the family. *Daedalus* 106 (spring) 115–25.

Siegel, H. 1986 Relativism, truth and incoherence. *Synthese* 68 (August): 225–61.

Stigler, G. J., and G. S. Becker. 1977. De gustibus non est disputandum. *American Economic Review* 67 (March): 76–90.

Strober, M. H. 1975. Formal extrafamily child care—some economic observations.

Sex, discrimination, and the division of labor. New York: Columbia University Press.

Thurow, L. C. 1985. *Dangerous currents: The state of economics.* New York: Random House.

Tversky, A., and D. Kahneman. 1981. The framing of decisions and the psychology of choice. *Science* 211 (January 30): 453–58.

UNESCO. 1983. *Quality of life: Problems of assessment and measurement.* Paris: UNESCO.

Walker, D. 1999. Fundamentals of curriculum. San Diego: Harcourt Brace Jovanovich.

Ward, B. 1972. *What's wrong with economics?* New York: Basic Books.

Webster's new collegiate dictionary. 1958. Springfield, MA: Merriam Co.

The Impact of Integrating Scholarship on Women into Introductory Economics

Evidence from One Institution

Maureen J. Lage and Michael Treglia

There is widespread agreement that women are underrepresented both in the economics profession and in the classroom (Ferber 1990; Phillip 1993). It has also been shown that male students generally perform better than female students in economics courses (Siegfried 1979; Heath 1989; Lumsden and Scott 1987; Watts and Lynch 1989). This situation has been attributed to such factors as a chilly classroom environment (Ferber 1984, 1990; Hall and Sandler 1982) and a lack of coverage of issues concerning women and minorities (Feiner 1993) as well as underlying cultural differences. Although much research has focused on whether gender-based differences in performance exist, relatively little is known about the efficacy of methods for mitigating these differences.

In this essay we empirically examine the effect of integrating the latest scholarship on women into the principles of microeconomics course.[1] The content of the introductory microeconomics course was modified to address economic issues in a gender-inclusive manner. In addition, the formats of the classroom and of examinations were changed in a manner consistent with hypotheses that explain why female students do not perform as well as male students in economics courses. Thus, we examine the extent to which observed differences in economics performance based upon gender can be modified. Our evidence suggests that all students perform significantly better in a gender-inclusive economics course. Furthermore, there is an additional increase in the performance of female students.

Integration of Gender Scholarship

The first step in integrating gender scholarship into the principles of microeconomics course was to determine how much time should be devoted to gender issues and what level of integration is appropriate for an introductory course. McIntosh (1983) describes five phases of integrating women's studies issues into a traditional curriculum. Although her discussion pertains to incorporating gender issues into the history curriculum the stages are not field specific and, therefore, could easily be applied to economics.[2]

The first phase is a traditional approach to economics in the sense that gender differences receive no attention. At this stage, for example, instructors would talk about "profit maximizing firms" and "utility maximizing consumers." In the second phase some time is devoted to women who have made substantial contributions to the field of economics but without mentioning any extraordinary difficulties that may have been encountered. Implicit in this stage is that women can succeed as long as they work hard. For example, at this stage a textbook may mention that in 1963 Anna Schwartz coauthored *A Monetary History of the United States, 1867–1960* with Milton Friedman and may even include a box containing a biography on Anna Schwartz. In phase 3 accepted economic theory is applied to, tested on, or extended to the realm of women. In this phase, however, women are generally treated as problems or anomalies. For example, the life-cycle model might be applied to the study of single female–headed households. The fact that this model does not typically hold for this segment of the population would be treated as a curiosity but not as evidence that the theory is invalid. In phase 4—*Women and Economics*—new material, theory, and methodologies are developed that help to explain the anomalies discussed in phase 3. An example of phase four would be a lecture examining the "natural" rate of unemployment and how it differs across gender lines.[3] In phase 5 economics is redefined or reconstructed into an all-inclusive vision. At this stage topics, methodology, and pedagogy would be examined from the perspective of women.

Using McIntosh's (1983) model as a frame of reference, the content of the principles of microeconomics course examined here changed from phase one to phase three. Before these changes, the course was a fairly rigorous yet standard introduction to microeconomics. After the course revision, a much greater emphasis was placed on gender issues, and students were encouraged to apply the tools of economic analysis to help explain some of the observed differences between the economic status of men and women. The remainder of this section briefly outlines the differences between the traditional and the gender-inclusive courses. The appendix provides a more detailed comparison.

In regard to coverage of the material, the textbook's chapters on poverty and income distribution and on labor market discrimination were covered in class for the first time. As the class worked through this material, the emphasis was on gender differences and the competing economic explanations of these differences. Outside reading that discussed gender issues was also assigned and discussed in class. For example, when covering comparative advantage and the gains from trade, the Becker model of specialization within the family was introduced. Additional readings addressed the topics of price discrimination based on gender, affirmative action in the labor market and in higher education, and comparable worth.

The classroom format was also modified. Ferber (1984, 1990) pointed out a need to reexamine how economics is taught at the introductory level in order to improve the classroom climate for women. Horvath, Beaudin, and Wright (1992) suggested that female students need more validation than men to persist in the study of economics. Erkut (1983) found that female students generally were less confident of success than male students. These findings suggest that changing the classroom format from an exclusively teacher-centered pedagogy to a more active, student-centered pedagogy would create a learning environment conducive to a wider array of learning styles. Thus, the classroom format was changed from one of entirely lecture to one where lecture was used along with discussion and group work in class. This change allowed the instructor to have more interaction with students in class and to provide quicker and more direct feedback.

Another aspect of male-female performance difference has been attributed to the type of examinations administered. Ferber, Birnbaum, and Green (1983) and Lumsden and Scott (1987), among others, have suggested that essay exams rather than multiple-choice exams would reduce the male-female differential in performance. Although this result is not conclusive,[4] this change was made in order to allow for the possibility of such bias existing. Thus, although quizzes in the traditional course were entirely multiple choice, in the gender-inclusive course a writing component made up approximately 66 percent of each quiz. In addition, a larger component of each exam consisted of short-answer and essay problems.

Data

The data set for this study was constructed from one instructor's principles of microeconomics course over a period of three semesters beginning in fall 1992 and ending fall 1993. During the first two semesters the classes fit the description of phase one, whereas during the third semester the course was modified as described in the previous section. By limiting the study to one instructor, we are able to abstract from how differences in faculty affect student performance.[5] For the most part students at Miami University are Caucasians who have entered the university directly from high school and attend on a full-time basis. The students were not aware of any change in the course; in all cases, they simply signed up for a section of Economics 201. Therefore, the study should be free from any self-selection bias that could have occurred had the students been able to enroll in a particular type of course.

We used the Test of Understanding in College Economics (TUCE) to measure the impact of covering material in a gender-inclusive fashion on student performance. Specifically, the third edition of the TUCE was administered as both a pretest and posttest. Only the first 31 TUCE questions (out of 33) were used because the material on exchange rate determination, which is covered by the last two questions of the TUCE, is typically not covered by the instructor in microeconomics but in principles of macroeconomics. POSTTUCE (the number correct on the posttest out of 31 questions) was the dependent variable in this study. The pretest score (PRETUCE) was used to control for prior economics knowledge. Neither the pretest nor posttest scores were used in any determination of students' grades. Although this use of the pretest and posttest may lead to downwardly biased results, there is no reason to think that such a procedure would result in bias in comparing the students in the traditional course with the students in the gender-inclusive course.

Additional variables used to control for students' ability included GPA and ACT.[6] GPA is the student's overall grade point average from the semester prior to enrolling in the principles of microeconomics course. ACT is the student's composite ACT score. Both variables measure the skills that the student brought to the course, and we hypothesized that each would have a positive impact on POSTTUCE performance. Although GPA and ACT are proxies for student ability, both were included in the regressions because they might be measuring different aspects of that ability. For instance, ACT is usually regarded as a measure of knowledge, whereas GPA may be measuring assiduity as well as knowledge.[7]

Dummy variables were used to capture differences between the traditional course and the gender-inclusive course and differences between male and female students. GENDER, a dummy variable that was equal to one for female students, captured any differential between male and female students. GI was a dummy variable that was equal to one for students who took the gender-inclusive course. We hypothesized that GI would have a positive effect on students' performance. Finally, GENDER*GI, the interaction term between GENDER and GI, captured any additional benefit of the gender-inclusive course for female students.

Summary statistics for all the variables used in this study are presented in table 1. The sample consisted of 164 students, 97 of whom took the traditional course, while the remainder took the gender-inclusive principles of microeconomics course.

Results

As a preliminary step, several diagnostic checks were run to test for problems in the data. The Spearman rank coefficient was calculated between the absolute value of the residuals and each of the explanatory variables. The results of this test indicate that heteroscedasticiy was not a problem.[8] Also,

TABLE 1. Descriptive Statistics for Student Groups

Variable	M	SD	Minimum	Maximum
Female Students ($n = 87$)				
POSTTUCE	13.2985	3.9773	5	26
PRETUCE	9.1719	2.7345	4	15
GPA	2.9520	0.5329	1.758	4
ACT	25.4815	2.4933	20	30
GI	0.4328	0.4922	0	1
Male students ($n = 77$)				
POSTTUCE	15.4737	5.2171	5	28
PRETUCE	9.9643	3.1332	5	19
GPA	2.8326	0.5509	1.5	4
ACT	25.3333	3.3544	18	32
GI	0.3793	0.4849	0	1
Students in traditional course ($n = 97$)				
POSTTUCE	14.2162	4.9856	6	26
PRETUCE	9.7639	2.8802	4	16
GPA	2.8632	0.5820	1.5	4
ACT	25.5620	2.9560	18	32
GENDER	0.5135	0.5033	0	1
Students in gender-inclusive course ($n = 67$)				
POSTTUCE	14.4200	4.2814	7	28
PRETUCE	9.2083	3.0314	4	19
GPA	2.9527	0.4828	1.8	3.7220
ACT	25.1578	2.7950	20	32
GENDER	0.5687	0.5002	0	1
All students ($N = 164$)				
POSTTUCE	14.2984	4.6973	5	28
PRETUCE	9.6517	2.9417	4	19
GPA	2.8978	0.5455	1.5	4
ACT	25.4167	2.8862	18	32
GI	0.4085	0.4934	0	1
GENDER	0.5305	0.5007	0	1

the correlation coefficients between all independent variables were calculated. The two variables that were most highly correlated were GPA and ACT, with a coefficient of .6637. For the reasons previously discussed, both variables were included in the regressions.[9] Finally, Chow tests were conducted to test the hypothesis that allowing the coefficients of all independent variables to differ between the students in the traditional course and the gender-inclusive course provided any additional explanatory power over that provided by the use of intercept dummy variables alone. The results of the Chow tests indicated that the students in the traditional course were not significantly different from the students who took the gender-inclusive course.[10] This result was not surprising, given the control for self-selection.

We report here the results of two tests of the impact of integrating the latest scholarship on women into the introductory microeconomics course. Model A was a pure stock equation in which POSTTUCE was regressed on all variables mentioned above except PRETUCE. Model B again used POSTTUCE as the dependent variable while including PRETUCE among the independent variables. This controlled for the level of economic knowledge students brought to the course.[11] The regression results are reported in table 2.

TABLE 2.   Ordinary Least Squares

Independent variable	Post-TUCE	
	Model A	Model B
INTERCEPT	−7.058	−8.543
	(−1.898)*	(−1.576)*
PRE-TUCE	—	0.296
		(1.925)*
GPA	2.243	1.524
	(3.282)**	(1.960)*
ACT	0.528	0.454
	(4.208)***	(3.327)***
GENDER	0.114	0.377
	(0.131)	(0.417)
GI	2.118	2.400
	(2.003)**	(2.230)**
GENDER × GI	2.360	2.468
	(1.888)*	(1.942)*
Adj. R^2	0.332	0.339
F	10.459***	8.60***

Note: t-statistics are given in parentheses; $N = 164$.

*Significant at the 10 percent level.

**Significant at the 5 percent level.

***Significant at the 1 percent level.

The first major result of this study was that the effect of the gender-inclusive course (GI) on all students' performance was positive and significant in both regressions. In the pure stock equation approximately 2.1 points were added to the POSTTUCE score for students who took the gender-inclusive course relative to those who did not. In model B 2.4 points were added to POSTTUCE for students in the gender-inclusive course. The second main result was that both equations showed that the interaction term between GENDER and GI was greater than zero at a 7 percent level of significance. In each model the performance of female students was enhanced by more than 2 points relative to male students' performance in the gender-inclusive course. This result implies that the performance of females in the gender-inclusive course was approximately 15 percent greater than that of comparable males. Note that these results were statistically significant, although the measure of performance was based on multiple-choice questions and some evidence suggests that multiple-choice questions may be gender biased.

The effect of the GENDER variable alone was not significantly different from zero in either model. Furthermore, in model A both GPA and ACT had the expected, significant, positive effects on students' performance on POSTTUCE. These results generally held for model B as well, although the significance level on GPA changed from 1 percent to 10 percent when PRETUCE was included. Both models yielded similar adjusted R^2s and F statistics that were significant at the 1 percent level.

These results suggest that a gender-inclusive course generally improves all students' performance with an additional increase in the performance of female students. The results, however, must be interpreted with caution. First, it may be argued that if the instructor was more enthusiastic about the new material, this enthusiasm may be at least partially the cause of increased student performance. There is some indirect evidence this is not the case. Specifically, Lumsden (1974) and Lumsden and Scott (1983) have shown that instructor enthusiasm is one of the major determinants that affect an instructor's evaluations. Although the instrument used by the students to evaluate the instructor did not have a direct question about the instructor's enthusiasm, it is revealing that there was not a dramatic change in evaluations of the instructor when comparing the results from the traditional course with those from the gender-inclusive course. On a nine-question evaluation form using a five-point scale, the average increase was 0.08; the largest improvement on any individual question was 0.2. Furthermore, the percentage of students commenting on the instructor's enthusiasm in the written portion of the evaluation form remained approximately constant for the two courses. These two pieces of evidence suggest that the increase in student performance was not attributable to a change in instructor enthusiasm.

The second caveat that applies to the results concerns the nature of the experiment. As outlined above and detailed in the appendix, the experiment consisted of a multi-part treatment in the gender-inclusive course. Recall that coverage of the material, the format of the class, and the methods of student assessment were all modified, consistent with hypotheses explaining why female students do not perform as well as male students in economics courses. As such, the results of this study only indicate the success of using this "package" to ameliorate previously documented differences based on gender. Further research is called for to determine the individual impact of each component of the package.

Conclusion

Generally, all students in this study performed better in a course that integrated gender issues into the curriculum. In addition, female students' performance was enhanced relative to men. These results were robust to alternative specifications of the education production function. Therefore, the results from Miami University suggest that documented gender-based differences can be ameliorated without sacrificing the performance of male students in the class.

APPENDIX: COMPARISON OF TRADITIONAL COURSE AND GENDER-INCLUSIVE COURSE

    I. Textbook assignments

    Both courses used as the primary test *Principles of Microeconomics,* 2d ed., by James F. Ragan and Lloyd B. Thomas. Fort Worth: Dryden Press, 1993.

    A. Material in the traditional course not included in gender-inclusive course

      1. Business firms in the American economy

      2. Increasing costs, perfectly competitive industry

      3. Decreasing costs, perfectly competitive industry

      4. Unions

      5. Antitrust policy

    B. Material in the gender-inclusive course not included in traditional course

      1. Discrimination in the labor market

      2. Poverty and income distribution

II. Outside readings
   A. Traditional course
   B. Gender-inclusive course
      1. "The Family as Economic Unit: The Division of Labor be-tween Husband and Wife." In *The Economics of Women, Men, and Work,* by Francine D. Blau, and Marianne A. Ferber, 34–48. Englewood Cliffs, NJ: Prentice-Hall, 1992.
      2. Price discrimination
         a. "In the Market." Chapter 1 in *Why Women Pay More* by Frances Cerra Whittelsey, 11–21. Washington, DC: Center for Responsive Law, 1993.
         b. Students also viewed a video segment from "Prime Time Live" in which gender discrimination was examined by showing the different experiences of a man and woman in similar settings, such as purchasing a car, taking shirts to be laundered, and so forth.
      3. Affirmative action
         a. "A Limit to Affirmative Action," by James Blanton. *Commentary* (June 1989): 28–32.
         b. "Saving Affirmative Action," by James Forman Jr. *Nation,* December 9, 1991, 746, 748.
         c. "How Is Affirmative Action like Crop Subsidies?" by Gary S. Becker. *Business Week,* April 27, 1992, 18.
         [*Note:* All these readings are available in *Race and Gender in the American Economy: Views from Across the Spectrum,* ed. Susan F. Feiner. Englewood Cliffs, NJ: Prentice-Hall, 1994.]
      4. Comparable worth
         a. "What's a Women's Work Worth?" editorial, *New York Times,* February 18, 1984.
         b. "Pay Equity—Surprising Answers to Hard Questions," by Barbara Bergmann. *Challenge* (May–June 1987): 45–51.
         c. "Equity and Comparable Worth," by Joseph McKenna. From the Newsletter of the Center for Economic Education, University of Missouri–St. Louis, May 1984.
         d. "The 'Comparable Worth' Trap" by June O'Neil, *Wall Street Journal,* February 20, 1984.
         [*Note:* All these readings are available in *Introduction to Microeconomics—Student Workbook,* by Phillip Saunders, 15th ed. (1993). Available from Phillip Saunders, 3725 Brownridge Road, Bloomington, IN 47401-4209.]

III. Classroom format
   A. Traditional course
      100 percent lecture
   B. Gender-inclusive course
      1. Approximately 65 percent lecture
      2. Approximately 35 percent discussion/group work
         a. Discussion of outside readings
         b. Group work/discussion of worksheet assignments

IV. Determination of grades
   A. Traditional course

Exam one	25 percent
Exam two	25 percent
Exam three	25 percent
Quizzes	10 percent
Homework	15 percent

   B. Gender-inclusive course

Exam one	25 percent
Exam two	25 percent
Quizzes	10 percent
Group homework	10 percent
Worksheets	5 percent

V. Format of assignments
   A. Exams
      1. Traditional course
         55 percent multiple choice
         45 percent short answer/problems
      2. Gender-inclusive course
         100 percent short answer/problems
   B. Quizzes
      1. Traditional course
         100 percent multiple choice
      2. Gender-inclusive course
         a) Quizzes on the outside reading
            Short-answer questions designed to test whether or not
            they had come to class prepared to discuss the material
         b) Quizzes on the textbook
            Multiple choice and explain—students receive two points
            for choosing the right answer to the multiple-choice question
            and up to four points for explaining why their answer
            was correct

  C. Homework
   1. Traditional course
    Homework was short-answer problems that must be completed independently.
   2. Gender-inclusive course
    Homework was short-answer/problems that were completed in groups of four. The instructor assigned the groups to diversify majors, mathematical background, and gender.
  D. Worksheets
   1. Traditional course
    No worksheet assignments
   2. Gender-inclusive course
    a) Worksheet assignments are from *Introduction to Microeconomics—A Student Workbook,* by Phillip Saunders.
    b) Worksheet assignments were to be attempted before the instructor lectured on the material.
    c) After a lecture on the material, students worked in groups on the work sheets to ensure that they understood the material. The answers were then covered in class by the students explaining them to the rest of the class.

NOTES

This essay originally appeared in *Journal of Economic Education* (winter 1996): 26–36. Reprinted by permission of the Helen Dwight Reid Educational Foundation. Published by Heldref Publications, 1319 Eighteenth St., NW, Washington, DC 20036-1802. Copyright © 1996.

1. This project is a result of one of the author's participation at a conference on Improving Introductory Economics by Integrating the Latest Scholarship on Women and Minorities—a faculty development project funded by the National Science Foundation. Although the focus of the conference was on race and gender issues, our research focused exclusively on gender issues because of the homogeneous student population at Miami University, where the research was conducted.

2. Bartlett (forthcoming) provides an excellent explanation of how the McIntosh model can be used to explain various phases of integrating new scholarship on women into economics.

3. Bartlett (forthcoming) provides an entire lecture of this topic.

4. For example, Williams, Waldauer, and Duggal 1992; and Caudill and Gropper 1991.

5. Data limitations restricted this study to only one instructor. Specifically, although other instructors have also integrated scholarship on women into their classes, they did not administer the pretest and posttest both before and after changing their classes.

6. In addition to GPA and ACT the variables SCHOOL (a dummy variable equal to one if the student was enrolled in the School of Business) and CALC (a dummy

variable equal to one if the student had successfully completed a calculus course prior to enrolling in the principles course) were originally included in the regressions. In all cases the latter two variables were insignificant. The result that students enrolled in the business school did no better than other students at the university is consistent with many previous studies (Van Scyoc and Gleason 1993; Lumsden and Scott 1987; and Siegfried and Fels 1979). In addition, these findings support previous research that found that enrollment in calculus did not have a significant impact on student performance in principles of microeconomics (Brasfield, Harrison, and McCoy 1993; and Siegfried and Fels 1979). In consequence, the variables SCHOOL and CALC were omitted in the reported analysis.

7. We thank the editor for this clarification.

8. The Spearman rank coefficient estimates ranged from 0.0007 to 0.002.

9. Running the regressions including GPA but not ACT, and vice versa, gave similar results to those reported.

10. The Chow tests yielded F statistics ranging from 0.449 to 1.712 for the models listed in table 2. The critical values for 164 observations and $k = 5$ or $k = 6$ ranged from 2.15 to 2.27.

11. Other specifications using direct measures of learning-flow variables were examined to test the robustness of our results. For instance, both an absolute improvement measure (DTUCE = POSTTUCE − PRETUCE) and a gap-closing measure of learning (GAP = DTUCE / [31 − PRETUCE]) were regressed on the explanatory variables. Because these alternative specifications gave similar results, they are not reported here. These results are available from the authors upon request.

REFERENCES

Bartlett, R. L. Forthcoming. Macroeconomics: An introductory lecture integrating the new scholarship on women. In *Teaching differently: Facing the biases of gender, culture and education,* ed. J. Bauer, J. Bransberg, and E. Maher. Albany: SUNY, Feminist Studies in Education.

Becker, G. S. 1991. *A treatise on the family.* Cambridge: Harvard University Press.

Brasfield, D. W., D. E. Harrison, and J. P. McCoy. 1993. The impact of high school economics on the college principles of economics course. *Journal of Economic Education* 24 (spring): 99–110.

Caudill, S. B., and D. M. Gropper. 1991. Test structure, human capital, and student performance on economics exams. *Journal of Economic Education* 22 (fall): 303–6.

Ekrut S. 1983. Exploring sex differences in expectancy, attribution, and academic achievement. *Sex Roles* 9 (February): 217–31.

Feiner, S. F. 1993. Introductory economics textbooks and the treatment of issues relating to women and minorities, 1984 and 1991. *Journal of Economic Education* 24 (spring): 145–62.

Ferber, M. A. 1984. Suggestions for improving the classroom climate for women in the introductory economics course: A review article. *Journal of Economic Education* 15 (spring): 160–68.

———. 1990. Gender and the study of economics. In *The Principles of economics course: A handbook for instructors,* ed. P. Saunders and W. B. Walstad, 44–60. New York: McGraw-Hill.

Ferber, M. A., B. G. Birnbaum, and C. A. Green. 1983. Gender differences in economic knowledge: A reevaluation of the evidence. *Journal of Economic Education* 14 (spring): 24–37.

Ferber, M. A., and J. A. Nelson. 1993. Introduction: The social construction of economics and the social construction of gender. In *Beyond economic man: Feminist theory and economics,* ed. M. A. Ferber and J. A. Nelson, 1–22. Chicago: University of Chicago Press.

Friedman, M., and A. J. Schwartz. 1963. *Monetary history of the United States, 1867–1960.* Business Cycle series no. 12. Princeton: Princeton University Press.

Hall, R., and B. Sandler. 1982. The classroom climate: A chilly one for women. *Project on the education and status of women.* Washington, DC: Association of American Colleges.

Heath, J. A. 1989. An econometric model of the role of gender in economic education. *American Economic Review* 79 (May): 226–30.

Horvath, J., B. Q. Beaudin, and S. P. Wright. 1992. Persisting in the introductory economics course: An exploration of gender differences. *Journal of Economic Education* 23 (spring): 101–8.

Lumsden, K. G. 1974. The information content of student evaluation of faculty and courses. In *Efficiency in universities: The La Paz papers,* ed. K. Lumsden, 175–204. Amsterdam and New York: Elsvier Scientific.

Lumsden, K. G., and A. Scott. 1983. The efficiency of innovative teaching techniques in economics: The U. K. experience. *American Economic Review* 70 (May): 13–17.

———. 1987. The economics student reexamined: Male-female differences in comprehension. *Journal of Economic Education* 18 (spring): 1–11.

McIntosh, P. 1983. Interactive phases of curricular re-vision: A feminist perspective. Working Paper. Wellesley College Center for Research on Women.

Phillip, M. C. 1993. Race, gender and economics in the classroom. *Black Issues in Higher Education* 10 (June): 14–18.

Siegfried, J. J. 1979. Male-female differences in economic education: A survey. *Journal of Economic Education* 10 (spring): 1–11.

Siegfried, J. J., and R. Fels. 1979. Teaching college economics: A survey. *Journal of Economic Literature,* 42 (September): 923–69.

Van Scyoc, L. J., and J. Gleason. 1993. Traditional or intensive course lengths? A comparison of outcomes in economics learning. *Journal of Economic Education* 24 (winter): 15–21.

Watts, M., and G. Lynch. 1989. The principles course revisited. *American Economic Review* 79 (May): 236–41.

Williams, M. L., C. Waldauer, and V. G. Duggal. 1992. Gender differences in economic knowledge: An extension of the analysis. *Journal of Economic Education* 23 (summer): 219–30.

PART 3

Alternative Pedagogies

Exploring the Gender Gap on the GRE Subject Test in Economics

Mary Hirschfeld, Robert L. Moore, and Eleanor Brown

On average women achieve lower scores on the Graduate Record Exam (GRE) Subject Test in Economics than men. From 1989 though 1992, 5,815 men and 2,164 women nationwide took the exam; the mean score for women was 603, in contrast to a mean score of 651 for men.[1] In this essay we look for explanations behind the gender gap in economics GRE test scores. Our data include GRE scores, overall college GPA as well as grades in all college economics and math courses, and Scholastic Aptitude Test (SAT) scores for economics majors at Occidental College, all of whom are required to take the GRE Subject Test. We also look at economics majors at Pomona College, who take an alternative standardized test, also produced by Educational Testing Service (ETS), known as the Major Field Achievement Test (MFAT) in Economics.

We find no easy answers. In particular, our results do not support the notion that men are simply better than women at economics; that the difference can be explained by such things as grades in economics courses, SAT scores, or even math backgrounds—or that women are substantially handicapped by a multiple-choice format alone.

We briefly review the GRE exam and the literature on gender and performance in economics, and preview our key empirical results. We then describe the Occidental data and estimate GRE score-generating functions for men and women economics majors. The Pomona College experience with the MFAT exam is contrasted with the Occidental GRE results. We then propose a possible explanation for our results.

The GRE and the Gender Gap

According to the descriptive booklet distributed to all economics GRE test takers by ETS, "scores on the test are intended to indicate students' abilities and their mastery of the subject matter emphasized in many undergraduate programs, with a focus on analytic methods for dealing with economic problems." The booklet goes on to describe the content of the exam:

> The committee of examiners has felt that the primary concern in most graduate school admissions is the student's aptitude for and competence in the basic skills of economic analysis. Of secondary importance is his or her knowledge of economic history, institutions, and terminology. Economic analysis is broadly defined. It includes interpreting and manipulating diagrams and simple mathematics; explaining and predicting economic behavior, given certain assumptions; prescribing appropriate action and policy; and drawing conclusions from specified economic information and data. (Educational Testing Service 1979, 5; and 1987, 6)

Given this orientation, some might conclude that the differential performance by gender must reflect the fact that men have better aptitude for, and competence in, the basic skills of economic analysis. The results we present using data from Occidental College indicate that this differential performance on the GRE persisted even when we controlled for undergraduate grades in economic courses and SAT scores.

Others might point to prior studies, most of which used results from principles of economics courses, that have found that women do worse on standardized multiple-choice exams. A good summary of these past studies on the effect of gender on scores on tests of economic understanding can be found in Williams, Waldauer, and Duggal (1992, 219–20). In general, such studies have used standardized tests to identify the determinants of such economic knowledge. The most comprehensive survey to date (Siegfried 1979) found that men performed better than women in a majority of cases. More recent studies (Anderson et al. 1994; Heath 1989; Soper and Walstad 1988; Walstad and Soper 1980; Ferber, Birnbaum, and Green 1983; Gohmann and Spector 1989; Lumsden and Scott 1987; and Watts and Lynch 1989) seem to confirm the previous findings. Evidently, these men-women differentials are reduced (Ferber, Birnbaum, and Green 1983) or even reversed (Lumsden and Scott 1987) when essay questions are used instead. The study by Williams, Waldauer, and Duggal (1992) extends the research to include intermediate theory and economic statistics courses, and includes essay questions. According to the authors, this provides better information on "the issue of whether observed differences in performance on economic exams are the result of greater male skills in quantitative and spatial relationships compared with greater female skills in verbal relationships" (220). Their study finds "no evidence to support the hypothesis that significant and consistent gender differences exist in college students' performances on economic exams" (229).

Our results, using data from Pomona College, where almost all economics majors take the Major Field Achievement Test in Economics, indicate virtually no differential performance by gender. The MFAT is a shorter and easier version of the GRE Subject Test in Economics prepared by ETS and contains some of the same GRE questions, but it has the same multiple-choice format.[2] Thus, a more complex set of considerations may lie behind the differential performance by gender on the GRE Subject Test than simply the multiple-choice format.

Gender Differences on the GRE Subject Test in Economics at Occidental

Since the early 1980s, every economics major at Occidental has taken the GRE Subject Test administered in February as one part of their comprehensive exam. In addition, each Occidental major takes principles of microeconomics, principles of macroeconomics, intermediate microeconomics, intermediate macroeconomics, a course each in statistics and econometrics, and at least three upper-division courses in economics. Two terms of calculus are also required as is the writing of a fifty-page senior thesis.[3]

The mean GRE score by gender at Occidental over the past five years is similar to the national averages of the eight thousand individuals who took the exam nationally over the 1989–92 period. In particular, the mean for men at Occidental was 646 (with a standard deviation of 73), while that for women was 598 (with a standard deviation of 58). Such scores are unadjusted and thus are of only limited usefulness. Yet they show that the forty-eight-point difference in the means of the men and women who took the exam nationally (651 vs. 603) is almost exactly the same for Occidental students over the past five years. In this sense the Occidental results are not an anomaly.

We were able to get detailed information about our economics graduates during the last five years, including their high school SAT scores, GPA in all economics courses taken at Occidental, and specific math and economics courses taken (and respective grades). The results of our basic equation are shown in table 1. We used OLS to regress the GRE Subject Test in Economics score (GRE) on a student's GPA in all economics courses taken at Occidental (GPA), Math SAT (SATM), Verbal SAT (SATV), a gender dummy variable (MALE), and a constant term (column 1). Separate OLS equations for men and women are also displayed in table 1. Presumably,

SAT scores allowed us to control for verbal and quantitative aptitude as of the senior year in high school as well as skills in taking standardized multiple-choice exams.[4]

The data in table 1 demonstrate that the differential effect of gender remains quite strong, even after adjusting for economics GPA and SAT scores. Women with the same GPA in economics and SAT scores as men scored about forty points lower, or about 94 percent of the score for men.[5] Further, this coefficient is significantly different from zero, with a t statistic of 3.6. The other variables were all significantly different from zero and of the expected sign.

Of course, we were implicitly assuming that this equation that translates relevant economics skills and knowledge (in the form of GPA), and math and verbal aptitudes plus standardized test-taking skills (in the form of SAT scores) into generating points on the GRE, was identical for men and women. The separate results by gender (second and third columns) allowed the coefficients on each of the independent variables to differ by gender. The Chow test resulted in a rejection of the null hypothesis that the regressions are the same.[6]

In general, following Oaxaca (1973), we could decompose the difference in the means for men and women in the GRE into two parts: (1) the portion that resulted from the difference in the returns of a student's investment in economics-relevant skills and knowledge in generating points on

TABLE 1. Results of Estimating Basic Equation for Occidental College Economics Majors (GRE Score = Co + C1 MALE + C2 GPA = C3 SATM + C4 SATV + error term)

Variable	All	Men	Women
MALE	39.7	—	—
	(10.9)		
GPA	78.9	77.2	85.8
	(10.4)	(12.1)	(20.3)
SATM	.203	.212	.162
	(.071)	(.084)	(.122)
SATV	.110	.125	.067
	(.058)	(.072)	(.087)
Constant term	172.40	202.60	199.70
Observations	149	118	31
% male	79	100	0
R^2	.46	.40	.47
Mean GRE	636	646	598
SEE	53.4	56.4	41.2

Note: Standard errors are in parentheses. MALE = dummy variable, male = 1. GPA = Grade point average of all economics courses (4 = A, 3 = B, etc.). SATM = score on mathematics portion of SAT. SATV = score on verbal portion of SAT.

the GRE, such as GPA in economics; and (2) the portion that resulted from the different skill levels. When we carried out the calculations, we found that only 13.8 percent of this difference was due to the different skill levels, while 86.2 percent was due to the different returns from these variables.

The approximately forty-point differential that remained after controlling for GPA and SAT scores turned out to be a remarkably robust result. Because prior studies showed that math courses taken and math course performance were sometimes significant variables explaining multiple-choice exam results (e.g., Anderson et al. 1994), we added variables to the basic equation to capture the number of math courses taken beyond calculus as well as the grade in calculus. The addition of such variables altered the basic equation only slightly, with the coefficient on MALE falling from 39.7 to 37.8, while all the other coefficients were hardly changed. The coefficient on MALE was also changed only slightly when we limited the sample to those students with an economics GPA of 3.5 or below. Because grades are truncated (there is no way to acknowledge better than A work), it has been suggested that such constraints could be masking differences among the very best students. Finally, the coefficient on MALE was little changed when we substituted overall GPA (for economics GPA) or substituted course grades in the three core courses of intermediate microeconomics, intermediate macroeconomics, and econometrics.[7] (Details of these results are available from the authors.)

Thus, the central question remains. Why do women do less well on the GRE, even after controlling for economics grades, SAT scores, the number of advanced math courses, and calculus grades? Of course, grades in economics courses could be measuring many other potential differences between men and women, such as writing skills or effort that the GRE test does not measure. We, therefore, turned to the results at Pomona College, where we had information on economics GPA and scores on the Major Field Test in Economics for a sample of Pomona economics majors.

The Pomona College Results with the Major Field Test in Economics

Although we knew that the gender difference in unadjusted test score means for Occidental students was in line with differences observed nationally, we wondered whether our results, controlling for grades in economics courses, could be replicated at a similar liberal arts college. Our search led us to Pomona College and a rather different piece of evidence. All senior economics majors at Pomona are required to take a standardized test.[8] Unlike Occidental students, however, most take the Major Field Achievement Test

(MFAT) in Economics, which like the GRE, is developed by ETS.[9] This test, according to ETS, is a shortened and easier version of the GRE. Although it includes some actual GRE questions directly, it is designed to be a better indicator of the knowledge that an undergraduate economics major has acquired.

The Pomona data had MFAT scores for ninety-three students from the graduating classes of 1990, 1991, and 1992. Of the sample 26 percent were female, compared to 23 percent in the Occidental sample. The Pomona men and women had remarkably similar performance averages: the women had a slightly lower MFAT mean, 169.8 versus 171.8 for men, and a slightly higher grade point average, 9.65 versus 9.58 on a twelve-point scale (A = 12, A− = 11, B+ = 10, and so on). Nationally, although the women/men ratio of MFAT test scores was a bit lower than at Pomona, it was still quite a bit above the ratio for the GRE Subject Test.[10]

Regressing MFAT scores on economics GPA and the gender dummy variable (MALE) yielded the results reported in table 2. (The results of a similar equation using the Occidental sample are also shown in table 2 for comparison purposes.) As in the raw data, the MFAT scores at Pomona did not seem to be much affected by gender. The regression of the full sample's test scores on GPA and MALE are reported in table 2, column 1; the MALE variable was not statistically significant at the .05 level. In this data set females scored only slightly lower than their male counterparts on the MFAT, with or without controlling for grades in economics courses.

TABLE 2. Results of Estimating Basic Equation for Major Field Test in Economics (MFAT) — Pomona College Economics Majors (MFAT score = A0 + A1 MALE + A2 GPA + error term)

Variable	Pomona College—MFAT			Occidental—GRE		
	All	Men	Women	All	Men	Women
MALE	2.53	—	—	46.5	—	—
	(1.89)			(11.2)		
GPA	6.77	6.83	6.52	94.0	93.2	98.3
	(.66)	(.76)	(1.39)	(10.1)	(11.6)	(19)
Constant Term	104.4	106.4	106.8	312.1	361.2	299.2
Observations	93	69	24	149	118	31
R^2	.53			.42	.35	.48
% male	74	100	0	79	100	0
Mean MFAT(GRE)	171.3	171.8	169.8	636	646	598.0
Mean GPA	9.60	9.58	9.65	3.05	3.06	3.04
SEE				55.7	58.7	42.7

Note: Standard errors are in parentheses. MALE = dummy variable, male = 1. MFAT = Major Field Achievement Test Score in Economics. The scale ranges from 120 to 200. GPA = Grade point average in all economics courses. Pomona uses a 12-point scale: A = 12; B = 9; C = 6, etc.

The regressions for Pomona men and women run separately are reported in columns 2 and 3 of table 2. The two groups had quite similar constants and intercepts. Indeed, the Chow test for comparing two regressions indicated that we could not reject the null hypothesis that the Pomona equations are the same.[11] The regression represented by column 1 in table 2 implies that women with the same GPA as men at Pomona scored almost as well on the MFAT.[12] The results made it clear that the Pomona-MFAT data and the Occidental-GRE data gave quite different pictures of the relationship between gender and test scores. It is possible, of course, that the difference arose from some sort of difference between the economics programs and economics students at Occidental and Pomona, but these schools have quite similar philosophies and attention to pedagogy, and in both samples women had slightly higher GPAs than men. In addition, the national averages on the GRE and MFAT tests mirror our results from Occidental and Pomona. As such, we feel that the interesting hypotheses link gender differences in performance to differences across the two tests.

A Possible Explanation with Testable Implications

In searching for an explanation of this persistent gender gap in test performance on the GRE, two hypotheses suggested themselves. First, it may be that on average men and women self-select economics with somewhat different interests, and the GRE is more nearly aligned with the subset of economics that appeals to men. If the GRE accurately reflects the skills and interests relevant to further productivity in economics, the gender gap is a signal that the areas of economics that attract women as undergraduates receive less emphasis in advanced study. Alternatively, the content and or structure of the GRE exam may have inherent biases that lead it to underestimate, on average, the potential of women economists. If, for example, some economists excel at manipulating analytical tools and others at connecting analytical techniques to important problems, a test that focuses on the first set of skills will underrate the second set of economists.

Under the first hypothesis the GRE is doing its job.[13] Under the second hypothesis the GRE is systematically misevaluating candidates for graduate school, with potentially costly implications for women and the economics profession. Because its consequences are more serious, we pursue the second hypothesis here. We offer a set of hypotheses about the potential sources of bias in the GRE, outline some potential tests (both informal and formal) of the hypotheses, and report some very preliminary results.[14]

Men also outperform women on the SAT exams. For example, in 1980 the average verbal score for men was eight points higher than that of women, and the gap between the means on the mathematical score was forty-eight points. Studies indicate that these results are biased in favor of men. An examination of the numerous tests of mathematical ability shows a slight advantage (which does not approach the difference measured by the SAT) for men that has been diminishing over time. There is a similarly slight advantage for women in tests of verbal ability. Thus, the SAT appears to overstate male abilities in both categories, and is considered by many psychologists to be a flawed instrument (Fausto-Sterling 1985, 262).[15] The GRE Subject Test in Economics is structurally similar to the SAT and may carry the same biases.

Our results have shown that even holding constant economics GPA and SAT scores (along with whatever bias inheres in those scores), men score on average forty points higher than women. A straightforward response to our results might be to ask whether any advantages enjoyed by men on the SAT exam are magnified on the GRE Subject Test in Economics. There are two obvious differences between the exams. First, the GRE exam is taken at the end of the college career, rather than at the beginning. Second, the GRE exam is in a field that continues to be dominated by men; in 1988, only 32.8 percent of all bachelor's degrees in economics were received by women, up from 9.8 percent in 1966 (U.S. Department of Education 1990).

Both the SAT and the GRE Subject Test are multiple-choice exams administered within a rigid time constraint. Both exams present some problems that appear unfamiliar, but that can be analyzed using familiar tools. Both reward a willingness to guess when some choices have been ruled out. On exams like this, confidence and competitiveness are two attributes that might enable students to get maximum scores for their ability level. There are several reasons for this. First, questions that appear unfamiliar may scare off students lacking confidence. In contrast, students confident of their abilities may be energized by the challenge. Thus, students with confidence would tend to answer more questions than students with less confidence. The confidence gap would be exacerbated by the time constraints of the exam. Students with less confidence may be more afraid of running out of time, and so might skip questions they are, in reality, capable of handling.[16] Students who thrive in competitive situations are likely to maintain a more confident attitude under the stress of the exam than those students who tend to avoid competition. The smaller gender gap on the MFAT, which allows more time per question and is a less intimidating exam, is consistent with this explanation.[17]

Differences in confidence might lead to differences in guessing strategies. On the SAT and GRE, students score a point for each correct answer and lose one-fourth point for each wrong answer. If one potential answer can be eliminated, guessing leads to a higher expected score. Students with confidence might be more willing to risk being wrong than students without confidence. In this light, it is interesting to note that the MFAT, which has a much smaller gender gap, has no penalty for wrong answers.

The gap in confidence and competitiveness is likely to greater when students take the GRE economics exam than when they take the SAT. The GRE comes at the end of the college career. It appears that women systematically lose confidence over the course of their college years, while men maintain or strengthen their confidence. For example, Karen Arnold studied a group of high school valedictorians through their college careers. The women earned higher grades than the men on average. However the men had sharply higher estimates of their own intelligence as they moved through college. The percentages are as shown in table 3 (Arnold 1992, 398). Hall and Sandler (1983) have also argued, based on substantial empirical work, that the classroom environment in college (differential responses from professors, harassment from male students) tends to discourage women.[18]

Pursuing this hypothesis in a highly informal manner, the two authors at Occidental tried to predict which students would have large residuals based on their personalities. This exercise was quite successful, including the identification of two women who had the type of confidence we have discussed.

We also wondered about the gender gap on the GRE Subject Test in other disciplines. The hypothesis above would suggest that this gap should be widest in those disciplines where there are fewer women relative to men, ceteris paribus. The gap should also be wider in those disciplines in which test problems appear unfamiliar but which can be analyzed using familiar tools.[19] It turns out that the gender gap is largest in math and physics (100 and 70 points, respectively), where men outnumbered women test takers by a 2 to 1 and 4 to 1 margin, respectively. The gender gap is smallest for psychology, education, and sociology where women score 10 points less, 5 points less, and 5 points more than men, respectively. In each of these latter three disciplines more women than men were test takers.[20]

TABLE 3

Intelligence Self-Estimate	High School Senior		College Sophomore		College Senior	
	Male	Female	Male	Female	Male	Female
Average/slightly above average	30	35	28	54	19	30
Above average	47	44	50	42	56	70
Far above average	23	21	22	4	25	0

More formal tests of the confidence gap hypothesis are theoretically possible. It would be useful, for example, to test the following predictions: (1) men attempt more questions and are more willing to make informed guesses, and therefore leave fewer questions unanswered; (2) the gender gap would be smaller if the GRE Subject Test were administered without, or with less severe, time constraints; and (3) correlation between reported self-esteem (or similar measures from the psychology literature) and GRE scores would be positive, all else held constant.

None of these tests lies within the scope of our data. We asked ETS if they could help us with the first prediction and they graciously agreed to run a limited test using data from one recent administration of the GRE Subject Test in Economics.[21] Specifically, the results show that of the 130 individual test questions, men left 17 percent blank, while the women left 20 percent blank. Unfortunately, we were unable to obtain the exact sample sizes used by ETS in calculating these figures, but on average about 500 men and 180 women would be taking the GRE Subject Test in Economics at any one administration. Because sample sizes of only 10 correspond to a t value of 1.97, we believe it is safe to conclude that this difference is significant.[22] The statisticians also calculated for each question the percentage of men who left it blank and the percentage of women who left it blank. For 117 of the questions the difference between these percentages was less than ten percentage points; for example, the percentage of men who left it blank might have been 6 percent, while the percentage of women, 8 percent, for a difference of two percentage points. For the remaining 13 questions, however, the difference in these percentage was greater than ten percentage points; 23 percent of the men left one of these questions blank, while 39 percent of the women did, for a difference of sixteen percentage points. In all these cases in which the difference was greater than ten percentage points, the men always had a lower percentage left blank.[23]

Conclusions and Implications

In trying to account for the fact that women score about fifty points lower than men on the GRE Subject Test nationally, we have tried to show that some of the more obvious explanations do not explain the differential. Our analysis of the data from senior economics majors at Occidental College over the past five years shows that although economics GPA and SAT scores are significant variables in predicting the GRE Subject Test score, women with the same economics GPA and SAT scores, and even math background and ability, as their male counterparts still score about forty points lower on the GRE Subject Test. Although earlier research has suggested that women do worse on standardized multiple-choice exams, our analysis of data from senior economics majors at Pomona College over the past three years indicates that this differential between men and women all but disappears on the Major Field Test in Economics, a shorter and easier version of the GRE Subject Test.

The explanation we offer suggests that the GRE Subject Test is a somewhat flawed instrument of measuring a student's aptitude for, and competence in, the basic skills of economic analysis. Because the GRE Subject Test is a multiple-choice exam administered with a rigid time constraint involving problems that appear initially unfamiliar but can be analyzed using familiar tools, confidence and competitiveness are two attributes that might be more important to GRE performance than to performance as an economist. We conducted several very informal investigations of our hypothesis and had ETS perform a more formal test of one of our predictions. All the results were consistent with our confidence gap hypothesis. Naturally, further investigation of this issue would be useful.

We hope our empirical results will spur further investigation by others. It would be useful to know if our findings at Occidental and Pomona can be duplicated at other institutions that require their students to take the GRE Subject Test or the MFAT. Perhaps just as important, we hope that graduate schools that currently use the GRE Subject Test as part of their admissions process, and undergraduate programs that, like Occidental, have used the GRE Subject Test as part of their evaluation of senior economics majors, might keep our results in mind when considering the scores of women that appear out of line with the other measures they use.[24]

NOTES

This essay originally appeared in *Journal of Economic Education* (winter 1995): 3–15. Reprinted by permission of the Helen Dwight Reid Educational Foundation. Published by Heldref Publications, 1319 Eighteenth St., NW, Washington, DC 20036-1802. Copyright © 1995.

1. This information comes from phone conversations with Dawn S. Robinson, Associate Program director of the GRE Program Staff.

2. According to the ETS (1990, 2), "the Major Field Achievement Tests are based on the GRE Subject Tests, but they are shorter and less difficult, making them suitable for all seniors majoring in the field, not just those planning graduate study." The MFAT results from Pomona College also make it difficult to accept an amended version of the first explanation. Such an explanation would start with the assumption that men have better aptitude for, and competence in, the basic skills of economic analysis but add that no independent variables, such as economics grades and SATs, can adequately control for such aptitude and competence.

3. Several individuals, including some at Educational Testing Service, wondered whether our results were due to the fact that there could be differences by gender in the economics courses taken. For example, it was suggested that a smaller proportion of women might take econometrics. Although such a conjecture might be important for a national sample, the breadth of the Occidental requirements, which require every major to take a course in statistics and another in econometrics, would seem to rule this out for our sample.

4. It should be noted that some psychologists contend that the SAT exam itself is biased in favor of men.

5. We obtained this percentage by subtracting the coefficient on MALE from the mean for men and then dividing this difference by the mean for men.

6. The F statistic was 3.32 with 4, 141 degrees of freedom. The critical F-statistic value at the .05 level for 4, 120 $d.f.$ is 2.45.

7. We also ran all equations in table 1 with additional dummy variables for the graduation year of each student. This was to control for the possibility that different classes that have slightly different means on the GRE also might have different proportions of men. The coefficients of these dummy variables never had significant t statistics, nor did their inclusion alter the coefficients of the independent variables in table 1 in any significant way.

8. All Pomona College economics majors take principles of macroeconomics, principles of microeconomics, statistics, intermediate microeconomics, intermediate macroeconomics, and one semester of calculus and must attend a senior colloquium. Students have the option of either taking five additional upper-division courses in economics or pursuing an alternative set of requirements that includes substantially more mathematics (one course beyond linear algebra and differential equations) and one fewer economics courses. Most Pomona economics students planning to go to graduate school take the GRE, and some of these students (three men and two women from the graduating classes in our sample) exercised their option to substitute the GRE for the MFAT in fulfilling their testing requirement.

9. The MFAT has only 90 questions and lasts 120 minutes (1.33 minutes per question), while the GRE Subject Test has 135 questions and lasts 170 minutes (1.26 minutes per question), according to the materials provided to test takers (Educational Testing Service 1987, 6).

10. Nationally on the MFAT, for the period 1989–92, the mean for 1,175 men was 154, and the mean for women was 148. Thus, the women's mean was 95.8 percent of the men's. For the Pomona students this ratio was a bit higher, at .988. Both are well above the .92 value nationwide on the GRE Subject Test.

11. The Chow test F statistic to determine if the regression for men is different than the regression for women has a value of only .016 with 2, 89 degrees of freedom. This is far below the critical value of 1.40 for the .25 level. Thus, we cannot reject the null hypothesis that the Pomona equations are the same. For the Occidental results, however, the F statistic was 8.52 with 2, 145 degrees of freedom. Thus, we could reject the null hypothesis that the Occidental equations are the same.

12. If we subtract the coefficient on MALE from the mean MFAT score for men and then divide by the mean MFAT score for men, the resulting percentage is 98.5. This compares with a percentage of 92.6 using the GRE results in table 2, column 4, at Occidental.

13. Schneider and Briel (1990, 9), in their most recent validity report of the GRE, find that the GRE Subject Test in Economics has an average correlation with first-year

graduate school grades of .42, while the average correlation between first-year graduate school grades and GRE Verbal, Quantitative, and Analytical test scores are .23, .26, and .27, respectively. Undergraduate GPA had a correlation coefficient of .34. This, by itself, does not mean that the GRE Subject Test is a good measure to use for admission, because graduate schools might have the same biases in terms of confidence and competitiveness that we suggest the GRE may have. Further, it may be that graduate schools themselves, especially in the first year, may be emphasizing a particular subset of skills that are not important for the ultimate success of Ph.D. economists.

14. We should briefly note that the Educational Testing Service uses a statistical procedure on the GRE General Test known as Differential Item Functioning Analysis (DIF Analysis) to test for bias on any specific question. In a technical report, *Sex, Race, Ethnicity, and Performance on the GRE General Test,* DIF Analysis is described as based "on a comparison between groups of test takers of the same overall ability, as determined by their performance on the test as a whole. A DIF statistic is computed for each test question, indicating the extent to which members of the focal group perform differently from members of the reference groups who have the same scores on the test as a whole. On the basis of this type of analysis, any questions that members of the focal group miss substantially more often than members of the reference group are deleted from the test scores used to match the two groups on ability" (Educational Testing Service 1989, 5). Upon closer questioning, it turns out that this DIF analysis is not performed on the GRE Subject Test in economics (although it is on some other Subject Tests such as in psychology), and the number of females taking the GRE Subject Test in economics on any given date is less than the two hundred necessary for statistical validity. Dawn Robinson, of ETS, did have the statisticians at ETS perform this analysis for us for the December 1992 and December 1991 administrations of the Subject Test, even though the number of women taking the test was too small for statistical validity. The results indicated that none of the questions would have been deleted based on the standard DIF analysis. A few were in the B, or second, category, in which there was some evidence of differential results but not serious enough to warrant deletion of the question (and some of these had women performing better than men). The failure of this DIF analysis to find evidence of a gender bias in any particular question does not necessarily imply, however, that there are not inherent biases in the content and/or structure of the GRE exam taken in its entirety, as our discussion will demonstrate.

15. It is worth noting that women outperform men in the classroom, as measured by GPA in both high school and college. This female advantage is observed in math courses (at all levels through graduate school) (Fausto-Sterling 1985, 266).

16. One of the authors teaches a mathematics course for economics majors who are intimidated by math. In this course students complain particularly about the deleterious effects of time constraints on their performance. The author has found that exams administered to students without time constraints tend to give a better reading of a student's ability (as demonstrated on problem sets and by the student's responses in class) than do exams with time constraints.

17. The only careful analysis of the time-constraint issue that we discovered was a 1979 report by ETS entitled *Effect of Increased Test-Taking Time on Test Scores by Ethnic Group, Age, and Sex* (Wild and Durso 1979). It investigated the effects of increasing the test time to reduce the time pressures of the verbal and quantitative experimental sections of the GRE Aptitude (but not Subject) Test. The results indicated that, "although the 20-minute experimental tests [are] generally more speeded [*sic*] than

the 30-minute tests, the 10 additional minutes resulted in a small score increase for all groups, and differential score gains were not found between the subgroups."

18. Of course, other more speculative reasons have been advanced for the type of confidence that enhances exam performance by men. For example, as far back as the turn of the century, Helen Bradford Thompson devised some early versions of IQ tests. On these tests she found that men and women performed equally well, except on puzzles. Her explanation for this disparity was that boys were "encouraged to independence and individuality, while girls were trained to 'obedience, dependence, and deference'—hardly the tools for effective problem-solving" (qtd. in Russett 1989, 168). Others (Siegfried and Strand 1977, 247) cite as a standard hypothesis (for the better performance of men on economics exams) that "women students have grown up in a cultural environment in which girls are not supposed to like business and thus have a disadvantage in business or economics courses." Still others would cite the fact that women tend to be a smaller proportion of economics majors and thus find themselves in the uncomfortable position of being in the extreme minority in their economics classes. Yet, while these last two rationales could easily have negative consequences for the self-confidence of the women who do persevere in the major, it is also possible that only confident women stick it out in this environment.

19. We thank Peter Kennedy, associate editor of the *Journal of Economic Education,* for directing our attention to this possible additional test of our hypothesis.

20. This information comes from a telephone conversation with Rob Dorso at ETS and is based on all students taking these exams during 1988–91.

21. The information reported here was based on a phone conversation with Dawn S. Robinson. She indicated that prior to our inquiry ETS had not investigated the number of questions left blank by gender.

22. Using a sample size of 500 men and 180 women, the t statistic for the difference between the means comes out to 10.075.

23. No further information was available in which to carry out a formal significance test. Further, we were not able to examine the thirteen questions where the difference in percentage left blank was greater than 10 percentage points to determine if there was any similarity in the type of question. We were informed that there was no discernable pattern about when in the exam these thirteen questions occurred. For example, it was not the case that the thirteen questions came toward the end of the exam. Note that the confidence gap hypothesis does not require or even predict that women will have more unanswered questions at the end of the exam because of time pressure. All that matters is a perception that time constraints will become binding.

24. Readers whose undergraduate or graduate departments compile statistics relating test scores to performance are invited to report to us what data are available. Correspondence should be sent to Professor Robert L. Moore, Department of Economics, Occidental College, Los Angeles, CA 90041.

REFERENCES

Anderson, G., H. Benjamin, and M. A. Fuss. 1994. The determinants of success in university introductory economics courses. *Journal of Economic Education* 25 (spring): 99–119.

Arnold, K. 1992. Academically talented women in the 1980s: The Illinois valedictorian project. In *Women's lives through time: Educated American women of the twentieth century*, ed. Kathleen Dan Hulbert and Diane Tickton Schuster. San Francisco: Jossey-Bass.

Educational Testing Service. 1979 and 1987. GRE: A description of the advanced economics test, 1980–82, and 1988–90. Princeton, NJ: Educational Testing Service.

———. 1989. Sex, race, ethnicity, and performance on the GRE general test: Technical report. Princeton, NJ: Educational Testing Service.

———. 1990. Major field achievement tests: Assessment in the major. Princeton, NJ: Education Testing Service.

Fausto-Sterling, A. 1985. *Myths of gender: Biological theories about women and men.* New York: Basic Books.

Ferber, M. A., B. G. Birnbaum, and C. A. Green. 1983. Gender differences in economic knowledge: A reevaluation of the evidence. *Journal of Economic Education* 14 (spring): 24–37.

Gohmann, S., and L. C. Spector. 1989. Test scrambling and student performance. *Journal of Economic Education* 20 (summer): 235–38.

Hall, R. M., and B. R. Sandler. 1983. The classroom climate: A chilly one to women. Washington, DC: Project on the Status and Education of Women. Association of American Colleges.

Heath, J. A. 1989. An econometric model of the role of gender in economic education. *American Economic Review* 79 (May): 226–30.

Lumsden, K. G., and A. Scott. 1987. The economics student reexamined: Male-female differences in comprehension. *Journal of Economic Education* 18 (fall): 365–75.

Oaxaca, R. 1973. Male-female wage differentials in urban labor markets. *International Economic Review* 14(3): 693–709.

Russett, C. E. 1989. *Sexual science: The Victorian construction of womanhood.* Cambridge: Harvard University Press.

Schneider, L. M., and J. B. Briel. 1990. *Validity of the GRE: 1988–89,* summary report. Princeton, NJ: Educational Testing Service.

Siegfried, J. J. 1979. Male-female differences in education: A survey. *Journal of Economics Education* 10 (spring): 1–11.

Siegfried, J. J., and S. H. Strand. 1977. Sex and the economics student. *Review of Economics and Statistics* 59 (May): 247–49.

Soper, J. C., and W. B. Walstad. 1988. What is high school economics? Posttest knowledge, attitudes and course content. *Journal of Economic Education* 19 (winter): 37–51.

U.S. Department of Education, National Center for Education Statistics. 1990. *Digest of Education Statistics.* Washington, DC: Government Printing Office.

Walstad, W. B., and J. C. Soper. 1989. What is high school economics? Factors contributing to student achievements and attitudes. *Journal of Economic Education* 20 (winter): 23–28.

Watts, M., and G. J. Lynch. 1989. The principles course revisited. *American Economic Review* 79(2): 236–41.

Wild, C., and R. Durso. 1989. Effect of increased test-taking time on test scores by ethnic group, age, and sex. *GRE Board Research Report No. 76-6R.* Princeton, NJ: Educational Testing Service.

Williams, M. L., C. Waldauer, and V. C. Duggal. 1992. Gender differences in economic knowledge: An extension of the analysis. *Journal of Economic Education* 23 (summer): 219–31.

Does Personality Type Explain the Gender Gap in Economics?

Analysis and Pedagogy

Andrea L. Ziegert and Dennis Sullivan

Nearly twenty years ago Siegfried (1979) reported that men outperformed women in introductory economics classes, and the existence of a "gender gap" became part of the professional literature. In a survey of more recent works, Ferber (1990) notes the importance of distinguishing between the stock of economic knowledge that a student has when they enter their first college economics course, and the flow or rate of learning that occurs during a college economics course. Two-thirds of the studies Ferber surveys found statistically significant stock differences in understanding economics which favored men, while men learned statistically significantly more than women in the classroom in one-third of the studies reviewed. In addition, the method of testing matters: men do better than women on multiple choice tests, while women do as well as men on essay tests.

This gender gap in learning, is attributed, in part, to a "chilly classroom climate" (Bartlett and Ferber [1998]; Ferber [1990], and Hall and Sandler [1982]). Evidence suggests that instructors view women as less dedicated and less promising students than their male counterparts, and that instructors reinforce stereotypes of gender differences in career aspirations. For example, instructors may be less supportive of further graduate or professional study for women rather than for men in their classes. Other researchers have suggested that the lack of balance in the content of introductory texts contribute to the gender gap in learning (Feiner and Morgan (1987) and Ferber (1990)).

Alternatively, Borg and Shapiro (1996) in a study of students in principles of macroeconomics courses, and Ziegert (1998) in a study of students in principles of microeconomics courses, find that differences in personality type partially explains the differences in learning between male and female students in both principles of economics courses. This essay builds upon the work on personality and learning, and poses the following research questions:

Do differences in personality temperament between men and women explain any of the gender gap in economics knowledge (stock) and learning (flow)? (between group variation); and

Is the effect of personality temperament on knowledge of economics and learning of economics the same for both women and men? That is, do men and women with identical personality temperaments learn economics equally well? (comparative within-group variation).

Because most economists are unfamiliar with the role of personality type in classroom learning, a brief introduction is presented.[1] That introduction is followed by an analysis of the two research questions. The essay concludes with some comments relating the answers to these two questions to their implications for pedagogy.

Personality Temperaments and Learning

The role of personality type and learning was developed by C. G. Jung and made operational by Isabel Briggs Myers and Katherine Briggs in the well-known Myers-Briggs (personality) Type Indicator (MBTI). While only Borg and Shapiro (1996) and Ziegert (1998) apply this information to economics courses in particular, considerable research has used the MBTI to examine the role of personality in learning in general (McCaulley (1976) and Center for Applications of Psychological Type). In addition, the MBTI is frequently studied and used in business settings to improve teamwork and worker productivity. Because many economists are unaware of this research, a brief discussion of personality types and learning in an economics classroom is in order.

Preference Scales

Jung classified all mental activity according to the four dichotomous personality preference scales found in table 1. The preference scales identify and describe an individual's preferences for relating to the world (I-E), processing information (S-N), making decisions (T-F), and lifestyle and time orientation (J-P). Each scale is a continuum: an individual can exhibit different degrees of these personality traits; an individual's Myers-Briggs (personality) Type Indicator can be measured as being closer (further) from either extreme on the continuum. In addition, the more a person reinforces a particular personality preference say, the feeling versus thinking preference, the stronger that preference (feeling) will be in his or her personality. Each individual can be described by his or her personality type, composed of one preference from each of the four preference scales (ENTJ, ISFP, ENSP, INTJ, etc.).

Introversion-Extroversion (I-E)

The most misunderstood of the preference scales, the introversion-extroversion preference does not describe an individual as either a wallflower or the life of the party. Instead this preference scale refers to *the focus of one's attention or source of energy.* Extroverts (E) are outward turning and are energized by the world outside of themselves. They can be characterized as sociable, action-oriented, and risk taking. In the classroom, extrovert students respond quickly to questions and often need to talk out loud to know what they think. Extroverts can handle multiple stimuli without losing focus and generally prefer talking rather than writing as a mode of communication. They have a broad breadth of interests. About 75 percent of the U.S. population are estimated to be extroverts and the remaining 25 percent are introverts.

On the other hand, Introverts (I) are inward turning and find the source of their energy in the inner life of ideas and concepts. They are private and reflective and often exhibit a depth (vs. breadth) of interests. In the classroom, introvert students need time to get to know their instructors and classmates, they need time for reflection before discussion, and prefer one-to-one rather than group activities. If introverts are silent in class, it does not necessarily mean they are uninterested, but rather they need time to reflect upon the information and place it in context before discussing it with other students. Introverts will often express an opinion only when asked. Introverts prefer writing rather than talking as a mode of communication.

At the end of the teaching day, an extroverted professor is likely to be "wound up" and energized by teaching. He or she often has difficulty unwinding and wants to talk about and process what happened in the classroom. An introverted professor, while often energetic in the classroom, is

TABLE 1. Personality Preference Scales

Introversion (I)	Extroversion (E)
Sensing (S)	Intuitive (N)
Thinking (T)	Feeling (F)
Judging (J)	Perceiving (P)

drained at the end of the day. Bringing out the connections in the classroom is often exhausting, and an introverted professor needs solitude to re-energize and process what happened in class. Research suggest, introverts outnumber extroverts on college and university faculties.[2] This may partially explain the prevalence of passive rather than active pedagogies in college classrooms, as professors teach in a manner more consistent with their own personality preferences.

Sensing—Intuitive (S-N)

The sensing-intuitive preference scale refers to the *way in which an individual takes in information.* Approximately 75 percent of the U.S. population prefer "S" while the remainder prefer "N." A sensing individual trusts the data and information that comes from his or her five senses. These students focus on details and specifics, often work sequentially, prefer experience-rooted learning, and value information that is practical and personally relevant. In an economics classroom, these students may focus on replicating graphs drawn on the board without understanding the underlying concepts (i.e., they know that MC crosses ATC at a minimum, but they don't know why).

Intuitives prefer to take in information through "intuition" or hunches. They like the "big picture," focusing on patterns and concepts first, rather then detail. They learn from insight and enjoy learning new skills. These students like solving problems, enjoy change, and are often innovative in their thinking though frequently they may make errors of fact. Students with an intuitive preference are likely to get bored with a professor who reviews problems in class that illustrate general concepts, through use of details, as they find such activities obvious and repetitive.

In the classroom a sensing professor may ask students for specific examples of economic phenomena (when you go to the store, how do you decide what to buy?) and then develop a concept or theory in terms of a concrete example or student experience. On the other hand, an intuitive professor will often present a theory or concept first, and may be frustrated when some students fail to see its relevance or to be able to generalize to specific facts or circumstances.

Thinking—Feeling (T-F)

Thinking does not imply intelligence, nor does feeling imply emotion; instead this preference scale describes *ways in which individuals evaluate information and make decisions.* Thinking—Feeling preferences are evenly divided among the overall population: 50 percent are "T," and 50 percent are "F." Thinkers tend to make decisions impersonally, making objective judgments that emphasize analysis and place a high value on fairness. Emotions and feelings are important to thinkers, but are valued as one of many aspects to be considered in the decision. In the classroom, thinkers love competition and debate and try to sway others to their position. The feeling person makes decisions on the basis of personal values and places a high value on harmony. Their decision making style is subjective and empathic. They like to give and receive affirmation. They do not like debate but prefer collaboration to competition in the classroom.[3] Feeling students learn best once they've developed a relationship with both their instructor and student colleagues.

Thinking versus feeling professors differ most on their approach to student evaluation. Thinkers are likely to have a grade distribution for the course on the syllabus on the first day of class. With few exceptions, grades are set easily by applying this predetermined distribution. A feeling professor, on the other hand, is likely to give more weight to individual student growth and circumstances.

The Thinking-Feeling preference is unique among the personality preferences: because it is the only preference scale that has significant differences in the distribution of preferences among men and women. Approximately 60 to 65 percent of women tested are classified as feeling, while 60 to 65 percent of men tested are classified as thinking.[4]

Judging—Perceiving (J-P)

The final preference scale, judging-perceiving indicates preferences in relating to the outer world: an *individual's need for order, closure, openness and adaptability.* This preference scale is evenly distributed among the population: 50 percent of the U.S. population is classified as perceiving and the remainder as judging. Judging individuals prefer an orderly and structured environment. They are goal oriented and often have detailed plans to achieve their goals. When a decision is needed, "Js" are often anxious until a decision is made; they seek closure. In the classroom these students often complete papers and assignments before their due dates and are very organized in their studying. They are often upset, however, if scheduled tests or assignment deadlines are changed.

Perceiving individuals prefer a spontaneous and flexible environment. They like to keep their options open and are often tentative in their decision-making and uncomfortable making decisions quickly. Often they will postpone decisions until the last possible moment to insure that all possible options have been explored. These students pull "all-nighters" to complete required assignments. Imposing structure on these students may actually be counterproductive, since they require a degree of flexibility to accomplish their tasks. This preference has important implications for active learning or group activities in the classroom. Combining "J" and "P" students on group projects can spell disaster unless the "J" students' need for structure and the "P" students' need for flexibility is discussed and some compromise reached.

A professor's office often betrays his or her classification on the J-P personality preference scale. Judging individual's need for order often translates into orderly files, and organized, clean desks: everything has a place and everything is in its place. On the other hand, a "non-P" observer may consider a perceiving individual's office a disaster area. Books, papers, and files are stacked everywhere and the desk surface hasn't been seen since the beginning of the term. Generally, however, "P" individuals know where things are and can operate successfully in such an environment.

Learning Theory, Personality Temperaments, and Economics

Understanding economics is a process of gathering information, making sense of information, building conceptual models, and using these models to evaluate and analyze different situations and alternatives. Jungian psychological theory suggests that people with different personality temperaments or types prefer to receive and process information differently. Personality type plays an important role in a student's understanding of economics. Given the more analytical nature of economics, some personality types may succeed in economics more readily than do others. Faculty personality type is also important in determining the way in which economic concepts are presented. Thus, if students and faculty have the same personality type, they are more likely to receive and process information in a similar fashion. In addition, understanding ways in which different personality temperaments gather and process information can lead to more effective pedagogies which will benefit all economics students. At a minimum, if a class contains students with a variety of personality temperaments with their own preferred methods of gathering and processing information, an instructor might increase the amount of learning that occurs by varying the way economic principles are presented and developed and how learning is evaluated.

Isabel Myers considered the S-N and T-F personality preference scales as most important for understanding how people learn.[5] These preferences relate directly to the learning process: S-N preference involves the gathering of information and the T-F preference involves decision making and problem solving. Learners can be classified as having one of four possible combinations of these preferences: SF, ST, NF, and NT.

Given the possible combinations of these preferences this research hypothesizes that, ceteris paribus, the more theoretical and technical characteristics of principles of economics will lead NT students to perform better and SF students to perform less well. This hypothesis has underlying gender implications. Because female students have a greater probability of being an "F" (60 to 65 percent chance versus a 35 to 40 percent chance for males) than a "T" (35 to 40 percent chance versus a 60 to 65 percent chance for males), women on average are expected to perform less well than their male counterparts, all else equal. Thus, personality temperament may explain some of the gender gap in learning in economics.

Table 2 summarizes the role of personality type in learning economic principles. In general, regardless of the performance measure employed, introverts outperform extroverts and thinking students outperform feeling students in the classroom. This latter result may be important for understanding the gender gap in learning since women are more likely to be classified as feelers while men are more likely classified as thinkers.

TABLE 2. Summary of Research on Personality Temperaments and Performance in Economic Principles

Performance Measure: Course Grade in Principles of Macroeconomics (Borg & Shapiro)
Course Grade in Principles of Microeconomics (Ziegert)
- Introverts (I) outperform extroverts (E)
- Sensing (S) students outperform Intuitive (N) students
- Ziegert finds Thinking (T) students outperform Feeling (F) students
- Ziegert finds ST students outperform all other students
- Borg & Shapiro finds SJ students outperform NF and NT students
- Borg & Shapiro find that students earn higher grades if their personality types match that of their instructors

Performance Measure: Post-TUCE Score (Ziegert)
- Introverts (I) outperform extroverts (E)
- Intuitive (N) students outperform (S) students
- Thinking (T) students outperform Feeling (F) students
- NT students outperform NF, and SF students

Performance Measure: Post-Pre TUCE Score (Ziegert)
- Introverts (I) outperform extroverts (E)
- Thinking (T) students outperform Feeling (F) students
- NT students outperform ST, SF, and SJ students

Data

The database for this study is a subset of that employed by Ziegert (1998). It consists of 323 observations of Miami University students from a fifteen-week semester. The 323 observations include 140 women and 183 men. All were enrolled in a Principles of Microeconomics course, taught by full time faculty with Ph.D. degrees in economics, in classes of thirty-five or fewer students. Ten different instructors participated in the study, three of whom were women. Every student in this sample took the Test of Understanding College Economics (TUCE) both at the beginning of the semester (hereafter referred to as the Pre-TUCE) and near the end of the course (the Post-TUCE.) Both students and faculty took the 70 question Keirsey Sorter, a Myers-Briggs type standard personality inventory.[6] The results of these instruments were then matched with each student's course grade, Grade Point Average (GPA) prior to the class, and ACT score (or its SAT equivalent), data obtained from university databases.

Gender Differentials in Measured Learning

Table 3 shows gender differentials in model variables. The first three variables are potential measures of a gender gap in "learning." Women received higher course grades than men, the difference being significant at a 10 percent level of significance but not at a 5 percent level. On the other hand,

TABLE 3.   Gender Differentials in Model Variables

	Women	Men	$|t|$
Mean Course Grade	2.69	2.51	1.64
Mean Post-TUCE Score	13.7	14.7	1.99
Mean Post-TUCE minus Pre-TUCE Score	4.0	4.4	0.95
Mean GPA	3.11	2.98	2.05
Mean ACT	26.0	26.1	0.47
Percentage Extrovert (E)	63.6	72.1	1.62
Percentage Intuitive (N)	35.7	29.0	1.28
Percentage Thinking (T)	42.1	51.4	1.65
Percentage Judging (J)	87.9	80.0	1.99
Percentage ST combination	32.9	42.6	1.80
Percentage NT combination	9.3	8.7	0.17
Percentage NF combination	26.4	20.2	1.30
Percentage SF combination	31.4	28.4	0.58

men scored about one answer higher on the TUCE exam given near the end of the course, a small difference but significant at the 5 percent level of significance. The gender difference in the improvement in TUCE score from beginning of class to end is also larger for men, but the difference is not statistically significant.

Gender Differences in Measured Personality Type

The remaining entries in table 3 show gender breakdowns of personality types for the students in our sample. In the sample of students studied, women are less likely than men to be extroverts and thinkers and more likely to have the introvert and feeling personality preferences. Furthermore, women are more likely than men to rely on intuition and to make decisions in the decisive fashion associated with the Judging preference. Ziegert (1998) argues that the N-S and T-F preferences are particularly important for learning in economics. The final four entries in table 3 shows the gender analysis of the four possible combinations. Women are statistically significantly less likely to be classified with a ST preference then are men, whereas the distribution of the remaining N-S and T-F preference combinations is similar for both men and women. Given previous work on personality temperament and learning in economics and this sample distribution of personality preferences, the question remains: do the differences in the distribution of personality preferences explain any of the difference in learning experienced by women and men?

Basic Regression Results

Basic OLS regression results are shown in tables 4 and 5. Three measures of student performance are employed: grade earned in microeconomic principles (GRADE), number of questions correct on the TUCE exam given at the end of the course (Post-TUCE), and the difference between the number of correct questions answered on Post-TUCE and Pre-TUCE exams (Post-TUCE minus Pre TUCE). Both GRADE and Post-TUCE are measures of the stock of economic knowledge while Post-TUCE minus Pre-TUCE is a measure of the flow of learning.[7] The coefficients and model statistics presented in tables 4–6 also reflect the inclusion of a series of faculty fixed effects variables to control for class specific differences for nine of ten participating faculty; the coefficients on these variables, however, are not reported. The results support four useful conclusions:

Consistent with Ziegert (1998), GPA and ACT scores are consistently significant and positive; both prior academic performance and measured "aptitudes" matter regardless of the measure of performance employed. The effects of GPA and ACT scores are similar for both genders (not significantly different).

Looking at the regressions using GRADE as the dependent variable, we see that the personality temperament variables do not add very much though an "F" preference and the NF and SF personality preference combination operates to the detriment of men.

The detrimental effect of the "F" preference is far more obvious when the TUCE outcomes are analyzed, with or without control for PRE-TUCE results. The "F" preference generally, and the SF and NF personality preference combinations particularly, work to the detriment of both men and women. In addition, men with "S" and "E" personality preferences also perform less well.

Comparing the regression results for men to those for women, we conclude that while the "F" and SF preference combination are detrimental for both men and women, the marginal detrimental effect is greater for men than for women.

Differences in the empirical results using the TUCE variables rather than course grade may reflect differences in the precision and consistency with which student performance in economics is measured. Differences in instructor grading scales make course grades relatively less consistent and precise measures of student performance than the number of questions answered correctly on either the Post-TUCE exam or differences in Pre-TUCE minus Post TUCE exam scores.

Matching Hypothesis

Borg and Shapiro (1996) find that matching of student and professor personality temperaments improves grade results. Consistent with the analysis by Ziegert (1998), we do not find statistically significant effects of exact (all four indicators) matching for either women or men. Recall that Myers-Briggs thought the S-N and T-F personality preference scales most important for understanding the learning process. The effects of matching on possible combinations of these personality scales (S-N and T-F) employed in table 3 is shown in table 6.

TABLE 4. Regression Results Using Individual Type Indicators

Regressor	Dependent Variable: GRADE		Dependent Variable: Post-TUCE		Dependent Variable: Post-TUCE minus Pre-TUCE	
	Women	Men	Women	Men	Women	Men
Intercept	−1.49*	−1.64**	−12.19**	−3.36	−15.19**+	−6.35*
GPA	.90**	.64**	1.43*	1.37**	1.19*	1.09*
ACT	.05*	.08**	.80**	.51**	.50**	.25*
E (vs. I)	.06	−.02	−.16	−1.41*	.35	−1.09
S (vs. N)	.09	.06	−.39	−1.34*	−.50	−1.34*
T (vs. F)	−.12+	.32**	1.52**+	2.96*	2.03**	2.66**
J (vs. P)	.07	−.13	.28	.48	1.71	.09
Adjusted R^2	.39	.37	.41	.40	.25	.28
F for Ho: personality coefficients = 0	.31	1.83	1.70	7.90**	5.45**	5.67**

Note: All regressions include variables for faculty fixed effects.

*Coefficient ≠ 0 at .10

**Coefficient ≠ 0 at .01

+Coefficients differ between genders at .10

TABLE 5. Regression Results Using Combinations of S-N and T-F (ST omitted category)

Variable: Regressor	Dependent Variable: GRADE		Dependent Variable: Post-TUCE		Dependent Post-TUCE minus Pre-TUCE	
	Women	Men	Women	Men	Women	Men
Intercept	−1.35*	−1.33*	11.32**+	−2.08	−12.13**	−5.52*
GPA	.91**	.64**	1.46**	1.50**	1.32*	1.18*
ACT	.04*	.08**	.81**	.49**	.49**	.23*
NT	−.14	−.06	.58	1.24	.62	1.83*
NF	.03	−.32*	−1.26*	−1.84*	−1.99*	−1.47*
SF	.10+	−.32*	−1.42*+	−3.10**	−1.93**	−2.52*
Adjusted R^2	.40	.38	.4	.39	.24	.28
F for Ho: personality coefficients = 0	.34	2.25*	2.27*	8.65**	3.67**	6.77**

Note: All regressions include variables for faculty fixed effects.

*Coefficient ≠ 0 at .10

**Coefficient ≠ 0 at .01

+Coefficients differ between genders at .10

Matching of personality type with faculty personality type does not seem to affect grades at all. It does, however, seem to have some effect on TUCE scores, particularly for men. NT men seem to receive a benefit from being matched with an NT instructor, while NF males are actually penalized for being matched with a NF instructor. Since there were only ten instructors, however, the effects of personality matching may in some cases be confounded with other faculty traits (such as predilection for multiple choice questions) which also affect measured student performance.

What If Women Had Men's Personality Types and Men Women's?

A comparison of the frequencies in table 3 suggests women are more likely than men to have the "F" and "NF" and "SF" personality preferences. The regression results in tables 4 and 5 suggest that students with these personality preferences ("F," "NF," and "SF") will perform less well on the TUCE exams. This implies that, on average, women will derive a TUCE score disadvantage and men a TUCE score advantage from the gender distribution of personality preferences. A review of table 3 suggests this is indeed so. On average, men score one question higher on the Post-TUCE exam and 0.4 of a question higher on the Post-TUCE minus Pre TUCE exam, than do women.

An interesting exercise in the spirit of the famous analysis of gender wage differentials by Ronald Oaxaca (1973) is to see what differences it would make if each gender retained its GPA and ACT scores (and instructors) but switched personality type. To implement this exercise we have used the personality type breakdown employed in table 3, but, given each gender, the personality distribution associated with the other gender. The results are shown in table 7.

TABLE 6. Coefficients of Matching Variable added to Model in Table 7

Effect of minus MATCH on	GRADE		Post-TUCE		Post-TUCE Pre-TUCE	
	Women	Men	Women	Men	Women	Men
MATCHNT	0.42	0.01	1.39	4.68*	0.55	5.52*
MATCHST	−0.03	−0.13	1.99	−0.72	0.95	0.13
MATCHNF	0.05	−0.46	1.40	−2.60	0.53	−4.87*
MATCHSF	−0.13	0.04	−0.52	−0.17	−1.62	0.84
F for Joint significance	0.24	0.58	1.14	1.50	0.28	3.12

*Coefficient $\neq$ 0 at 0.10

TABLE 7.   Effect of Gender Patterns of Personality Distribution on
Measured Learning

	GRADE	Post-TUCE	Post-TUCE–Pre-TUCE
Effect on women of men's type distribution	0	+0.12	+0.17
Effect on men of women's type distribution	−0.2	−0.21	−0.16

Given the gender differences in measured learning displayed in table 3, we can develop estimates of the gap in both the stock and flow of economic knowledge that is attributed to differences in personality type. We have already seen that personality type has no statistically significant result on women's grades, so the result in the first column of table 7 is not surprising. Ceteris paribus, if women had men's personality distribution, 12 percent (0.12) of the one question gap on the Post-TUCE exam and 42 percent (0.17/0.4) of the 0.4 question gap on the Post-Pre TUCE exam would be eliminated. If men had women's personality distribution, they would earn lower scores on the TUCE exam: 21 percent (0.21) of the one question gap on the Post-TUCE exam and 40 percent (0.16/0.4) of the 0.4 question gap on the Post-Pre TUCE exam would be eliminated. Thus table 7 can be interpreted as showing that 12 to 21 percent of the "gap" in mean Post-TUCE score, or about 40 percent of the "gap" in mean Post-TUCE minus Pre-TUCE score can be attributed to the gender pattern of personality type.

Conclusions and Recommendations

The gender gap in both the stock and flow of economic understanding can, in part, be explained by differences in personality preferences, and furthermore, personality preferences sometimes affect men and women differently in the classroom. In particular, both male and female students with the "feeling" preference rather than the "thinking" preference are at a statistically significant disadvantage in introductory economics courses and men more so than women. This result has several important implications for pedagogy in introductory classes in economics most of which have already been discussed under the rubric of feminist pedagogy (e.g., Bartlett and Ferber 1998; Bartlett 1996; and Ferber 1984).

First, we need to make our classrooms more hospitable for *all* learners regardless of their personality type—those who are thinkers *and* those who are feelers. Students with the feeling preference learn best when they've developed relationships with their instructor and other members of the class. It often benefits these students to take time at the beginning of the term to allow students to get to know one another and their instructor through any of a variety of "ice-breaking" exercises. Second, we need to provide a human face to the economic analysis and content of our introductory courses. Recall that feeling students learn best when they can relate to people through empathy. This suggests a discussion of income distribution, for example, would be more meaningful to feelers if different demographic groups were discussed as likely belonging to different quintiles in the distribution rather than the more traditional approach often taken in the texts. Third, students need opportunities to both cooperate *and* compete with one another on learning tasks in the classroom. Feelers are naturally more cooperative rather than competitive in group situations and place a high value on harmony. Opportunities to work together on learning objectives would enhance a feeler's performance. And, finally, instructors should portray students as being evaluated on the basis of their performance against predefined learning objectives rather than just "grading on the curve" or evaluating a student's performance relative to other students. This emphasis on the cooperation between instructor and student in achieving learning objectives rather than on competition with other students will enhance feeling students' comfort with the evaluation process and may enhance performance.

The original motivation for this essay was the desire to analyze the gender gap in economics and consider its implications for pedagogy. In particular, we hypothesized that the well-known gender difference in the Thinking-Feeling personality temperament would account for some proportion of the observed gender gap in measured performance. In addition to calibrating that effect, however the analysis generated an unexpected result. While the effects of the feeling personality temperament indeed play a role in the gender gap, the magnitude of the actual effect on an individual's performance is larger for men than women. As a group, women are more affected by the relatively poor performance of the feeling temperament in economics, because women are more likely to have a feeling temperament, but men who have a feeling temperament suffer a greater detrimental effect. Therefore, the pedagogical suggestions made in the previous paragraphs may not only mitigate the gender gap in performance, but also benefit a group of men whose performance seems to be affected adversely affected by their personality preferences. Feminist pedagogy may benefit more women, but it may also benefit (selected) men more.

NOTES

Helpful comments from the faculty of the Economics Department at Denison University are gratefully acknowledged. All errors of commission and omission remain those of the authors. Please contact Professor Ziegert concerning any comments or questions.

1. For more details on the distribution of personality type in the U.S. population and the date used in this analysis, see Ziegert 1998, for details.

2. Center for the Applications of Psychological Type 1993.

3. Indeed, Nelson (1996) has suggested that the very content of economics with its focus on competition rather than cooperation may be difficult for some individuals.

4. Center for the Application of Psychological Type 1993.

5. *MBTI: Introduction to Type in Organizational Settings,* 11.

6. Research by Tucker and Gillespie (1993); and Quinn, Lewis, and Fischer (1992) have shown better than 80 percent concurrent validity between the MBTI and the Keirsey when administered to college students.

7. These results were obtained by adding four dummy variables (NT, ST, NF, and SF) to the empirical models presented in table 7. If both a student and his or her instructor shared the same combination of the S-N and T-F personality preference scale—for example, NT—then a match occurs, and the dummy variable NT would take a value of one (1). If a student and his or her instructor did not share the NT combination, then the dummy variable NT would be set equal to zero (0).

REFERENCES

Anderson, G., D. Benjamin, and M. A. Fuss. 1994. "The Determinants of Success in University Introductory Economics Courses." *Journal of Economic Education* 25 (spring): 99–119.

Bartlett, R. L. 1996. "Discovering Diversity in Introductory Economics." *Journal of Economic Perspectives* 10 (spring): 141–53.

Bartlett, R. L., and M. A. Ferber. 1998. "Humanizing Content and Pedagogy in Economics Classrooms." In *Teaching Undergraduate Economics: A Handbook for Instructors,* ed. W.B. Walstad and P. Sanders, 109–25. New York: McGraw-Hill.

Becker, W. E., Jr. 1983. "Economic Education Research: Part III: Statistical Estimation Methods." *Journal of Economic Education* 14 (summer): 4–15.

Borg, M. O., and S. L. Shapiro. 1996. "Personality Type and Student Performance in Principles of Economics." *Journal of Economic Education* 27 (winter): 3–25.

Center for Applications of Psychological Type. 1993. "An Assortment of Facts about Type in Education." Gainesville, FL.

Feiner, S., and B. A. Morgan. 1987. "Women and Minorities in Introductory Economics Textbooks." *Journal of Economics Education* 18 (fall): 376–92.

Ferber, M. A. 1990. "Gender and the Study of Economics." In *The Principles of Economics Course: A Handbook for Instructors,* ed. P. Sanders and W. B. Walstad, 444–60. New York: McGraw-Hill.

———. 1984. "Suggestions for Improving the Classroom Climate for Women in the Introductory Economics Course." *Journal of Economics Education* 15 (spring): 160–68.

Hall, R. M., and B. R. Sandler. 1982. "The Classroom Climate: A Chilly One for Women?" Washington, DC: Project for the Status and Education of Women, Association of American Colleges.

Keirsey, D., and M. Bates.1984. *Please Understand Me: Character and Temperament Types,* 5th ed. Del Mar, CA: Prometheus Nemesis Book Co.

Lawrence, G.D. 1993. *People Types and Tiger Stripes: A Practical Guide to Learning Styles.* Gainesville, FL: Center for Applications of Personality Type.

McCaulley, M. 1976. "The Myers-Briggs Type Indicator and the Teaching-Learning Process." Gainesville, FL: Center for Applications of Psychological Type.

Myers, I. 1975. *Manual: Myers-Briggs Type Indicator.* Palo Alto, CA: Consulting Psychologists Press.

Myers, P., and K. Myers. 1991. *MBTI: Introduction to Type in Organizational Settings.* Palo Alto, CA: Consulting Psychologists Press.

Nelson, J. A. 1996. "The Masculine Mindset of Economic Analysis." *Chronicle of Higher Education,* June 28, B3–4.

Oaxaca, Ronald. 1973. "Male-Female Wage Differentials in Urban Labor Markets." *International Economic Review* 14 (October): 693–709.

Quinn, M. T., R. J. Lewis, and K. L. Fischer. 1992. "A Cross-Correlation of the Myers-Briggs and Keirsey Instruments." *Journal of College Student Development* 33 (May): 279–80.

Siegfried, J. J. 1979. "Male-Female Differences in Economic Education: A Survey." *Journal of Economic Education* 10 (spring): 1–11.

Siegfried, J. J., and R. Fels. 1979. "Research on Teaching College Economics: A Survey." *Journal of Economic Education* 17 (summer): 923–69.

Tucker, I. E., and B. V. Gillespie. 1993. "Correlations among Three Measures of Personality Type." *Perceptual and Motor Skills* 77 (October): 650.

Wetzel, J. N., W. J. Potter, and D. M. O'Toole. 1982. "The Influence of Learning Styles and Teaching Styles on Student Attitudes and Achievement in the Introductory Economics Course: A Case Study." *Journal of Economic Education* 13 (winter): 33–39.

Ziegert, Andrea L. 1998. "The Role of Personality Temperament and Student Learning in Principles of Economics: Further Evidence." Working Paper. Granville, OH.: Denison University.

The Road Not Taken

Service Learning as an Example of Feminist Pedagogy in Economics

KimMarie McGoldrick

Two roads diverged in a yellow wood and I—
I took the one less traveled by,
And that has made all the difference.

—Robert Frost

In 1988 the Association of American Colleges (AAC) and the American Economic Association assembled a task force to study the "Status and Prospects of the Economics Major." This report, by Siegfried et al., suggests that more needs to be done to teach our students to think like economists. Further, it indicates that lecturing emphasizes "passive learning, narrow forms of evaluation, few or no writing assignments, and a reliance on textbooks (rather than real books) and routine problem sets; all of these practices limit intellectual stimulation" (Siegfried et al. 1991, 206). The report outlines a number of approaches and changes that have the potential for improving undergraduate economic education by providing opportunities for students to practice thinking like economists.

Among the suggested changes are expanding the writing across the curriculum program, encouraging cooperative learning, developing hand-on experiences (emphasizing context rather than the abstract), and including more applications of active learning. The report also recommended that educators be aware of the changing gender makeup of our audience. The chilly climate toward women in the classroom and lack of gender-neutral examples must be addressed. To the extent possible, educators must also recognize that students evolve in their educational process, as suggested by Perry (1970). Although not specifically expressed in their report, many of the changes outlined by the AAC are consistent with the ideals expressed in feminist pedagogy.

Feminist pedagogy and its application in economics have received recent attention in the literature (e.g., see Shackelford 1992; and Bartlett and Feiner 1992). They suggest a more inclusive presentation and practice of the economic way of thinking through challenging patriarchal structures, recognizing alternative ways of knowing, and emphasizing process in addition to outcomes. While these may be applied in the classroom through the application of active learning, cooperative learning, in-class writing assignments, and alternative evaluation techniques, they can be extended to include out-of-class projects and papers. One such out-of-class experience is service learning.

Service learning is an educational tool that relies on the combination of community volunteer service and classroom theory. Its goal is to allow students to have the opportunity to be active participants in their education. David Kolb (1976, 1984) suggests that learning is a cycle that incorporates a person's concrete experience through active reflection to the formation of abstract concepts and generalizations; these concepts and generalizations may then be used to test implications of concepts in new situations leading to a new concrete experience. Economics classes tend to begin this cycle of learning with abstract concepts and generalizations, while often neglecting altogether any concrete experience. If students cannot relate to these concepts through the learning cycle they are less likely to remember them or be able to put them into practice. It has been argued that information gained through concrete experience and processed by observing and reflecting is more likely to be retained and thus become useful knowledge.[1]

Projects incorporating service-learning experiences help inform student understanding of classroom theory, the abstract concepts, and generalizations. Likewise, classroom theory can be used to help students develop a greater understanding of real-life experiences gained through service learning. This linking process can be developed through a variety of exercises including journal writing, classroom presentations and discussions, and term papers. Thus, this unique educational tool creates a process that empowers students by making them experts through their experiences while reinforcing the relevance of economics theory.

This essay details the consistency of service learning with the ideals of feminist pedagogy. While there are many different interpretations of how teaching techniques may be consistent with feminist pedagogy, this chapter uses the work of Shackelford (chap. 2 in this volume) as its model to show that service learning has the potential of achieving a more inclusive classroom. The discussion will begin with a brief description of the various applications of service learning and will then use one of these forms to demonstrate how service learning is consistent with three themes of feminist pedagogy as outlined by Shackelford.

Models of Community Service Learning

It is often easy to lecture on and discuss detailed economic theory while neglecting applications to the world outside the classroom. While some of our students may be able to draw on limited work experience, many do not recognize that there are links between economic theory and their everyday lives. There are a variety of forms of community service learning that can provide a vehicle for discussing these links, each having a different focus, degree of time commitment, and applicability to theories discussed in economics courses. These differences allow for a number of alternatives in the integration of service learning into any course within the discipline. The models discussed in the remainder of this section are based on those detailed at the Learning in Community Settings (LINCS) Program at the University of Richmond. These models include community service, student-based instruction, action research, and community problem-solving (COMPS) seminars.

Community Service

The first stage of integrating service learning into a class often includes requiring some level of community service as a component of the required course work or as an option in place of another assignment in the class. This implies direct contact, on an individual basis, with a single community organization. Over the semester, students typically volunteer ten to thirty hours providing valuable assistance to the organization in a variety of ways. For example, students exploring issues of poverty may volunteer at the local homeless shelter. The integration of this work with course content may occur through class discussion, journal writing, class presentations, or a formal paper. The combination of service hours and assignments promoting class content integration generally makes up 10 percent of the students' course grade.

Student-Based Instruction

This form of community service learning has many similarities to basic community service. It also suggests a time commitment of ten to thirty hours over the course of the semester and accounts for approximately 10 percent of the students' final grade. Student-based instruction provides students with the opportunity to teach and provide mentorship for those in need. This service might be provided in the form of after-school programs, seminars, or presentations. For example, principles students may teach basic economic concepts such as scarcity, choice, and opportunity cost to grade school students. The integration of this work with course content may be demonstrated through class discussion, journal writing, a on-site evaluation of each students' work, or a formal paper.

Action Research

On a slightly more intensive scale of service, action research is most like the concept of an internship or independent study. The main difference is in the focus of the work to be accomplished during the project. Action research involves a project that will benefit the targeted organization as opposed to the internship focus on skill acquisition.[2] Students apply the theory and information taught in the classroom to their projects, thereby grounding a course's subject matter in a real-life experience. In this case, a number of students design and implement a project with the goal of aiding the organization. For example, students tackling the impact of minimum-wage law changes on employment may volunteer at a local unemployment office. They might use this opportunity to develop a survey to determine the causes of unemployment and thus be able to identify programs (education, training, etc.) that would help alleviate some of the joblessness. To demonstrate their ability to link theory with practice, students compile reports based on their research that are professionally bound and presented to the organization at the end of the semester. This form of service learning can be expected to require twenty-five to thirty hours during the semester and account for up to one half of the students' final grade.

COMPS

Finally, community problem solving (COMPS) seminars are probably the most in-depth and time intensive integrations of service learning into course work. Students attend a seminar class with assigned readings specific to a particular problem of the community. As a group, students work up to thirty hours a week with a single organization to address this problem and come up with a plan of action to resolve it. A topic such as welfare policies would be appropriate for students reading about alternative proposed welfare reform policies during the class portion of the seminar. Volunteering at local welfare offices would allow groups of students the opportunity to assess the impact of these programs on welfare recipients. The time-intensive nature of this form of service-learning suggests that the entire course be focused on the volunteer component and thus the entire grade would be linked to this service. Assessment is generally based on a presentation to the organization's board of directors that includes an assessment of the magnitude of the problem, overviews of related issues, and a plan for eliminating or reducing the problem.

The differences among these various methods are obvious and each has advantages and disadvantages. While community service provides the most simple, straightforward method of integrating service learning into the course, the connection between course content and volunteer services may not be made. Student-based instruction necessitates a translation of economic knowledge, implying a mastery of economic theories. The more time-intensive action research directly applies economic theories to a limited experience. The major down side to student-based instruction and action research is the extent of work required of the instructor in setting up community links. Finally, COMPS seminars provide the ultimate in structure and integration. These alternatives include the use of complete projects (from start to finish) whereby students generally will have the opportunity to see the impact of their work. However, these projects are time intensive and focus on a single problem, so students do not have the opportunity to learn about many topics that a less service-intensive class would address.

Is Service-Learning Consistent with Feminist Pedagogy?

Based on the above described models, I have incorporated both student-based instructions and a project that is a cross between community service and action research (McGoldrick 1998; and McGoldrick, Battle, and Gallagher forthcoming). I began using these alternative techniques in my classroom because I wanted to show the relevance of the theories we were discussing to the students' lives in a way that was participatory. Only later did I discover that much of what I was doing, and the motivations for such exercises, were generally consistent with the process and outcomes generated by incorporating feminist pedagogy ideals into course work.

My personal exploration into recognizing the link between service learning and feminist pedagogy began with a comparison of the three-theme approach taken by Shackelford (1992) to the community service/action research project I have incorporated into a "Women and Gender Issues In Economics" course.[3] Women and Gender Issues in Economics is an upper-division elective course requiring both micro- and macroeconomic principles. It is designed to point out differences in economic circumstances between men and women. Various theories are provided in order to explain these differences, and students are expected to understand as well as contrast neoclassical, Marxist, institutionalist, and feminist perspectives on each topic covered.

Students were given three project options for earning fifteen percent of their grade: participating in the service project, doing a traditional research paper, or writing a biography of a female economist. Both the traditional research paper and the biography were expected to be ten to fifteen pages in length and structured in a format with which students would be familiar. Seventeen of the nineteen students in this course chose the service project; each of the other options was chosen by a single student.

The community service project required each student to identify an organization that has an economic impact on women in the local community. Fifteen hours of community service were required. One question that may be raised relates to the depth of experience that may be obtained with only fifteen hours of required service. Training time, for instance, may cut into the hours of actual service to the program participants. The organizations identified for this application were chosen with these constraints in mind. Each organization identified practical tasks that required little training yet gave students the opportunity to interact and make an impact on program participants. In addition, much of the information students needed for the written component of their project was provided in the organizational brochures and records. Thus, fifteen hours of community service provides a minimal but sufficient experience for students to draw upon. This is especially the case because students are expected to complete outside research about the economic issues identified to supplement their service experiences.

Throughout the remainder of this essay I argue that service-learning is consistent with feminist pedagogy by showing that (1) it may be used to dismantle patriarchal structures and help empower those disempowered in such structures; (2) it allows students to better develop and express their ideas including exploring their own biases and assumptions; and (3) it focuses on the construction of knowledge and the process of learning. The remainder of this section will elaborate on each of these three themes, explore how they manifest themselves in economics, and show how service-learning may be used to move the discipline toward a more egalitarian epistemological approach in the study of human behavior.

Patriarchal Structures

At the very heart of feminist critiques of the discipline is the patriarchal structure embedded in nearly every fiber of economics. The key to the continuation of this patriarchal structure is the classroom. This is the first arena in which students interact with the purveyors of the discipline and the topics that economists investigate. They are confronted with a teaching style that most likely is in the form of lecture, presented with materials that are formulated in terms of abstract mathematical modeling (as opposed to contextual modeling), and are subject to male domination in class expression (by students and instructors).

The lack of a significant female representation in the discipline is generally argued to be the result of differential mathematical abilities or background. But there appears to be little statistical evidence to support this theory: "female undergraduate students tend to do less well in economics courses than male students, even though females' overall grade point averages tend to be higher" (Ferber and Nelson 1993, 3). Instead, many argue the source to be gender differences in learning styles. Ferber and Nelson (1993) also find that women and men do not score significantly different, for example, when essay questions (as opposed to multiple-choice questions) are used for grading purposes. The failure of the discipline to recognize these differences and its continuation of antiquated teaching methods that perpetuate the low female representation in economics contributes further to the patriarchal structure.

If one also considers the treatment of women and minorities in textbooks to be reflective of what is taught in the classroom, a patriarchal structure is easily documented. Feiner and Morgan (1987) suggest that introductory textbook treatment of women and minorities is less than sufficient. Feiner (1993) further documents the presentation of such material as biased, based on Guidelines for Recognizing and Avoiding Racist and Sexist Biases in Economics.[4] Even in labor economics textbooks, questions have been raised about examples and contexts in which gender-specific findings are included and the subsequent generalizations that are made based on gender-lopsided data. For example, Gray (1992) documents the extent to which women are included in generalized discussions, the biased treatment of women's issues, and unwarranted inferences made about women's choices based on raw data.

Feminist pedagogy suggests a method of presenting materials that gives equal voice to all participants in the economy. Thus, even if a class is dominated in numbers by a gender or racial group, alternative perspectives of economic issues should be raised. Service learning provides an opportunity to develop these materials and encourages a basis for discussion consistent with feminist pedagogical goals. This is accomplished by taking the subject material authority away from the instructor and giving students ownership of the development and application of economic theory, providing a common experience among the students, and exposing students to the realities of theory.

In order to provide details of the link of service learning and feminist pedagogy, the following discussion focuses on the community service experiences of students enrolled in a gender issues in economics course. Students were required to volunteer fifteen hours at a preapproved community agency; a number completed their service at the Emergency Shelter, a homeless shelter for women. They were then required to link this to economic theory through class discussions, journal entries, a term paper, and a poster presentation to the faculty.[5]

Each student benefited from different firsthand experiences with women who were affected by welfare policies. They learned about the processes these homeless women went through to obtain benefits for themselves and their children. They were also able to gather relevant statistical data about these women's experiences including how long they stayed at the shelter, which services they took advantage of, how long it took them to locate employment, and so on. This breaks down the patriarchal structure by empowering students through their own experiences. They are not confined to the instructor's determination of what is fact or fiction when relating issues of welfare and poverty, but rather the knowledge is constructed through their direct experiences.

Students are also empowered through the commonalities of their experiences. They have a basis for conversation that does not center on a single student having authority. My experiences with service learning suggest that students are more likely to discuss their experiences if they know some of their classmates have been experiencing similar issues. This is especially true for students who are uncomfortable speaking in front of their classmates. They generally begin with simple statements in agreement with generalities expressed by their classmates. The instructor can take this opportunity to encourage the description of student- specific experiences, which will draw out shy students, giving them a voice when they might otherwise be silent.

Finally, community service provides an avenue for the presentation of nontraditional theories and topics. Since each experience will be unique, a single economic theory will generally not satisfy all students. Theories describing the causes of and policy solutions for poverty provide a good example of this conflict. Many students volunteering at the homeless shelter discovered various aspects of environment and family history that contributed to the current circumstances of these homeless women. Others found lack of education and training to be the root of the problem. Still others grappled with discrimination. These differences lead students to develop very different policy implications with respect to work fare programs, for example.

Expression

Feminist pedagogy recognizes the importance of the diverse set of experiences each student brings to the classroom. Indeed, these are valued precisely because they provide perspectives that identify the existence and extent of the patriarchal structure under which our experiences develop. The objective, mathematical, and empirical components of the discipline have been promoted to the extent that recognition of a patriarchal history has been neglected. "An operative feminist pedagogy allows students, through open dialogue and conversation, to compare, contrast, and connect their views and ideas with those of others toward a goal of achieving a greater understanding of the subject" (Shackelford 1992, 371). This problem may be documented in the teaching styles of instructors as well as the evaluation methods used.

The key to expression is the opportunity for interaction within the classroom. But as Bartlett and King so aptly describe, it is only in the upper-division seminar classes that students have the opportunity to "be more than mere receptors of economic knowledge and manipulators of contrived exercises" (1990, 182). The reasons most often provided in defense of this trend include the overwhelming material that *must* be covered in lower-division classes necessitating a "time efficient" lecture format, the lack of training and comfort on the part of instructors that feeds the fear of allowing the class to get on *tangents,* and large class sizes that make discussion *impossible.* This last supposition is reinforced by the findings of Siegfried and Kennedy suggesting that "the time a student is involved in active recitation declines sharply with class size" (1995, 348–49).

An alternative form of expression occurs during the evaluation process. The vast literature exploring gender differences in knowledge range from those who found males outperform females on standardized tests (Gohmann and Spector 1989; Watts and Lynch 1989; Lumsden and Scott 1987; Ferber, Birnbaum, and Green 1983), to others who found no gender differences in standardized test results (Williams, Waldauer, and Duggal 1992; Rhine 1989; Watts 1987; Buckles and Freeman 1983; Kelley 1975), and to yet others who found these gender differences disappearing or even that females outperformed males when essay questions were used (Ferber and Nelson 1993; Lumsden and Scott 1987; Ferber, Birnbaum, and Green 1983). These differences in economic knowledge are compounded given the overwhelming use of multiple-choice questions as the main evaluative method. Indeed, Siegfried and Kennedy found that "multiple-choice questions account for about two-thirds of total assessment" (1995, 349).

These traditional methods of accessing economic knowledge neglect accounting for differences in personal history. All multiple-choice questions and most essay questions implicitly assume each student has the same life experiences. They do not allow the opportunity for students to identify and express how their environmental circumstances influence their economic education.

Service learning, on the other hand, requires students to identify and confront life circumstances outside their own experiences and as a result most students are motivated to explore their own biases and the construction of those biases. They are in control of their education to the extent that they choose a project that has personal meaning.[6] Students are more likely to be expressive about a topic of their own choosing or that has some personal meaning to them. Students may also be asked to formulate a comparison of alternative theories, considering the realistic nature of assumptions in traditional economic models, based on these experiences. My observations of this process indicate that the "rational self-interested man" assumption is questioned extensively, for example. In this process, service learning is consistent with feminist pedagogy because it recognizes that "the transformation of facts into social problems and curricula is not an objective, rational, scientific process, as we have been led to believe. Rather, the process of problem definition and selection of areas for study are always subjective, shaped by values, interests, and ideologies" (Bricker-Jenkins and Hooyman 1987, 39).

Process

Feminist pedagogy suggests that the construction of knowledge is as important as the knowledge itself. Thus, instructors should be concerned with the process of teaching as well as the topics included in their courses. Service learning provides a venue to teach our students to apply and critique theories in light of race, class, and gender implications. Yet if one still relies on standard course materials for the presentation of economic theory, this task is complicated in that research and textual materials do not necessarily present materials in an unbiased fashion (Bell 1974; Feiner 1993; Feiner and Morgan 1987).

Shackelford (1992) suggests a number of venues for change in the economics classroom that are appropriate for describing the impact of service learning on the process component of feminist pedagogy. In particular, she discusses issues related to course content and materials, classroom environment and attitudes, assignments, and evaluation.

Content and Materials
The student-centered nature of experiences inherent in service learning suggests that students will have control over the content covered. This implies the use of nontext sources of economic readings. These readings should provide economic content as well as examples of criticism in order to give students a model for the content and theory critiques they are expected

to pursue in their service-learning projects. In addition, the instructor should be prepared to provide a model of critique and problems or exercises that promote an understanding of this process during the semester.[7] Thus, when students put their service-learning experiences in economic context, they have been trained to be critical of the economic theories typically used in conjunction with their economic issue. The service-learning project causes students to identify an economic issue, consider relevant theories, critique these theories, and formulate policy implications.

Classroom Environment

Service-learning promotes an atmosphere conducive to the sharing of experiences among students. An instructor need not explicitly set aside class time to discuss each service-learning project. Theories discussed in class will naturally be challenged, critiqued, and supported by students familiar with the first-hand (personal and service learning–generated) experiences related to the economic issue. Although some of the more basic theoretical details may be presented by the instructor, the experiences of students will generally lead the class to a student-centered discussion. This style promotes the process of learning in addition to factualized memorization. "Student-centered, rather than teacher-centered, discussion allows students to understand that the way they explore and construct their views may have to do with their experiences as workers, as students, as members of families, as union members, as women, or as men and women of color" (Shackelford 1992, 573).

Assignments

The use of journals, papers, and poster sessions will, to differing degrees, link economic theory to reality and challenge assumptions of these theories within the context of each students experience. Weekly journal writing can develop these skills when the instructor takes the time to develop the process of applying course content rather than allowing students to just regurgitate it. When service-learning experiences are related, questions may be raised in response that promote the students' development of critical thinking about what they are experiencing as opposed to simple description of these experiences.

The second stage of this process may be encompassed by a ten to fifteen page report requiring an introduction of the organization, details of its goals and programs, and proof of at least two economic impacts related to their service. At least one of these impacts should be quantitative in nature, to avoid relying solely on anecdotal analysis, and students should be required to link their work with the theories discussed during the semester. This is the point at which their experiences are compared to a spectrum of economic theories proposing to explain the issue. Students are then able to determine which theory best fits the problem they confronted and explain the inconsistencies of other theories.

In addition, students could be asked to create a poster including a description of their organization, the programs provided, any pamphlets relating relevant information, and the economic impacts identified. These posters may be reviewed by invited faculty of the economics department and the business school, and others involved with service learning. The purpose of the poster session is to provide an opportunity for conversations that allow for a more complete communication and comparison of student experiences. Students continue the process of learning as they compare their findings with classmates. If we consider an economic problem to be a jigsaw puzzle of complex assumptions, theories, and policy implications, we can only realistically expect our students to understand parts of this puzzle through their direct experiences. The poster session is one way of bringing the other pieces together in order to allow the class to complete the puzzle.

Evaluation

Service learning provides many modes of evaluation that are both content and process oriented. Many of the traditional methods of content evaluation easily apply to service learning. Descriptive journal entries, essays, exams, and projects are tools by which students may be assessed on their knowledge of economic principles. These should satisfy any administrative stress on the teaching of content. In addition to these content-oriented methods of evaluation, service learning allows for process-oriented evaluation based on the Kolb learning cycle. A description of various assignments that may be used as either content- or process-oriented evaluation tools follows.

The success of service-learning in economics depends greatly on the ability of the instructor to promote the integration of student experiences with class or course materials. The first stage of this process could include a written journal or paper that reflects the Kolb learning cycle described above. Recall that the cycle combines a concrete experience through a reflective stage to an analytical stage to a stage of application of new ideas, which, when tested, provides a concrete experience that begins the cycle again. One might begin this by asking students a few questions that will guide them through this process. Having students describe the events that took place (who, what, when, and where) satisfies stage one of the learning process. Next, students should react to these events (the why). Were the experiences what the student expected? Were students able to meet their goals?

In moving to the analytical stage of the process, students should consider what economic theories and assumptions they have challenged or addressed. Students should also describe what they have learned about learning, thus validating the learning process. Finally, each student should address how this experience has changed them beyond the class. Are the economic theories they have learned during this process applicable to other areas of their education and life? How have other areas of their education impacted their service-learning experience? These questions should be of particular interest to economics faculties since one of the goals of this learning process is to show that economics is "real world." In addition, it would be valuable for students to discover that economic issues surface in many other disciplines as well.

For the more project intensive service-learning applications, a formal report should also be required. The intent of this would be to provide descriptions of economic theories and summarize results of their applications to the community or agency with which the students are working. An obvious way to evaluate their report is to assess whether it is presentable for distribution. If, as turned in, the document is not presentable outside the classroom, students should have the responsibility to further develop it into a polished product. Such a process will then stress competency and reinforce process in addition to grades.

It is also important that students share their experiences with classmates. Sharing can be accomplished through an informal discussion or formal presentation. The use of this process will expose students to alternative applications of economic theory. Peer evaluation can be included as students assess one another's contribution to the learning environment.

Conclusion

The purpose of this essay was to link service learning with feminist pedagogy. If we, as feminists, are to suggest that the economics discipline is biased, we must also suggest methods of providing a more equitable playing field. I have argued here that the source of our efforts to transform the discipline should not rest solely on the incorporation of feminist perspectives within the economics literature. Indeed, incorporating student experiences in a systematic way has the potential for developing interest, relevance, and inclusivity through the materials covered in typical economics classes. Since many of the biases within the discipline are perpetuated through the content and processes developed for the classroom, targeting these areas may allow for changes parallel to those being called for with respect to research agendas as noted in the literature.

Shackelford's identification of three recurrent themes in feminist pedagogy provide a model for the changes necessary to move the economics classroom toward a more inclusive environment. I use this approach to show that service learning is consistent with this process. Namely, it can be used to create an educational setting that is more egalitarian in treatment of issues, is democratic in classroom environment, allows for individual student expression based on background and experiences, and stresses the learning processes in addition to content.

NOTES

1. This learning theory as it relates to the practice of service learning in economics is further detailed in McGoldrick 1998; and McGoldrick, Battle, and Gallagher forthcoming.

2. Although internships also provide such experiential learning experiences, these differ substantially from service-learning experiences. Internships are often applications of skills already acquired or of learning new skills. But they often neglect the integration of theory and practice that the service-learning experiences provide.

3. The description of this course is taken verbatim from McGoldrick 1998.

4. As developed by the Committee for Race and Gender Balance in the Economics Curriculum.

5. For further details, see McGoldrick 1998.

6. For example, in this project students were provided a list of acceptable service organizations, including some details of the expected activities. Students were also encouraged to explore alternative organizations and discuss with the professor potential links to economic theory. In this way students had a number of opportunities to choose a topic and organization with which they had personal interests.

7. In my class I assign reading from two texts: *Women, Men and Work* by Blau, Ferber, Winkler; and *Women and Economics* by Charlotte Perkins Gilman. I also assign thirty additional readings from a variety of sources ranging from the *Wall Street Journal* and *Signs* to *Race and Gender in the American Economy: Views from Across the Spectrum,* ed. Feiner, and *Beyond Economic Man* by Ferber and Nelson. I also use a version of Bloom's *Taxonomy* and Perry's *Framework* to develop critical thinking skills in my students. (This information is available upon request.)

REFERENCES

Bartlett, Robin, and Susan Feiner. 1992. "Balancing the Economics Curriculum: Content, Method, and Pedagogy." *American Economic Review (Papers and Proceedings)* 82 (May): 559–64.

Bartlett, Robin, and Paul King. 1990. "Teaching Economics as a Laboratory Science." *Journal of Economic Education* 21 (spring): 181–93.

Becker, William, and Michael Watts. 1995. "Teaching Tools: Teaching Methods in Undergraduate Economics." *Economic Inquiry* 33 (October): 692–700.

Bell, Carolyn Shaw. 1974. "Economics, Sex, and Gender." *Social Science Quarterly* 55 (December): 615–31.

Blau, Francine D., Marianne A. Ferber, and Anne E. Winkler. 1998. *The Economics of Women, Men, and Work.* 3d ed. Englewood Cliffs, NJ: Prentice-Hall.

Bricker-Jenkins, Mary, and Nancy Hooyman. 1987. "Feminist Pedagogy in Education for Social Change." *Feminist Teacher* 2 (fall): 36–42.

Buckles, Stephen, and Vera Freeman. 1983. "Male-Female Differences in the Stock and Flow of Economic Knowledge" *Review of Economics and Statistics* 65 (May): 355–58.

Feiner, Susan. 1993. "Introductory Economics Textbooks and the Treatment of Issues Relating to Women and Minorities, 1984 and 1991." *Journal of Economic Education* 24 (spring): 145–62.

Feiner, Susan, ed. 1994. *Race and Gender in the American Economy: Views from across the Spectrum.* Englewood Cliffs, NJ: Prentice Hall.

Feiner, Susan, and Barbara Morgan. 1987. "Women and Minorities in Introductory Economics Textbooks: 1974 to 1984." *Journal of Economic Education* 18 (fall): 376–92.

Ferber, Marianne, Bonnie Birnbaum, and Carole Green. 1983. "Gender Differences in Economic Knowledge: A Reevaluation of the Evidence." *Journal of Economic Education* 14 (spring): 24–37.

Ferber, Marianne, and Julie Nelson, eds. 1993. *Beyond Economic Man: Feminist Theory and Economics.* Chicago: University of Chicago Press.

Gilman, Charlotte Perkins. 1898. *Women and Economics.* Boston: Small, Maynard, and Co. Reprinted by Prometheus Books.

Gohmann Stephan, and Lee Spector. 1989. "Test Scrambling and Student Performance." *Journal of Economic Education* 20 (summer): 235–38.

Gray, Tara. 1992. "Women in Labor Economics Textbooks." *Journal of Economic Education* 23 (fall): 362–73.

Kelley, Allen. 1975. "The Student as Utility Maximizer." *Journal of Economic Education* 6 (spring): 82–92.

Kendall, Jane, ed. 1990. *Combining Service and Learning: A Resource Book for Community and Public Service,* vols. 1–3. Raleigh, NC: National Society for Internship and Experiential Education.

Kolb, David. 1976. *Learning Style Inventory: Technical Manual.* Boston: McBer and Co.
———. 1984. *Experiential Learning: Experience as a Source of Learning and Development.* Englewood Cliffs, N.J.: Prentice Hall.

Lumsden Keith, and Alex Scott. 1987. "The Economics Student Reexamined: Male-Female Differences in Comprehension." *Journal of Economic Education* 18 (fall): 365–75.

McGoldrick, KimMarie. 1998. "Service Learning in Economics: A Detailed Application." *Journal of Economic Education* 29 (fall): 365–76.

McGoldrick, KimMarie, Ann Battle, and Suzanne Gallagher. Forthcoming. *American Economist.*

Perry, William. 1970. *Forms of Intellectual and Ethical Development in the College Years: A Scheme.* New York: Holt, Rinehart and Winston.

Rhine Sherrie. 1989. "The Effect of State Mandates on Student Performance." *American Economic Review* 79 (May): 231–35.

Shackelford, Jean. 1992. "Feminist Pedagogy: A Means for Bringing Critical Thinking and Creativity to the Economics Classroom." *American Economic Review (Papers and Proceedings)* 82 (May): 570–76.

Siegfried, John, Robin L. Bartlett, W. Lee Hansen, Allen C. Kelley, Donald N. McCloskey, and Thomas H. Tietenberg. 1991. "The Status and Prospects of the Economics Major." *Journal of Economic Education* 22 (summer): 197–24.

Siegfried, John, and Peter Kennedy. 1995. "Does Pedagogy Vary with Class Size in Introductory Economics?" *American Economic Review* 85 (May): 347–51.

Watts, Michael. 1987. "Student Gender and School District Differences Affecting the Stock and Flow of Economic Knowledge." *Review of Economics and Statistics* 65 (May): 355–58.

Watts, Michael, and Gerald Lynch. 1989. "The Principles Course Revisited." *American Economic Review* 79 (May): 236–41.

Williams, Mary, Charles Waldauer, and Vijaya Duggal. 1992. "Gender Differences in Economic Knowledge: An Extension of the Analysis." *Journal of Economic Education* 23 (summer): 219–31.

Use of Structured Peer Review in Writing-Intensive Courses

Helping Students Comprehend the Evaluation Process

Joyce P. Jacobsen

This case study provides a concrete example of how economics courses might begin moving, at least on the margin, toward some of the principles advocated in the feminist pedagogy literature (cf. Schniedewind 1987; Shrewsbury 1993; other essays in the section on Alternative Pedagogies), in particular toward empowerment of students through use of alternative evaluation practices. I suggest specifically that the technique of structured peer review is a valuable way to show students how the evaluative process operates and that it allows them to participate in this process in an illuminating way. While many feminists might well regard this as only partial reform, within the economics discipline partial reforms are far more likely to become accepted and widespread, and the willingness of instructors to try one new method may lead to their being willing in future courses to attempt additional reforms that move the classroom environment in a more inclusive direction.

In the structured peer review exercise described herein, the students, after each writing a short (about five pages) paper, are asked to evaluate another student's paper, using a double-blind procedure. They are encouraged to provide comments regarding content, style, and grammar directly on the paper. Handing in a completed evaluation constitutes part of their class participation grade, although the evaluation itself is not graded. I read both the papers and the peer reviews and assign tentative grades for the papers. Then the peer reviews are handed to the students, and they are encouraged to rewrite the papers; finally, they hand them in for regrading.

How might this method fit within the rubric of "feminist pedagogy?" Gore (1993, 18) points out that the question of what is feminist pedagogy has been approached differently by the two main groups interested in the topic. One group, writing about feminist pedagogy from the context of

Women's Studies, has emphasized the pedagogy, in other words, "What is feminist *pedagogy?*" as opposed to discussing feminist theory or feminist methodology. The other group writes from the context of the educational establishment, that is, academicians within schools of education, and reworks the question into: "What makes pedagogy *feminist?*" In other words, if pedagogy is the craft of teaching, then is feminist pedagogy the feminist craft of teaching or the craft of feminist teaching?

Even though there is some question about what feminist pedagogy is, both groups would probably agree that one important goal of feminist pedagogy is to empower students. Shrewsbury (1987, 9) discusses empowering strategies and points out that such strategies entail "the implicit recognition that [students] are sufficiently competent to play a role in course development and are able to be change agents." To the extent that an activity, including peer review, gives students a voice in the course, it is empowering and thereby fits under either rubric as helping to achieve this goal.

An integral part of the empowerment strategy for many practitioners is to involve students actively in the evaluation processes of the course, particularly regarding their own grade. Shrewsbury argues that as students "struggle with evaluation methods, they learn how to evaluate actions and the connection between objectives and achievement" (1987, 11). She implies that it may be good to have multiple evaluation methods, so as to allow students to compare outcomes across methods. Therefore, allowing students to have a voice in determining course grades—and contrasting such a grading procedure to earlier paper grading procedures used in the course (where I have a student "writing tutor" mark comments on the paper and suggest a grade in conjunction with my own reading of the paper and final grade determination)—is helpful in reaching this goal as well.

It is clear that the method outlined here is critically dependent on the instructor's willingness to structure the course, at least partially, around writing assignments. This does not mean, however, that the instructor is giving up some pedagogical advantage by shifting some assignments, say, from problem sets to short papers. Indeed, there is evidence that students who have writing assignments in their classes learn the course material more effectively than those who do not (Langer and Applebee 1987).

Notably, the two economists who made early contributions to the feminist pedagogy literature both discuss the role of writing assignments in enabling professors to reach the goals of feminist pedagogy. Shackelford (1992; reprinted in this volume) views students as actively engaged with knowledge rather than being merely passive recipients of knowledge, emphasizing the view that knowledge comes out of process. She points to the essential role of writing assignments that include collaboration and peer review (1992, 573) in bringing about active engagement. On the other hand, Shackelford also discusses the hazards of the evaluation process (1992, 574). Beckman (1990) considers the three pedagogical philosophies of Pedagogy of the Oppressed, Feminist Pedagogy, and Writing across the Curriculum (WAC). Similar importance is placed on process in the three pedagogical methods, particularly the importance of maintaining a collaborative or co-operative process and the importance of sharing control and empowering students. Beckman points out that WAC shares key elements with the other two philosophies that are not explicitly stated as goals for WAC but often occur due to the way that writing assistants interact with students. Reflection and action are not integrated explicitly in WAC, however, as they are in the other two philosophies. Therefore, creating a writing-intensive economics course—an approach that is now used to a somewhat greater extent than previously, at least in introductory and elective economics courses—without reflection on how the writing is used in the structure of the course will not fully achieve the empowerment goal of feminist pedagogy.

In order to realize the benefits of written exercises in conjunction with furthering the goals of student empowerment through participation in and comprehension of the evaluation process, I devised the structure described in this essay. In both cases described here the peer-reviewed assignment follows three writing assignments of similar length, each of which was read both by one of the two writing tutors associated with the class and by myself. Writing tutors are a specialized type of teaching assistant, generally students who have taken the class the previous time it was offered and have per-formed strongly on written assignments; the tutors take a tutorial through the English department on how to serve as tutors and receive ungraded course credit for their work. The writing tutor marks the papers and sug-gests a tentative grade; I also mark on the paper, writing the summary comments at the end and making the final grading decision. Then the student meets individually with each of us during the semester to receive the three papers back and discuss writing and content (for approximately fifteen minutes per interview). The student has the option of rewriting once any or all of these three papers as well as rewriting the peer-reviewed fourth paper. This creation of an environment where students have the opportunity to discuss their writing and analytical skills with the professor and other stu-dents (i.e., the tutors) is designed to help them see how one might evaluate a paper; therefore, it would clearly be optimal to embed the peer-review exercise in this format.

Here I will give two examples of how the fourth writing assignment was used, one from an urban economics course and one from a course on the economics of gender. The relevant handouts for a paper on rent control in an urban economics course are displayed in Exhibit 1. Part 1 is the urban economics paper assignment. Part 3 is the guide that is handed out a week later, when students bring their papers to class marked with their university identification number and I distribute them randomly. The relevant handouts for a paper in the economics of gender course are displayed in Exhibit 1, parts 2 and 3. One additional set of questions is added to the top of the peer review sheet for this course: "Were the results of the interviews described clearly? Was all relevant information included (e.g., the different majors chosen, differences by sex, summaries of answers to the different questions) in the paper?" During the next class I collect the papers as well as the peer review sheets and use the latter along with my own evaluation to determine the grade for the paper. In the following class I hand back the papers, along with the relevant review sheets, to the students who wrote them.

The reason for this exercise is that it opens up the learning process in two ways. First, students become aware of how others in the class work, both through seeing another paper and through seeing the peer review of their own paper. Second, students become aware of how the evaluation process works, both by working through an evaluation themselves and by seeing the peer review sheet of their own paper. Those students who generally work in isolation are often particularly surprised to see how another person approaches the same assignment.

In addition to letting students see the evaluation of their own work, I pool information on the evaluation process and on outcomes (in the gender case) and present it in class. This presentation includes information on what proportion of the class rated the other person's paper better, the same, or worse than their own and what proportion made the same judgment as I did. In each course I had previously presented summary information on content from earlier papers. For example, on policy issue papers where the student is asked to decide by the end of the paper whether she or he is for or against implementation of the policy, I indicate what percentage of the class has taken each viewpoint.

The written assignments could vary along many dimensions from the ones presented herein. Regarding the more novel structure of the economics of gender example, which includes data collection and pooling of results for the class, I have written a previous paper arguing that there is value in incorporating data collection assignments into economics courses (Jacobsen 1994). In this paper I have focused on the writing and review process. It is helpful, however, to use an assignment where all students write on the same topic, although they can have variations in their approach to the topic (e.g., the urban economics assignment). That way they all understand the topic and have some opinion about it from having completed their own paper.

An important question, given the empowerment goal implicit in much of feminist pedagogy, is whether students view actions by those practicing

Fig. 1. Part 1. Urban economics paper assignment

Urban Economics

4th paper
3–5 pages, double-spaced, due in class one week from today
papers are graded on writing quality as well as on content

Consider the articles on rent control. Feel free to supplement these
readings with your own research. Write a paper on either:

  i) for a particular city that does not have rent control, what do you
     think would happen to its housing market if rent control were
     instituted in that city

  ii) for a particular city that does have rent control, what do you think
     the effects of the policy have been on that city's housing market

The "housing market" includes both owner-occupied and rental
housing, and you will probably want to talk about distributional
issues as well as overall housing supply and demand effects.

You may also want to suggest ways in which the policy could be
structured (for (i)) or restructured (for (ii)) so as to reduce negative
effects and increase positive effects.

**Note: This paper will be peer reviewed. In order to maintain a
double-blind procedure, put only your student ID number on this
paper, not your name. Give no details in the paper that would
identify yourself to your peer reviewer.**

Part 2. Economics of gender paper assignment

Economics of Gender

<u>4th paper</u>
3–5 pages, double-spaced, 1-inch margins, due in class one week
from today
papers are graded on writing quality as well as on content

Interview at least 8 Wesleyan students, divided equally by sex, who
have a declared major or definite plans to declare a particular major.
They must not have already been interviewed by another person
from our class, and must not be in our class.

Ask them the following questions:

1) How did you decide whether or not to attend a 4-year college?

2) How did you decide which college to attend?

3) How did you decide what major to choose?

4) What are your career plans, including possible graduate
training?

5) What are your family plans, as in are you planning to have
children, and if yes, do you plan to quit or reduce paid work
when they are young?

6) Ask them directly, if they haven't already discussed this,
whether their choice of major was influenced by their family
plans.

Summarize your findings, particularly with regard to differences by
sex, and discuss whether or not they lend support to the human
capital model. Also discuss whether or not you think your results are
similar to what a survey of all U.S. college students would find.

**Note: This paper will be peer reviewed. In order to maintain a
double-blind procedure, put only your student ID number on this
paper, not your name. Give no details in the paper that would
identify yourself to your peer reviewer.**

Part 3. Peer review handout

Peer Review for Paper #4

Please make marks directly on the paper indicating spelling errors, grammatical errors, awkward phrasings, incorrect assertions, or unclear points as well as writing your general impressions on this sheet.

1. What is your impression of the structure of the paper? Did it have a well-defined introduction and conclusion? Did the paper flow well from paragraph to paragraph? If not, how could it have been improved?

2. What is your impression of the general quality of the writing? Comment both in terms of technical problems and style. Were there many careless grammatical and spelling errors? Were there many awkwardly-constructed sentences?

3. What is your impression of the general quality of the analysis? Did the writer make any interesting points? Did the writer draw on economic theory to support his/her arguments?

4. Do you think the paper is better or worse than your paper? Why?

5. What grade would you give the paper? _____

6. What is your student id number? _____

7. Do you want to see the peer review of your paper?   YES   NO
   (the answers to Questions 4, 5, and 6 will not be shown)

If you have other comments to make regarding the paper or have suggestions as to other questions I should have included on this form, please write them below. If you need more space to answer any of the above questions, attach additional paper to this form.

feminist pedagogy as either inherently feminist or inherently good pedagogy. Bignell (1996), interviewing a sample of women's studies students in the United Kingdom, points out students may not "get" what is feminist about the methodology of women's studies classes; they may find the academic environment inherently intimidating (especially compared to women's support groups); or they may expect more support from women's studies tutors than they get, perhaps due to the marginalized positions of the tutors in the academic system (often part-time teachers or nontenured ones). Bignell comments that the writing on feminist pedagogy appears to be focused on the academics' view of the system. I noted this as well in my reading of the pedagogy literature; few examples reflect a social scientist's interest in actual impact of the pedagogical practices on any measure of either student satisfaction or performance. One simple way to approach the satisfaction measure is to read the student evaluation forms following the course and see how the students react to the practices presented in the course. Given the various problems associated with interpretation of student evaluation forms, such as the inability of instructors to control various factors that will influence the evaluations (including expected grade, class size, and whether or not the course is required), the best comparison to draw may be to similarly structured courses that the instructor is teaching concurrently or has taught in the recent past.

Given the general practice of teaching economics using a "top-down" lecture format rather than as either a lab science or a discussion format, students are likely to find this exercise novel in the context of an economics course, though they may have encountered it in other departments' courses. The students treat the peer evaluation exercise very seriously and, in general, make extensive markings on the drafts and peer review forms. I have used this format in each of the last four years while teaching at Wesleyan and used approximately the same format at other schools in the preceding five years. In each course the students have commented in the end-of-term evaluations that they value being able to treat their papers as essentially first drafts and being able to rewrite them for reevaluation (although not all students make use of this option; generally 30 to 40 percent of the papers are turned in for reconsideration). In addition, they comment that they find the grading to be fair (in these courses part of the course grade is also determined by the students' performance on two in-class exams, class participation, and a final research paper, which is not rewritten). This last point appears to be the main benefit of this exercise: it opens up the evaluation process, and it makes clear that evaluation of written work is a difficult procedure that necessarily involves the instructor's making comparisons across different students' work and weighing a number of factors in arriving at a grade. As such, this process does not cede final authority from the teacher but helps the student to understand the process the teacher goes through in deliberation.

A potential pitfall involved in using this exercise is some students' not taking the review seriously enough to do a good job. I simply assign a set number of points toward the course grade for completion of the peer review rather than assigning differential points (and therefore grades) depending on how good a job I think the student did on the peer review. This has proved to be sufficient motivation, but, if one is concerned about this, grades could be assigned.

The use of this exercise is one example of how economists might move on the margin toward feminist pedagogy. An obvious extension of this exercise is to cast it as a more group-oriented learning exercise. For instance, students could form groups, read through a paper and its accompanying peer review, and comment on the two documents. Another possibility is to have students form teams to write the papers and/or review them. I look forward to continuing to adopt and extend pedagogical innovations in my economics courses and hope that others will be stimulated in a similar fashion by descriptions of concrete examples such as this essay has attempted to provide.

REFERENCES

Beckman, Mary. 1990. "Classroom Methods Mirroring Workplace Values: Pedagogy of the Oppressed, Feminist Pedagogy and Writing Across the Curriculum." *Review of Radical Political Economics* 22:139–57.

Bignell, Kelly Coate. 1996. "Building Feminist Praxis out of Feminist Pedagogy: The Importance of Students' Perspectives." *Women's Studies International Forum* 19: 315–25.

Gore, Jennifer M. 1993. *The Struggle for Pedagogies: Critical and Feminist Discourses as Regimes of Truth.* New York and London: Routledge.

Jacobsen, Joyce P. 1994. "Incorporating Data Collection and Written Reports in Microeconomics." *Journal of Economic Education* 25:31–43.

Langer, J. A., and A. N. Applebee. 1987. *How Writing Shapes Thinking: A Study of Teaching and Learning.* Urbana, IL.: National Council of Teachers of English.

Schniedewind, Nancy. 1987. "Teaching Feminist Process." *Women's Studies Quarterly* 15:15–31.

Shackelford, Jean. 1992. "Feminist Pedagogy: A Means for Bringing Critical Thinking and Creativity to the Economics Classroom." *American Economic Review* 80: 570–76.

Shrewsbury, Carolyn M. 1993. "Feminist Pedagogy: An Updated Bibliography." *Women's Studies Quarterly* 21:148–60.

———. 1987. "What Is Feminist Pedagogy?" *Women's Studies Quarterly* 15:6–13.

Internships for Economics Students

Experiments in Feminist Pedagogy

Mary E. Young

American college educators have recently shown renewed interest in expanding programs that encourage students to learn through real-world experiences. These programs cover many forms of experiential learning, from voluntary community service to foreign exchange programs. It is increasingly recognized that one way to strengthen liberal arts education is to "encourage students to enhance their learning by involvement in their local and global communities through such activities as service learning, study abroad, and community internships" (American Council of Learned Societies 1994, 3). Supporters of this view include the late Ernest Boyer, former president of the Carnegie Foundation for the Advancement for Teaching, who argued that "higher education must pay much more attention in preparing students to be responsible citizens, and not strictly scholars and professionals" (1994, A48). Johnetta Cole, president of Spelman College, said that "she is trying to strengthen the 113-year-old legacy of her historically black, women's college by producing leaders" and "that . . . requires more than simply scholarly instruction" (qtd. in Marriott 1996, 38).

The idea of service-based learning is not a new concept in the United States, nor is its practice restricted to a small subset of colleges and universities. McGoldrick (1998) provides a concise history of service-based learning in the United States, and McGoldrick and Sanborn (1995) also discuss its use among economic educators. Some of the many schools that have already added community service as part of their graduation requirements include Portland State University, Stanford University, and Trinity University in Connecticut, San Francisco State University, the University of Pennsylvania, and the University of Denver (Marriott). The National Society for Experiential Education (NSEE), founded in 1971, is a key resource for such programs and offers a number of publications as well as national and regional conferences (Kendall, Duley, Little, Permaul, and Rubin 1986).

Experiential Learning in Economics

Most of the recent discussion about improving pedagogy in economics, even among feminist economists, has focused on how to develop more inclusive course contents and how to incorporate teaching methods that are effective for a wider variety of students (Aerni et al. 1999). Other discussions among economists concerned with pedagogical issues have explored how the use of computer-assisted learning can enhance learning (Young 1997). Despite these recent efforts to make economics more relevant and accessible, very few professional economists have taken the next step of urging that experiential learning be an integral component of earning an undergraduate degree in economics. Even feminist economists have been slow to recognize the importance of experiential learning as a valuable pedagogical tool. They have generally focused on the restructuring of economic research, while very few have made contributions to pedagogy (McGoldrick 1996).

Internships, in particular, may have been avoided by some liberal arts institutions because of their historical inclination to shun emphasis on selfish skill acquisition or technical training, as well as the difficulty of monitoring the quality of this type of experiential learning. Hence, there is a tendency to distinguish a service-learning method called "action research" from internships. "Action research involves a project that will benefit the targeted organization as opposed to the Internship focus on skill acquisition" (McGoldrick and Sanborn 1995, 8–9). Only the former is viewed as a part of selfless service-based learning. A major goal of this essay is to show how internships can become an integral part of efforts to improve pedagogy in the undergraduate economics curriculum by connecting theory with the "real world" as well as helping students add important experience to their resumes.

Exploring the Links between Feminist Theory, Pedagogy, and Experiential Learning

What does experiential learning in economics, particularly internships, have to do with feminist pedagogy? One way to address this question is first to discuss some relevant characteristics of feminist economics, on the assumption that feminist pedagogy is guided by feminist economic theory. Albelda has stated that

> economics in a feminist perspective is concerned with human well-being. It is not a game. This gives an emphasis to application and to the real world effects of economic theory; and it implies that the reason any

methodology is important is because of how its use may affect under-standing . . . feminist economics is overtly concerned with the GOALS of economics. (1995)

The belief that the integration of activism and scholarship is essential to feminism is not new; some feminists would go so far as to suggest that research can only be feminist if it is linked to action (Reinharz 1992). Ruth (1990, 41) describes the philosophy of the National Women's Studies Asso-ciation: "feminist education is a process that is deeply rooted in the women's movement and remains accountable to that community . . . the uniqueness of Women's Studies has been and remains its refusal to accept sterile divi-sions between academy and community." For feminist economists teaching activities that have activist goals are at least as valuable, if not more, than "basic research." In sharp contrast to this view, mainstream economists most often differentiate, rather than integrate, knowledge and action; the latter is considered to be political and polemical.

The following observations about feminist research methodology are equally applicable to students involved in experiential learning:

> Although changing the researcher is not a common intention in femi-nist research, it is a common consequence. . . . By this I mean that the researcher would learn about herself, about the subject matter under study, and about how to conduct research. Many feminist researchers report being profoundly changed by what they learn about themselves. Changes may involve completely reconceptualizing a phenomenon and completely revising one's worldview . . . Some feminist researchers dis-cover . . . that their research has sustained their lives. (Reinharz 1992, 194–95)

Another powerful voice for a feminist pedagogy that recognizes the valuable links between theory and action is bell hooks. hooks claims that "within revolutionary feminist movements, within revolutionary black liberation struggles, we must continually claim theory as necessary practice within a holistic framework of liberatory activism . . . we must actively work to call attention to creating a theory that can advance renewed feminist movements (1994, 69–70).

Most feminist economists would agree that there is a direct link between the intrinsic values of feminist economics and the use of action-oriented experiential learning as a pedagogical tool to make connections between classroom theory and the real world. Nevertheless, this link has not been developed as a pedagogical tool in economics to the extent this has been done by feminists in other disciplines. The remainder of this essay will focus on the practical aspects of developing one type of experiential learning, the academic internship for undergraduate economics majors (or minors), in a manner that is consistent with feminist economics and pedagogy.

Developing an Economics Internship Program: A Case Study

Background

Southwestern is a nationally ranked undergraduate liberal arts school of approximately thirteen hundred students located in Georgetown, Texas, approximately thirty miles north of the state capital of Austin. The university is loosely affiliated with the Methodist Church and places emphasis on offering a "value-centered" education that will prepare students to take their place in the global community. The large majority of Southwestern students are from Texas. The student body is approximately 83 percent white, 13 percent Hispanic, 1 percent African American, and 3 percent "other" or international students.

Georgetown, Texas, has a population of approximately twenty-five thousand. There are few "traditional" employment opportunities for economics students within Georgetown and only a limited number in nearby Austin; most of the "traditional" options would be in state or local governments. There are no large economic consulting firms, nor is there a large financial sector, as there would be in a bigger city.

The Department of Economics and Business is the third largest department on campus in terms of numbers of majors (economics, business, and accounting). Prior to the development of the new program, internships for academic credit in the department were negotiated on an ad hoc basis. There were no guidelines about what constituted an acceptable arrangement, and faculty were not given any "credit" for supervising internships in addition to their regular course loads. As a result, internships taken for academic credit varied widely in the hours of work and additional reading or writing they were expected to do. Further, there was little explicit effort to connect them to course material. In general, students were responsible for finding their own internships, although a few employers requested interns on a regular basis. No one from the University Career Services Office was assigned to help students with academic internships, although they did offer skill-building workshops and information regarding employment opportunities.

New Initiatives

Concern about student retention was a major factor in encouraging the university to take a more active approach with respect to experiential learning. Internships, with or without academic credit, were seen as acceptable; other possible arrangements included foreign exchange programs, exchange programs within the United States, community-service work, applied research with faculty and part-time and summer employment. Because the university did not have adequate personnel to implement all of these plans, departments began looking at ways to improve their own experiential learning programs.

The Department of Economics and Business was one of the first to move forward, primarily because of the author's participation in a National Science Foundation project that sought to improve course content and teaching methods, especially for women and minority students (National Science Foundation). Also, the department graduated an average of nine to twelve majors each year, a very reasonable number to become a "pilot group" for an expanded internship program.

Details of the Program

As of the 1997–98 academic year, it was strongly recommended that students majoring in economics take an internship for academic credit. It was originally approved as a requirement by the department; however, it quickly became apparent that some students, due to either academic or personal reasons, were not adequately prepared for an internship so that requiring one could reflect poorly on the student and the university. The internship is listed as a course during each semester and during the summer. In general, students are advised to take it in their junior year. By then they should also have completed two intermediate theory classes (usually taken their second year), Research Methods for Economics (usually taken in the fall of their junior year), and probably at least one advanced elective. A maximum of three academic hours is given for internships, and all are graded on a pass/ fail basis, although there may be extenuating circumstances in which exceptions are approved.

Students registered for the internship are expected to complete a minimum of 120 on-site hours during the semester. This time does not include hours required for group or class meetings, writing or reading assignments, and so forth. The total time (excluding travel time) that a student would spend at their internship and fulfilling additional responsibilities would be approximately 150 to 180 hours for three hours of academic credit. Such a structured and rigorous "internship course" for students with similar academic backgrounds was expected to lead to greater understanding of the relationships between theory and real economic problems in the community. It should also improve the quality of the required "Senior Capstone" course that all majors are required to take during their senior year.

The supervising faculty member is responsible for developing and maintaining approximately ten to fifteen internships (open only to students in the department) as well as supervising the students throughout the semester. It is recommended that the faculty member make at least one on-site visit to each student during the internship period; a total of three contacts between the sponsoring agency or firm and the faculty member are required. Thus, the faculty member will have significant influence on the content of the internships and will receive credit equal to that of a standard course. The faculty member will be under no obligation to assist other students in finding internships or in developing not-for-credit internships or employment possibilities. In the event that fewer than six students register for an internship in a particular semester, the faculty member can accumulate internships until the total number reaches the university's required minimum for a course.

There are a number of other issues that should be addressed by any department or institution offering such an internship program. For instance, it should be decided if monetary compensation will be allowed. The policy of this department is that compensation may be given even if the student is also receiving academic credit. A simple but legally sound contract between the university, the student, and the participating agency or employer is also necessary to clarify obligations and liabilities of all parties involved. The department or the university should develop a set of written guidelines that outline: (1) program (course) objectives; (2) responsibilities of the sponsoring agency, including the intern's direct supervisor; (3) the intern's responsibilities with respect to work hours, reporting requirements, etc.; and (4) how the student will be evaluated.

Developing Appropriate Internships

One of the most difficult challenges of such an internship course is the identification and development of appropriate, high-quality internships, if they are to be used as a means of exposing students to diverse perspectives. This is a particularly challenging problem in the case of internships for academic credit, because they involve a great deal of time and have substantial influence on a student's further academic decisions and future career.

Another concern arises when internships are to be used as a feminist pedagogical technique because of the way students and their parents are likely to react if the students are offered internships that do not fit traditional patterns. There may well be a backlash if students are placed in internships with community service groups, which may not be seen by everyone as appropriate places for "skill acquisition" or "job training." The fact that this type of backlash has been experienced by many faculty members who have altered course content to include a greater diversity of perspectives suggests that this problem may be expected to arise. Even hooks (1994, 202–6) notes that "profound commitment to engaged pedagogy is taxing to the spirit . . . the choice to work against the grain, to challenge the status quo, often has negative consequences. . . . Students do not always enjoy studying with me. Often they find my courses challenge them in ways that are deeply unsettling."

One way to forestall such criticism is to explain in advance that the departmental goal for internships is to challenge students to make connections between economic theory and real problems in the community and not primarily to gain employment experience. It also could be emphasized that there is much value in interacting with people who do not have training in economics as long as this presents an opportunity for students to strengthen their skills as budding economists and to analyze situations even though relevant data are not readily available.

The academic internship should also have rigorous expectations about reading, writing, and presentation assignments (which would usually be conducted outside of the internship on-site hours); in particular, presentations should involve other students, faculty, or members of the community. For example, a student working at a program that provided assistance to the homeless could simultaneously do research on the economics of homelessness. A student working with poor children could analyze the economics of poverty and poverty-aid programs. Such work will enhance the quality of the internship experience enormously as well as give it greater legitimacy among students, parents, other faculty, and administrators.

The location and content of the internship may be critical to determining whether it is simply one component of a fairly standard economic major or minor or a unique opportunity for students and faculty to explore economic policy and feminist economics, including feminist pedagogy. It is certainly possible, however, to employ feminist pedagogical techniques for students who are working in positions that use more common microeconomic and macroeconomic methods and data (e.g., economic research for a governmental agency). Colleges and universities that are in small cities or in rural areas would also be able to offer more internships if they expanded their definitions of appropriate location or content to include the myriad of community service agencies that often provide economic assistance.

Conclusions

Internships for academic credit are probably too time and labor intensive to be adopted as a requirement by institutions that graduate large numbers of students in economics. Yet their potential as a powerful pedagogical technique for urban, suburban, and even rural colleges and universities deserves attention. This potential will be further enhanced if "nontraditional" internships are offered to students trained primarily in mainstream economic thinking, allowing them to explore connections between the textbook and important economic problems, especially those facing people of color, women, children, and other groups that have traditionally received scant attention from mainstream economists. It is for this reason that feminist economists have been pioneers in promoting internships as a useful pedagogical tool.

REFERENCES

Aerni, April L., Robin L. Bartlett, Margaret Lewis, KimMarie McGoldrick, and Jean Shackelford. 1999. "Toward Feminist Pedagogy in Economics." *Feminist Economics* 5(1): 29–44.

Albelda, Randy. 1995. "What Is Intrinsic to Feminist Economics?" E-mail to fem-econ list. November 5.

American Council of Learned Societies. 1994. "Re-thinking Liberal Education." Symposium proceedings, April.

Boyer, Ernest. 1994. "Creating the New American College." *Chronicle of Higher Education,* March 9, A48.

hooks, bell. 1994. *Teaching to Transgress.* New York and London: Routledge.

Kendall, Jane, John Duley, Thomas Little, Jane Permaul, and Sharon Rubin. 1986. *Strengthening Experiential Education.* Raleigh, N.C.: National Society for Experiential Education.

Marriott, Michael. 1996. "Taking Education beyond the Classroom." *New York Times,* August 4, sec. 4A.

McGoldrick, KimMarie. 1996. "Special Issue Proposal." E-mail to fem-econ list. July 10.

———. 1998. "Service-learning in Economics: A Detailed Application." *Journal of Economic Education* 29 (fall): 365–76.

McGoldrick, KimMarie, Ann Battle, and Suzanne Gallagher. Forthcoming. " Service Learning and the Economics Course: Theory and Practice." *American Economist.*

McGoldrick, KimMarie, and Robert Sanborn. 1995. "Experiential Learning: An Application for Economics Students." Paper presented at the Eastern Economic Association Meetings, New York, March.

Reinharz, Sheila. 1992. *Feminist Methods in Social Research.* New York: Oxford University Press.

Ruth, Sheila. 1990. *Issues in Feminism.* Mountain View, CA: Mayfield Press.

Young, Mary. 1997. "Computer-Assisted Learning in Undergraduate Economics: Equity Considerations." Paper presented at the Southern Economic Association meetings, Atlanta, November.

Teaching Case Studies in the Principles of Economics Classroom

One Instructor's Experience

Amy McCormick Diduch

Most economics instructors are concerned about the quality of learning in their classrooms. Are students learning to "think like economists" through development of their analytical skills? Are they able to apply what they learn to a variety of more or less realistic problems? Are they becoming interested in the subject—interested enough to continue their studies? Is the content of most economics courses reflective of the experiences and interests of all students?

Not all the instructors who ask themselves these questions will find that they can be answered to their satisfaction. Many of our students are not learning to "think like economists." Many find the subject difficult, unrealistic, and narrowly focused at best. Many "otherwise bright" (Bartlett 1995) students, male and female, Caucasians and people of color, middle class and working class, come to feel that they just can't "do" economics. The "Sage-on-the-Stage" method of teaching economics does not reach all of our students, many of whom do not see their experiences acknowledged by traditional neoclassical models. Instructors who want to see all students learn will start to seek out alternative teaching methods. This essay suggests one possible alternative approach to the principles of economics course: case study analysis.

Can case study analysis be successfully introduced into the principles of economics classroom? Should it be? Can it address some of the differences in learning styles among students? Can it generate interest in economics among students who in the past have been marginalized? This essay explores the practical questions of whether and how case studies may be used at the principles level to help more students successfully learn economics. Case studies provide the opportunity to move the classroom beyond the Sage-on-the-Stage method of teaching toward one that develops groups and community learning.

Case Studies and Feminist Pedagogy

A major goal of many instructors in principles of economics courses is to teach students how to "think like economists." They do this by teaching models and methods of logical thinking; through examples in lectures and through problem sets and exams they ask students to apply these models and methods to situations of varying degrees of realism. Although the use of realistic problems serves to alert students to the various uses of economic thinking, the examples are often devoid of institutional details and rarely are used to point out the limitations of economic thinking. Lecture-based teaching supplemented with problem sets suits some students very well but others have difficulty learning the subject. Case studies are one means of addressing this issue.

The reasons case studies may be expected to accomplish this fall into two categories. These are similar to those described in the first essay in this volume as instructors move away from "Lecturing on the Received Neoclassical Canon." The first change is largely a matter of content—structuring materials in a way that promotes understanding the real-world setting for economic decision-making and the breadth of economic applications. The second change is a matter of pedagogy. Different teaching methods are needed to reach different types of students. Some students learn best through lectures, others through small group discussions, still others through research and writing. Bartlett (1995) suggests that among the main reasons why few women and people of color become economics majors, and why the number of economics majors has recently declined, are that they find both course climate and content discouraging. She further argues that changes in introductory course content and pedagogy in classes as well as cooperative learning, more inclusive material, and more connections to students' lives would attract many bright students to economics. The inclusion of case studies in the principles class is one means of diversifying teaching techniques to reach all types of students.

Case study discussions allow students to work together in small groups where students learn through teaching one another. Many instructors find that they finally master economic theory when they must present it in their lectures; students involved in case study discussions can have the same opportunity to improve their understanding of economic theory. Moreover, students work together to actively "produce" an analysis of the case that reflects their own experiences and understandings and gives them a sense of their ability to "do" economics rather than simply "learn" economics. An added benefit is that students who first have the opportunity to express their views in small group settings subsequently are more willing to offer input to the larger class discussions. In my experience, this has been particularly true of female students.

For most instructors, the opportunity cost of introducing case study analysis in any economics course (in terms of lost lecture time) must be justified by better student performance in the course. Several instructors have attempted to quantify and demonstrate the effectiveness of case study teaching by focusing on student test scores and student satisfaction with a course. In his assessment of alternative instructional methods in agricultural economics courses, Steven Blank (1985, 59) found that case study analysis increased student test scores significantly and that students reported enjoying the challenge of working with cases. In other research, surveys of students in advanced economics courses using case studies revealed that students believed cases contributed substantially to their learning and significantly enhanced class discussion (Carlson and Schodt 1994). In their study of the impact of integrating scholarship on women in introductory economics courses, Lage and Treglia (1996, 26) found that "all students perform significantly better in a gender-inclusive economics course" in which teaching methods, as well as course content, are changed to include the diverse interests and learning styles of female students. Women, in particular, improved their performance significantly in the gender-inclusive course.

How does a principles course instructor incorporate case study analysis into principles courses? There are many possible ways, and this essay does not exhaust all the options. The following sections provide interested instructors with several ideas about how the case study approach might be used; creative instructors will likely have additional ideas.

Types of Case Studies

The usual case study presents information about a problem faced by a policy-making body or business firm. Students must use economic theory and the data provided to analyze the issues involved and make recommendations about possible courses of action. This approach can be used successfully in the principles course but does not represent the only possible option. There are at least two alternative methods for organizing discussion about a real-world "case": writing one's own and using a series of newspaper or journal articles as the basis for discussion.

No matter which of these formats suits their needs and tastes, instructors thinking about including cases in their course should have a particular goal in mind. Some cases allow students to test their understanding of one theoretical concept; others require them to synthesize several. Some case studies present a limited range of alternative viewpoints; others include a wide range. Some cases introduce more institutional detail and political realism than others. Additionally, instructors at many business schools use case studies to teach, rather than apply, theory. For example, an instructor could use a case detailing consumer response to price changes to allow students to discover the concept of elasticity. Although this approach may be difficult to employ at the principles level, some instructors might feel that it can be successfully used and will want to choose their cases accordingly.

Instructors interested in teaching the traditional case study method may want to choose from among the many offerings of the Harvard Business School, the Kennedy School of Government, and other sources of prepared cases. Many business schools now place their catalogues on the Internet and instructors can search for cases on various topics. My experience with teaching economics as a graduate student included the use of Harvard Business School's *Crown Cork and Seal and the Metal Container Industry* to address the issues of fixed and variable costs, the adoption of new technology, the determinants of demand for an industry's products and the effects of consumption on the environment, as an example of externalities. I continue to use this case in the firm behavior section of my principles course. The advantage of using prepared case studies is that it frees instructor time for focusing on the theoretical issues to be addressed and on the organization of class discussion. Cases are available for many interesting and relevant policy issues; students may be particularly interested in the Kennedy School's case on *The Urban League and the Youth Subminimum Wage* which addresses, among other issues, racial disparities in unemployment rates and whether the minimum wage does more harm than good to low-income groups. Many of these prepared case studies are well-suited to the skills of the principles level student; the instructor can guide student attention to those portions of the case that are most relevant for the questions at hand. Many of these case studies also come with teaching notes which review the details of the case, suggest a plan for class discussion, and include questions for students to consider.

There are, however, some disadvantages to using prepared case studies. It can take a great deal of time to locate suitable cases, particularly on issues of interest to the instructor and to principles of economics students. Although business school publishers provide catalogues of case studies that give some indication of case content, there is no way of being certain that the case will be applicable until one has a chance to read it. Anyone who has contemplated the long lists of available case studies from all sources will appreciate the difficulty involved. A second potential disadvantage of using some of these prepared case studies is the level of economic sophistication required for successful analysis. Instructors whose students are struggling with the more basic theoretical concepts may prefer to tailor their own case studies to the needs of their students. Moreover, prepared case studies will not often illustrate or support nonmainstream viewpoints, creating difficulties for instructors who want to offer diverse views in their classrooms. For these reasons, I offer two alternatives to the prepared case studies.

One possibility is for the instructor to prepare his or her own cases, using news reports, interviews, economic data and other sources of information about an issue of interest. An obvious advantage is that the cases can be tailored directly to the particular course. In addition, these cases are likely to be more up-to-date and can address economic questions that interest the students in that class. An obvious disadvantage is the time involved in writing a truly good case study from scratch. Therefore this approach is not likely to appeal to instructors who are untenured, as well as those who have a heavy load of teaching and/or committee responsibilities.

A less time-intensive alternative is to move away slightly from the traditional case study approach and think about a "case" as a set of related economic questions to be addressed rather than as a situation faced by one particular individual, firm, or policy group. The goal in this type of case is not usually not to reach a single decision or course of action but rather to understand how economic analysis can help shed light on an important public policy or business decision. While not a pure "case" in the business school sense, this type of analysis can help instructors accomplish many of the goals of traditional case study analysis.

Instructors focusing on an economic question can pull together journal articles that are not too technical for students in a principles course (e.g., articles in the *Journal of Economic Perspectives, Challenge,* and similar sources) and from newspaper and magazine articles (from the *Wall Street Journal, Economist, Dollars and Sense,* and others). For example, an instructor could take articles on the recent debate over the increase in the minimum wage from the *Wall Street Journal* and the *Economist,* pair them with articles from the *Journal of Economic Perspectives* and *Dollars and Sense,* and place students in the role of policymakers addressing the question of whether the minimum wage should be increased. Instructors can include estimates of elasticities of demand for labor and on the likely impact of a change in the minimum wage law on various groups of workers. Many viewpoints can be represented. It is much easier for an instructor to organize this type of case than to write a full case study. Instructors may, however, find it difficult and time consuming to provide the complexities of economic decision-making and the full institutional details that make case studies so interesting.

Once an instructor has decided upon the form of case study to use, there are several alternatives for using them in the classroom. Some of the options are presented in the next section. Instructors will also want to review some of the papers listed in the bibliography for other ideas.

How to Teach Case Studies in Introductory Economics Courses: One View

Instructors at business schools tend to use one of four approaches in teaching case studies (Rangan 1996). Rangan terms these approaches "lecturing a case," "theorizing a case," "illustrating a case," and "choreographing a case." *Lecturing a case* involves the instructor leading students through a series of questions and emphasizing points that are most relevant from the instructor's point of view. *Theorizing a case* refers to the use of cases to teach theoretical concepts. *Illustrating a case* refers to the use of a case to demonstrate ideas or concepts important to the course. *Choreographing a case,* Rangan's preferred method for business school classrooms, refers to case discussions that are more student-centered and less controlled by the instructor. Rangan argues that these discussions are more likely to allow for alternative viewpoints and lead to more learning by students.

In a principles of economics classroom, the two most relevant styles of case study presentation appear to be "lecturing the case" and "choreographing the case." Lecturing the case will be chosen by instructors who fear losing control over the class discussion and think that the opportunity cost of a poorly managed discussion is quite high. This format is also likely to be chosen by instructors whose students are unfamiliar with case study discussions and who are less sophisticated in their application of theoretical concepts. I tend to use this style of presentation at the principles level because I want to give students a solid idea of how economic concepts can be applied in real-world situations without having to spend too much class time correcting their economic analysis.

Instructors can use Rangan's preferred "choreographing the case" presentation style at the principles level if they have students who have enough confidence in their analytical abilities to be able to discuss appropriate applications and to draw conclusions. Students must be able to respond to comments made by other students, point out errors, and be willing to offer alternative viewpoints. Rangan's note on "Choreographing a Case Class" will be of use to instructors who want to pursue this presentation style; this note can be downloaded from the Harvard Business School web site or the hard copy may be ordered.

There are several steps to preparing and implementing a case study discussion. Roughly speaking, they can be broken down into preparation of the instructor and students before the discussion and management of the discussion with a summary and conclusion at the end.

Preparation of Students Prior to Case Discussion

For a case study discussion to work well, students need to be excited about their participation. If it is presented as just another assignment in an already busy semester, students are unlikely to appreciate the experience. Thus, it is worth the instructor's time to create interest in the case. Students may be motivated solely by the idea that they get to apply what they've learned in the classroom to a topic of interest to them. Other students will be interested to hear that case study analysis is used heavily in MBA programs, to which many of them aspire.

Most student preparation for a case study discussion takes place outside of class, although I have occasionally used class time for students to prepare answers to short cases in small groups. Students in a principles-level course generally need to be guided by a fairly extensive and specific set of questions that point them toward the appropriate economic tools to use and the more important themes of the case. My preference is to ask a mix of easy and difficult questions, some fact based and most requiring the use of graphs or other economic tools for a full answer. Several questions calling for opinions based on economic analysis, rather than objectively right-or-wrong answers, add interest to case discussions.

I strongly encourage students to work on the answers to case questions in small groups and sometimes assign students to them. I explain to the students that the questions are intended to challenge them and that using the resources of a group will make the analysis easier. I mention that there is real value in learning from one another and explain, for the benefit of the business-oriented students, that this is the way students in business schools prepare their cases.

Participation in the discussion can be encouraged in several ways. First, students who are required to hand in written answers to the case study questions or a short paper are more likely to be prepared for the class discussion. I emphasize to my students that I will not be looking for correct answers so much as effort and thorough analysis. Second, participation itself may be graded. I have found this does encourage some of my quieter students to speak up.

Preparation of the Instructor Prior to Case Discussion

The main determinant of the success of a case study discussion is the preparation of the instructor. It may be obvious, but bears mentioning anyway, that the instructor must have thorough knowledge of case and articles used for discussion. Students will garner evidence from all sections of the readings or case, and an instructor can be helpful in sorting out the relevant from the irrelevant only if she or he knows the context in which evidence is presented.

Before the discussion begins, the instructor should have in mind an outline of how the discussion will likely progress. Gomez-Ibanez and Kalt (1990) suggest that, for most case study discussions, no more than three key themes can be covered and that an instructor would do well to have in mind specific amounts of time to devote to each theme.

Management of the Case Discussion

The discussion needs to progress fairly rapidly to keep the attention of students. The instructor may decide to begin the class discussion by having several students summarize the important issues in the case. I play a relatively active part in discussions; I ask students questions, respond to incorrect answers if other students do not after being urged to do so, summarize student answers and sketch all graphs on the board as they come up. I also make sure that analysis is correct but try not to reveal my own opinions. This encourages students to offer alternative views and lets them participate in discussions about economic issues when there is room for legitimate disagreement.

During the discussion, I call on as many different students as possible; since all have had the opportunity to prepare answers ahead of time, I find that students are more willing to respond than in other classes. I do not, however, call on students unexpectedly unless I know they are fully prepared and are comfortable speaking in front of the class because I want students to get a good sense of just how much they have learned in their principles course and to gain confidence in applying that knowledge to analysis of economic events.

Beyond these general rules, two situations, in particular, may require specific instructor management. First, students may be tempted to discuss issues that do not advance class understanding of the case or, at any rate, have too high an opportunity cost given more important themes to be covered. In such a situation it is necessary to gently help students return to the main thread of the discussion, perhaps by asking specific questions. Second, students sometimes get bogged down trying find the answer to a particular question. Gomez-Ibanez and Kalt (1990) suggest asking a few rhetorical questions to point them toward an appropriate solution.

Summary and Conclusion of Case Discussion

At the end of the discussions the instructor may want to ask several students to offer summaries of what they learned from the particular case. This avoids having the instructor offer the "correct" view of the case. She or he may, however, need to focus attention on some minor or forgotten points and acknowledge alternative opinions that were not included in the summaries. I also point out to students all they have accomplished in applying the tools of economics they have learned in the course to an analysis of important issues involved in a real-world situation.

A Sample Case Study: Discrimination in Mortgage Lending

I developed a case study on discrimination in mortgage lending (see appendix for case readings and questions) for several reasons. First, it responds to the need to add material relevant to under-represented students in economics. Second, it allows students to use basic supply and demand analysis and to speculate about how to apply more advanced techniques while at the same time encouraging them to think about whether the standard economic theory adequately addresses all of the issues involved. Third, it allows for classroom debate over appropriate remedies for discrimination in mortgage lending, giving students the experience of using economic theory to make informed judgments. Fourth, the focus of the case can change over time as follow-up studies on mortgage lending are issued.

I address three main issues in discussing this case. First, students testify about the supply and demand effects of mortgage discrimination and on the increased mortgage lending, explaining their answers by sketching the relevant graphs on the board. Second, this case provides the opportunity to introduce a discussion of the economics of discrimination and the difficulties associated with measuring discrimination. Third, students analyze the policy options presented in the readings and suggest some of their own. The discussion concludes with the most current data and the effects of the actual policies chosen. The discussion tends to be lively and generates interest in the process of economic analysis.

Conclusion

Reasons for using case studies fall into two separate categories. The first, the focus of this essay, is pedagogical: cases provide an effective means of teaching students who are not well served by the traditional lecture method. The second is related to course content. Case studies may be a means of introducing students to nontraditional or less-apparent applications of economic theory. For example, the case study does allow an instructor to "Find and Add Women" to a course (Phase 2 in changing course contents). Used in this manner, the case acknowledges the separate interests of some students in the classroom and encourages all students to take seriously the analysis of these issues. This is also a relatively easy way for instructors to begin changing their teaching methodology, since case study analysis and discussion can be slipped into any economics course. Potential topics for analysis might include child care, allocation of time at work and in the home, discrimination, or comparable worth policies. But the real-world details included in some case studies can also be a starting point for challenging received neoclassical models and proposing alternative analytical methods (Phase 3 in designing course contents). In discussing comparable worth policies, for example, an instructor can direct students' attentions toward questioning whether markets work perfectly and whether market mechanisms can be expected to eliminate economic disparities. An instructor who uses a case study to challenge traditional models must be prepared, however, to change other components of the course as well. Otherwise, students will rightfully question the usefulness of either the material taught in the course or the case study itself.

Two other content-related reasons for using case studies in the principles of economics classroom come to mind. First, case studies can be used to point out the strengths and limitations of economic data and analysis. Students learn that the data they need to make a decision or predict an outcome may often be incomplete, unavailable, or flawed in some important way. Second, case studies can broaden student awareness of economic institutions, teaching students that economic decisions are not made solely in the realm of economic theory and that theory itself can be hard to apply in a world of imperfect information and uncertainty. Nevertheless, students can see that the theories learned in the principles course can give them insights into policy decisions and events in the news.

I use one or two case studies each semester in my principles of economics courses. I invariably find that some of the strongest participants in case study discussions are students who have appeared weaker on exams and quizzes; this reinforces the idea that teaching *all* students effectively requires the use of several different teaching methods. Further there is usually a very lively discussion and most students appear to be excited about the activity. My management of class discussion has improved as I have used cases and I enjoy the change from lecturing. Although I began using case studies in courses where I usually acted as the Sage-on-the-Stage lecturer, the positive experiences generated from the case study classes have emboldened me to pursue more active learning strategies and to include more alternative viewpoints throughout the course.

APPENDIX: A SAMPLE CASE STUDY ON DISCRIMINATION IN MORTGAGE LENDING

Students are assigned the following readings, which I include with their course reading packet at the beginning of the semester:

Bloomberg Business News. "Fleet Agrees to Settle Accusation of Loan Discrimination." *New York Times,* May 8, 1996, C4.
Bradsher, Keith. "A Second Fed Bank Study Finds Disparities in Mortgage Lending." *New York Times,* July 13, 1995, C1.
Hirsch, James. "Critics Say a Well-Intentioned Loan Plan Helped Minorities Buy Overpriced Homes." *Wall Street Journal,* July 20, 1995, B1.
Passell, Peter. "Race, Mortgages and Statistics." *New York Times,* May 10, 1996, C1.
"New Data on Mortgage Lending." *Chicago Fed Letter,* July 1997, no. 119.
Simmons, Jacqueline. "Home Prices Soar in Unexpected Places." *Wall Street Journal,* February 13, 1996, C4.
Wilke, John. "Home Loans to Blacks, Hispanics Soared in '94." *Wall Street Journal,* July 19, 1995, A2.
———. "Giving Credit: Mortgage Lending to Minorities Shows A Sharp 1994 Increase." *Wall Street Journal,* February 13, 1996, A1.

Instructors can also incorporate questions based on information found at the Department of Housing and Urban Development web site, http://www.hud.gov (check the URL before assigning to students), for lending practices of banks, credit unions, thrifts, and mortgage companies, by race, national origin, sex and income of applicants.

Student interest in this material may be increased by inviting them to be economic policy advisors to a government panel on disparities in mortgage lending. Students are asked to work in small groups to prepare written answers to the following questions, to be handed in after the class discussion. Students are encouraged to work in small "consulting" groups to prepare themselves for the hearing. I use the following set of questions which can certainly be tailored to meet the needs of many instructors:

MEMO
TO: Policy Consulting Group of Staunton, Economics Division
FROM: President, PCG
RE: Hearing on Disparities in Mortgage Lending
The Chair of the House Banking Committee has requested that we send a consulting team to the upcoming hearings on progress in eliminating disparities in mortgage lending. PCG has been asked to provide the economic analysis of mortgage discrimination and to provide its opinion on the policy options. I am asking your group to prepare answers to the following questions as preparation for testifying. Please return your answers to me in writing so I can assess your preparedness for the hearing.

1. Will discrimination in mortgage lending affect primarily the supply of or the demand for mortgage loans? Using a supply and demand diagram for mortgage loans (with the mortgage interest rate as the price), show the effect of discrimination on the quantity of loans made to minority applicants and the interest rate charged.

2. Is demand for mortgage loans likely to be elastic or inelastic? How does this interact with discrimination in mortgage lending? Demonstrate using a second supply and demand diagram.

3. On average, what percentages of white and black mortgage applications are rejected by lenders? Does the difference in rejection rates necessarily mean there is discrimination in mortgage lending?

4. How have researchers assessed the prevalence of discrimination in mortgage lending? What information do they need?

5. Explain the criticisms of the research conducted by the Federal Reserve Bank of Boston. Are any of the criticisms justified? How can they be addressed?

6. Explain the results presented in the study by the Federal Reserve Bank of Chicago. How does discrimination in mortgage lending occur?

7. Why did home loans to minority applicants increase in 1994? For which racial and ethnic groups did lending increase the fastest? The

slowest? Which mortgage lenders made the greatest improvement in lending to minority applicants? Which lenders were most likely to target loans to areas with heavy concentrations of minorities?

8. Using a supply and demand diagram and words, explain the effect of the increase in mortgage lending to minorities on home prices. Can this be considered a positive or negative development?

9. Of what interest is the loan/income ratio? Which mortgage lenders are most likely to make loans with high loan/income ratios?

10. What are some of the remedies available to policy-makers who wish to address the problem of discrimination in mortgage lending? Does economic analysis help us choose among the policy options? Which option would you choose and why?

REFERENCES

Blank, Steven. 1985. "Effectiveness of Role Playing, Case Studies, and Simulation Games in Teaching Agricultural Economics." *Western Journal of Agricultural Economics* 10(1): 55–62.

Boehrer, John, and Marty Linsky. 1983. "Teaching with Cases: Learning to Question." In *Learning in Groups,* ed. Clark Bouton and Russel Garth. New Directions for Teaching and Learning 14. San Francisco: Jossey-Bass.

Carlson, John A., and David W. Schodt. 1995. "Beyond the Lecture: Case Teaching and the Learning of Economic Theory." *Journal of Economic Education* (winter): 17–28.

Gomez-Ibanez, Jose, and Joseph Kalt. 1990. *Teaching Notes to Accompany Cases in Microeconomics.* Englewood Cliffs, NJ: Prentice-Hall.

Lage, Maureen, and Michael Treglia. 1996. "The Impact of Integrating Scholarship on Women into Introductory Economics: Evidence from One Institution." *Journal of Economic Education* 27 (winter): 26–36.

Liao, Ziqi. 1996. "A Co-operative Group Learning Strategy for Teaching Case Studies to Business Students." *Economics and Business Education* 4 (spring): 35–37.

Marks, Stephen G., and Michael G. Rukstad. 1996. "Teaching Macroeconomics by the Case Method." *Journal of Economic Education* 27 (spring): 139–47.

Ng, Maureen. 1996. "Teaching about Currency Exchange Rates with Case Studies of the US Dollar and Mexican Peso Depreciation." *Economics and Business Education* 4 (spring): 19–22.

Rangan, V. 1996. "Choreographing a Case Class." Harvard Business School Case Note 9-595-074, April 19.

Sykes, Gary. 1990. "Learning to Teach with Cases." *Journal of Policy Analysis and Management* 9(2): 297–302.

E-Mail Discussion Lists and Feminist Pedagogy in the Economics Classroom

Meenakshi Rishi

Since the 1980s there has been a dialogue in economic education on alternative pedagogical practices that would enable students to learn critical and creative thinking (Bok 1986; Siegfried et al. 1991). Some of these dialogues suggest that feminist pedagogy is especially suited to the fostering of such skills because it emphasizes cooperation, community, and conversation rather than passive note taking. In the spirit of developing a feminist pedagogy in economics, this essay examines the way in which e-mail discussion lists can be used to foster a nonhierarchical forum for topical discussions.

The following section describes the use of an e-mail discussion list in an introductory classroom including a short discussion of the mechanics as well as the goals of this project. Then, two specific examples are used to indicate how this technique can promote open dialogue. Finally, potential advantages as well as disadvantages of such discussion lists for the introductory economics classroom are summarized in the conclusion.

E-Mail Discussion Lists in the Economics Classroom

The use of e-mail is becoming increasingly widespread among institutions of higher learning. E-mail can function as an effective classroom tool because it enhances communication and facilitates information provision (Harasim 1989; Manning 1996). An e-mail discussion list is an electronic mailing list that combines standard e-mail technology with an automatic administrative process. An administrative program such as "listserv" or "majordomo" is used to subscribe members to a common list, handle information requests, and route messages among list members. Subscribed members can communicate to the list by sending e-mail to the program, which passes it onto all list members. Interactions between list members are therefore quick, automatic, and can take place at any time of day, provided list members frequently check their e-mails and respond.

During the winter quarter of 1996–97 I subscribed my introductory economics class and myself to Econ 100-d, an economics discussion list. The class was composed of thirty-two students, twenty-three males and nine females. The class was informed that a weekly list participation grade of B or better would be determined by their ability to analyze and discuss at least one classroom topic on Econ 100-d. I supplied the first list posting on the subject of appropriate e-mail etiquette, or "netiquette."

Econ 100-d was developed to fulfill several goals. First, the list was to be a mechanism for disseminating information on upcoming tests, allocating reading assignments, and providing study tips to the class. I hoped that this would allow for more class time to be devoted to lecture and discussion. Second, this exercise was designed to provide an open forum where students could communicate with one another and me to clarify points not understood, raise questions, and more generally comment on topics from class discussion. Finally, the list was intended to provide a nonthreatening environment for students to enter into open and frank dialogue.

Literature has documented that the traditional classroom climate can be a threatening one for certain students who may feel alienated because of their race, gender, and/or economic class (Hall and Sandler 1982; Ferber 1984). E-mail discussion lists can be useful in dispelling the exclusionary classroom environment of the traditional classroom in many ways. Hawisher and Moran (1993, 22) suggest that "the lack of paralinguistic cues" such as appearance, voice, and facial expression invites participation in e-mail discussions from those who normally refrain from speaking face-to-face. Moreover, students may feel more comfortable talking on e-mail discussion lists since they cannot be interrupted and have more time to gather and organize their thoughts.[1] Thus, an e-mail discussion list has the potential of encouraging a nonhierarchical and nonintimidating classroom environment. In this regard the operation of an e-mail discussion list is consistent with an effective feminist pedagogy that is predicated on promoting an egalitarian and democratic classroom environment (Shackelford 1992).

Conjecturing about the benefits of e-mail discussion lists is easier than putting such lists into actual operation. While there were no problems with the information dissemination aspect of Econ 100-d, student inertia and absence of conversation on the list soon emerged as serious issues. For this reason, I assumed a more active role on the list and posted questions at frequent intervals. I selected specific real-world problems on topics that I thought would provoke discussion. This interventionist technique produced encouraging results, and the students became more responsive. About 40 percent of the class posted at least one relevant (analytical) message on the discussion list in an average week. Furthermore, participation rates almost doubled during discussions of topics such as the student bookstore as a monopoly, poverty and welfare, social security, the budget deficit, and free trade. In some cases students who said little in class but were frequent participants on Econ 100-d started to participate on a more regular basis in class as well. My strategy of posting more questions also facilitated the introduction of more inclusive subject matter into the course as documented by the following examples.

Poverty and Welfare

In traditional principles courses there is scant attention paid to the topic of poverty and welfare. Often this is a direct result of the corresponding small coverage of these topics in standard economics textbooks.[2] Insofar as poverty is a social phenomenon that has a disproportionate impact on women, minorities, and children, I felt that it was an important issue for the class to discuss. To facilitate in-class debate and list conversation, students were provided with supplementary readings that examined poverty from a critical, historical perspective.[3] Current income and poverty statistics were also distributed and list members were asked to analyze the topic on Econ 100-d. The ensuing interactions on the discussion list were animated, lasted over one week, and involved 85 percent of the class. More than half of these postings were authored by female students with no one woman dominating the conversation. This involvement far outweighed their representation in the class. Interestingly enough, list interactions went beyond the poverty debates and developed into a discussion incorporating related topics such as profiles of welfare recipients, equity considerations, and welfare reform. The following (sequential) dialogue is illustrative.

Female student 1: I am amazed by the statistic mentioned in class today. Women maintained 86 percent of the 10.5 million single-parent families with children in the United States in 1992. I think these women chose to have children because of the welfare benefits. What do you say?

Male student 1: I agree, they have too many kids and are extremely lazy . . . if these welfare benefits are stopped then they will find work and not be poor any longer.

Female student 2: . . . Here is something that has been sitting on my mind. As usual I know a girl (a single mother) who used assistance for a while. But now she and her HEALTHY baby are on their own. She is in community college and is working two jobs. Not everybody abuses the system.

At this point I distributed some Census Bureau statistics in class that focused on the profile of welfare recipients. The data helped debunk popular stereotypes of welfare recipients by underscoring that more than 80 percent of U.S. families on welfare have only one or two children and that poverty is not confined to the unemployed. As the comments provided here will demonstrate, subsequent list postings (and class debates) revolved around a discussion of these statistics and welfare critiques.

Female student 3: I have a point to make about the figures presented in yesterday's lecture. As mentioned in class, U.S. teenagers have a higher pregnancy rate compared to some industrialized countries, yet our welfare system provides fewer benefits than any of these nations. So, I feel that welfare benefits do not encourage unintended pregnancies. I think that morals are to blame for unintended pregnancies.

Female student 4: I do not believe that morals are an issue . . . fairness is. I think a lot of you guys feel that welfare provides no incentive to work. On the other hand, how do you expect people to go out and seek a job without a fair chance to compete with people who have the money to be educated? Therefore, we need to think about welfare reform more realistically.

Female student 5: . . . Are the rich not lazy themselves? Some were born into wealth and some stay poor in spite of working hard. . . . I think that this welfare reform business is basically good. But it will not work if we do not create educational opportunities for people to at least gain a high school diploma.

These comments are indicative of student critical thinking that goes beyond the standard coverage of the topic of poverty and income distribution in introductory economics textbooks. Such discussions also suggest an operative feminist pedagogy that "allows students, through open dialogue and conversation, to compare, contrast, and connect their views and ideas with those of others toward a goal of achieving a greater understanding of the subject" (Shackleford 1992, 571).

Additional proof of the nonthreatening atmosphere created by these list postings arrived unexpectedly. Michelle, a quiet student in class, used Econ 100-d to "speak" about her family's eleven-month experience with federal assistance. Her personal account emphasized that poverty is not confined to single-parent households and that some recipients can use welfare as an effective short-term safety net. Michelle's postings also highlighted specific societal prejudices against the poor and became a learning experience for the class (and the instructor).[4] The e-mail discussion list was thus able to create opportunities for the instructor and the students to interact as co-learners, enabling a greater comprehension of the topic.

Free Trade, the Girdle Factory, and the Broom Business

The in-class discussion of free trade and its consequences was preceded by a PBS video presentation that surveyed two manufacturing plants (a girdle factory and a broom business) whose workers were about to be displaced by the North American Free Trade Agreement (NAFTA). The video report stated that the U.S. garment industry could lose almost a million jobs as a consequence of NAFTA. At the same time, the report also mentioned the positive impact of NAFTA in generating net exports. For example, the report noted that displaced broom factory workers could find alternative employment in a fire extinguisher factory that was experiencing a boom in export sales as a direct consequence of NAFTA. Following this video presentation, students were asked to consider the nature of economic theory and the conduct of economic policy. Within this context, students were asked to discuss whether the theoretically welfare-enhancing impact of free trade could have different policy implications for various groups of people. As the following summary indicates, list postings around this theme were lively and indicative of critical thinking.[5] A few comments also suggested that some list participants were able to make connections between the video report and previous class discussions on poverty.

Female student 1: I do not personally like what NAFTA is doing to all those women in the garment factory. You did notice that all the employees in the girdle factory were female? My question is whether this will worsen the statistics of women in poverty.

Male student 1: I think that if NAFTA causes the garment industry to lose jobs and if most of these jobs were held by women or poor Americans, it will worsen the statistics on poverty and unemployment in this country. The impact will be worse on certain groups—women, children, etc.

Female student 2: I was just reading an article in *U.S. News & World Report* on NAFTA. It said that so far the impact of the trade pact

has been minimal. I will mention some statistics . . . the net gain in
U.S. jobs before NAFTA was 2.8 million jobs and the net gain in
U.S. jobs after NAFTA has been 2.2 million.

Male student 2: I think that NAFTA is good because it also creates jobs.
Like in the broom factory case where workers could get jobs in
another factory. Also do not forget that we are creating jobs in
Mexico with NAFTA.

Male student 3: I feel that there is no "one size fits all" situation here and
that NAFTA will affect different people differently.

Creative reasoning, critical thinking, and the ability to "see the world
through many different sets of eyes" are central to the agenda of developing
an operative feminist pedagogy (Rothenberg 1996, 67). These interactions
suggest that an e-mail discussion list is one pedagogical strategy that can
promote the operation of feminist pedagogy in the economics classroom.

Evaluating Econ 100-d

It is not simple to assess the efficacy of alternative pedagogical strategies
(Kurfiss 1998). Econ 100-d was evaluated via standard departmental evaluation forms as well as by a survey designed to gauge student reaction to the list.
On a scale of 1 (lowest) to 5 (highest), students on average rated the course
4.3 and the instructor 4.2. Evaluations of the same course taught without
the use of e-mail discussion lists in the previous quarter averaged 4.0 for the
course and 4.1 for the instructor. Students gave Econ 100-d an overall mean
score of 3.5 on the additional appraisal survey conducted at the end of the
course. Written comments solicited from the class on the same survey form,
were perhaps more instructive. On the positive side most students liked "the
informal atmosphere of the list" and felt that Econ 100-d was "an excellent
way to keep informed with opinions of the class." On the negative side
students (and the instructor) found the list to be very time-consuming and
there were occasional lapses in conversation. A possible solution to this latter
problem may be to assign students as moderators on specific topics.

Summary and Conclusion

As Becker and Watts (1996) have noted, a majority of introductory economics
classes use lectures to transmit neoclassical materials to students. Feminist
pedagogy would suggest that educators promote creative and critical thinking

via methods that are nonhierarchical and allow for inclusive course contents. The use of an e-mail discussion list is one alternative that has the potential for contributing to the development of feminist pedagogy in economics. The examples provided earlier indicate that students used this informal forum to compare ideas, discuss readings, document personal experiences, and explore alternative theories to a depth not found in a standard principles text.

Instructors wishing to employ feminist pedagogical strategies in the economics classroom can certainly benefit from the use of e-mail discussion lists to enhance the learning environment. Discussion lists created for smaller groups of students can facilitate the collaboration that is required for team projects. By dissolving the boundaries of time and space, e-mail discussion lists can promote greater interaction not only among students, but also between the instructor and the class. Further, the nonthreatening environment fostered by an e-mail discussion list can give a "voice" to certain students who are silenced in more traditional class settings.

Despite all the advantages associated with the operation of e-mail discussion lists as pedagogical tools, instructors need to be aware of the problems involved in this endeavor. Sproull and Kiesler (1991) have documented several research studies to support the thesis that people tend to express more opinions and vent more emotion in an electronic discussion than when they are face-to-face. This may lead to the transmission of nasty and hurtful language as a part of the e-mail message. Such breaches of *netiquette* usually can be overcome by assigning students as discussion moderators on particular topics. Another disadvantage associated with the operation of such lists is the amount of time they take. The reading load created by e-mail discussion can easily overwhelm the instructor. Students also, can feel burdened by the volume of messages on an active discussion list. This problem too, may be avoided by the use of students as moderators on specific discussions.

In summary, as our campuses become increasingly reliant on e-mail as a principal mode of communication, instructors should recognize the usefulness of e-mail discussion lists in generating an informal space for debate and dialogue. This instructor, for one, is convinced of the value of e-mail discussion lists as effective feminist pedagogical tools and will continue to use them in the economics classroom.

NOTES

I wish to thank J. Emily Hershey for invaluable research assistance with this essay.

1. In a series of experiments designed to study group decision making, Sproull and Kiesler (1991) discovered that participants in networked groups, linked via e-mail and computer conferencing, were able to talk frankly and openly. Further,

networked groups generated more proposals for action than traditional groups because, "instead of one or two people doing most of the talking as happens in many face-to-face groups, everyone had a more equal say" (119).

2. The essay by Janice Peterson in this volume provides an excellent example for incorporating poverty issues into a principles course.

3. For instance, Albelda and Folbre (1996) and readings contained in Feiner (1994) provide good content for a debate on poverty and income distribution.

4. Michelle mentioned that an English teacher was reluctant to give her details on an essay competition because he thought that poor students were (mentally) inferior. Michelle described feelings of frustration and anger when a Medicaid doctor misdiagnosed her fever and "quarantined" her. The family could not afford a second opinion.

5. List response rates on this topic were not significantly different by gender.

REFERENCES

Albelda, Randy, and Nancy Folbre. 1996. Welfare and Welfare Reform. *The War on the Poor: A Defense Manual.* New York: New Press.

Becker, William E., and Michael Watts. 1996. "Chalk and Talk: A National Survey on Teaching Undergraduate Economics." *American Economic Review* 86(2): 448–53.

Bok, Derek. 1986. *Higher Learning.* Cambridge, MA: Harvard University Press.

Feiner, Susan F., ed. 1994. *Race and Gender in the American Economy: Views from across the Spectrum.* Englewood Cliffs, NJ: Prentice-Hall.

Ferber, Marianne A. 1984. "Suggestions for Improving the Classroom Climate for Women in the Introductory Economics Course: A Review Article." *Journal of Economic Education* 15 (spring): 160–68.

Hall, Roberta M., and Bernice R. Sandler. 1982. "The Classroom Climate: A Chilly One for Women?" Washington, DC: Project for the Status and Education of Women, Association of American Colleges.

Harasim, Linda M. 1989. "On-Line Education: A New Domain." In *Mindweave: Communication, Computers, and Distance Education,* ed. Robin Mason and Anthony Keye, 50–62. New York: Pergamon Press.

Hawisher, Gail E., and Charles Moran. 1993. "Electronic Mail and the Writing Instructor." *College English* 55 (October): 6–27.

Kurfiss, Joanne G. 1988. *Critical Thinking: Theory, Research, Practice, and Possibilities.* ASHE-ERIC Higher Education Report no. 2. Washington, DC: Association for the Study of Higher Education.

Manning, Linda M. 1996. "Economics on the Internet: Electronic Mail in the Classroom." *Journal of Economic Education* (summer): 201–4.

Rothenberg, Paula. 1996. "The Politics of Discourse and the End of Argument." In *Creating an Inclusive College Curriculum: A Teaching Sourcebook from the New Jersey Project,* ed. Ellen G. Friedman, Wendy K. Kolmar, Charley B. Flint, and Paula Rothenberg, 59–69. New York: Columbia University Teachers College Press.

Shackleford, Jean. 1992. "Feminist Pedagogy: A Means for Bringing Critical Thinking and Creativity to the Economics Classroom." *American Economic Review* 82(2): 570–76.

Siegfried, John., Robin L. Bartlett, W. Lee Hansen, Allen C. Kelley, Donald N. McCloskey, and Thomas H. Tietenberg. 1991. "The Economics Major: Can and Should We Do Better than a B-?" *American Economic Review (Papers and Proceedings)* 81 (May): 20–25.

Sproull, Lee, and Sara Kiesler. 1991. "Computers, Networks, and Work." *Scientific American* 265 (September): 116–23.

Putting Economics to Work

Robin L. Bartlett

Students are rarely given an opportunity to put the economics they learn in college to work. Instead, they are given the opportunity to apply economic principles to contrived problem sets, case studies, or even actual cases after the fact. The content of most economics courses is prescribed. In addition, students rarely get a chance to learn economics in a way similar to how they will learn and work together in their jobs. Instead, in most classes they sit passively listening and working alone. This essay will describe a course in which students have an opportunity to study a wrongful death case using information about another student in the class and to do the economic analysis of the case as a member of a team. The effectiveness of this approach will be demonstrated during the term by the ability of these students to work effectively on an actual divorce case and present an economic brief to a judge. The impact of this experience on the students will be summarized in their own voices.

The Course

Economics 325, Women in the Labor Force, is similar to many introductory level and advanced courses that examine the economic position of women in the economy. "Econ 325" examines the forces that determine women's decisions to go into the paid labor force, to enter certain occupations, and to settle for lower wages and benefits. The course is an advanced area course. Students taking the course have had intermediate micro- and macroeconomics. The text is Joyce Jacobsen's *Economics of Gender* (1994). The theoretical material in her text is neoclassical economics applied to the various issues and problems associated with women's entry into the labor market.

Three aspects of the course, however, make it unique and make it easier for students to apply what they will learn to situations that might arise in their lives. First, the course fulfills the Women's Studies / Black Studies General Education requirement for graduation. Courses that fulfill this requirement focus on the consequences of discrimination and the relative position of women and/or African Americans in the United States. While there are ample introductory Women's Studies and Black Studies courses to fulfill the requirement, Economics 325 is an upper-level economics course that also fulfills it.

The second aspect of the course that makes it unique is its lecture/laboratory format. Denison University's Economics Department adopted a lecture/laboratory format in 1989 for its entire undergraduate curriculum (see Bartlett and King 1990). The purpose of the lecture/laboratory format is to give students a simultaneous "hands-on" applied experience with the theoretical material they are leaning in lectures. The significance of "hands-on" learning for certain groups of students has been demonstrated by Kolb (1981). In order to add a two hour laboratory component to traditional economics courses without having to either make the unnecessary trade-off between theory and application and without having to increase the staffing needs of the department, the senior seminar (which was not a capstone course) was eliminated and a two-hour laboratory component was added to the core courses of the major and several advanced courses.[1] While senior seminars still exist, they may or may not have laboratory components.

Third, while the teaching technique is basically lecture during the traditional class component of the course, some of the lectures are given by the instructor and others are given by students. Lectures occur three days a week. The material in the book is covered sequentially. The instructor lectures for fifty minutes one or two days a week and students give a series of ten-minute mini-lectures one day a week. These mini-lectures are developed by teams of six students in response to a question posed by the instructor.[2] After fifteen minutes of discussion a team member is randomly selected by the roll of the die (see Bartlett 1995b). The randomly selected student comes to the front of the class, tapes a sheet of paper from an easel pad to the board, and presents the team's answer. The grade she or he gets on the presentation is given to each of the other team members.

Groups of students are not necessarily cooperative learning teams, and cooperative learning teams are not necessarily teams. The random selection of a team member to present the material motivates a cooperative learning environment within the team. Every team member must be prepared to present the team's work. Better prepared students are motivated to teach since they may not be giving the team's answer and weaker students are motivated to learn as best they can because they may be giving the team's response. During the allotted fifteen minutes students teach one another. Teams make students truly responsible for one another's performances, and thus students are more motivated to read in advance, come to class, take good notes, and discuss the material with other team members outside of the classroom. In addition, teams build self-confidence (see Bartlett 1995c).

While Economics 325 focuses on the economic position of women and the "good and bad" forces that are at work in U.S. labor markets, its unique content and pedagogy helps to better prepare students to put their economics to work. The content ensures that they understand the different sources of labor market discrimination in the United States and how they affect individuals and groups. The team learning components ensure that students have experience working in groups and learn how to get along with different people to accomplish a task. The educational and psychological literatures also suggest that some students, particularly women and students of color, learn better in tightly knit groups (see Anderson and Adams 1992; Belenky et al. 1986; Ginorio 1995; Musil 1992; Sandler, Silverberg, and Hall 1996; Light 1990; Nieves-Squires 1991; Schoem 1993; Smith and Kolb 1985; Tobias 1990; Treisman 1992). Finally, the laboratory component gives students the opportunity to develop their abilities to use and manipulate data so that they can put their economics to work.

After what normally occurs during the semester is presented, the unusual opportunity that presented itself during the semester will be discussed. Then several student comments will document the significance of this experience for them.

What Normally Occurs during a Semester

The lecture component of the course progresses through the course material: what do we mean by gender differences, work, leisure, family, occupational segregation, human capital, and discrimination. For the students' portion of the lecture component, students form teams the first week of school and stay with their team throughout the semester.[3] Teams are arbitrarily formed by grouping students who happen to be sitting in a reasonable proximity to one another. The laboratory component of the course progresses with a series of weekly two hour labs devoted to the estimation of the economic worth of a victim of a wrongful death. Students are paired in lawyer/client relationships during which each has the opportunity to play the other role. Typical lawyer/client privileges extend to this relationship and confidentiality is extended only to include the instructor. The pairings are not arbitrarily chosen. Each student is paired with another who is different from him- or herself in at least one respect—either race/ethnicity/ nationality, gender, or class. Finally, it is assumed that each member of the pair has met an untimely death due to the negligence of the university.

Acting as someone else's attorney or being the family of a victim in a wrongful death case is a valuable personal and economic experience for students. In a personal sense they see a person's life story develop from his or her perspective and take twists and turns as a result of his or her place in society. They acquire information that would actually be used in a wrongful death case. Second, students get to deal with the issue of confidentiality and what that means in dealing with clients. Confidentiality is an important notion for college students to develop. In an economic sense, students learn the value of time, compounding, and discounting. In addition, students have the opportunity to examine the very real effects of race, gender, and class on the economic worth calculations of another student's life as compared to his or her own calculations.

The tangible outcome of the fourteen-week laboratory project is to develop a fifteen-page economic brief estimating the economic worth of a victim of a wrongful death case (their partner's hypothetical death). The labs are designed to produce a document that could actually be presented in a court of law. The following labs illustrate how students progress through the necessary economic analysis. Leslie Doe is a hypothetical victim used throughout the labs.[4] Her economic background and vital statistics are used to exemplify the various labs for the students. Student, however, must insert their client's information into the exercises.

Lab One—Leslie Doe's Economic History

The student acting as the first attorney interviews a member of the deceased's family (played by the hypothetically deceased student). The purpose of the interview is to obtain an economic history of the client. What was the educational level of the deceased's parents and grandparents? What were the occupations of the deceased's parents? How much education did the deceased have? What were the deceased's interests? How well was she or he doing in school? Did she or he have any work experience—held summer jobs or jobs during the school year? What were they? How much did she or he earn? At the end of the two hours the attorneys turn in two-page economic histories of their clients.

Lab Two—How to Find Vital Statistics in the Library

Students attend a class in the library conducted by library staff on how to find the necessary vital statistics for a wrongful death case such as life expectancies by gender and race (and in some cases for students of a different nationality), rates of return on various financial instruments over time, the inflation rate over time, and the starting wage for workers with similar education and work histories as those of the deceased. Following the introduction to data sources and access, students are sent on an economic scavenger hunt to find the necessary data for their clients. Each attorney turns in a referenced fact sheet on his or her client with copies of the source material attached.

Lab Three—Leslie Doe's Vital Statistics

In this lab, students input the information gathered during the economic scavenger hunt into a spreadsheet program in the computer lab to sketch out a timeline of their client's prematurely shortened lives. Although Excel is used in this project, any simple spreadsheet program will provide students with the computational and graphical tools they need. By the end of the lab period, each student produces a chart describing the victim's actual life events as ascertained in the economic history interview and their expected life events as ascertained from statistical tables.

Lab Four—Lifetime Earnings, or the Wonders of Compounding

In this lab students use the information they acquired during the personal interviews and at the library to estimate what their clients could have earned over their expected life spans. Students are shown how to calculate growth rates for earnings using historical inflation indexes and how to apply it to the victim's personal information in calculating his or her expected lifetime earnings. Each attorney produces a chart with his or her client's actual lifetime and expected lifetime earnings.

Lab Five—Which Compounding Rate?

In this lab students use different assumptions about starting salaries and inflation rates to examine a set of relevant expected earnings profiles. They compare the expected lifetime earnings profiles of their client with those calculated by their lab partners. Any observed differences based on race, gender, or class are discussed in a brief lab report.

Lab Six—Present Value, or What a Promise Is Worth

Students are introduced to the notion of discounting and instructed on how to calculate the discounted present value of future income. They are asked to develop a spreadsheet and to determine the effect of various discount rates on the present value of their client's worth.

Lab Seven—Which Discount Rate?

Various rates of returns to a range of financial instruments are examined. Students use information from the *Statistic Abstract* or the World Wide Web to find information to calculate the rates of return and the standard deviations of returns for stock issues, and government and cooperate bond issues for the last twenty years. Students then trace out the trade-offs between the risk and return associated with each investment. Finally, each attorney is asked to argue for a particular discount rate in his or her lab report.

Lab Eight—The Net Effect of Inflation and Discount Rates

This lab focuses on how the choice of reasonable compounding and discounting rates can affect the discounted present value (DPV) of their clients' lives. Students are asked to consider both the plaintiff's and the defense attorney's perspectives. Using their Excel worksheets, students calculate the DPV of their clients' lives using three different inflation and discount rate assumptions to circumscribe a reasonable settlement for the jury's deliberations.

Lab Nine—The Value of Nonmarket Work

To this point each attorney has focused on the market worth of their client's loved one. Each attorney makes another appointment with a member of the victim's family during lab time and discusses the victim's nonmarket production. The client's family representative is asked to list the victim's nonmarket activities. To calculate the value of the victim's nonmarket worth, the number of hours she or he spent at these tasks is multiplied by the hourly rate for a comparable service in the market place. Earnings estimates for these services are found in the appropriate *Employment and Earnings* collected by the U.S. Department of Labor. Each attorney produces a chart of the value of his or her client's lifetime nonmarket production.

Lab Ten—Total Market and Nonmarket Worth

The expected lifetime market and nonmarket production of each client is added together under the three different sets of inflation and discount rate assumptions from lab eight. A table is then constructed with all the scenarios and the nine different discounted present value for each.

Lab Eleven—The Effects of Race/Ethnicity, Gender, and Class

To understand how much of the observed differences in the above calculations are the result of discrimination and not just differences in abilities, educational levels, and experience, the class as a whole collects information on the incomes, educational levels, age, race, gender, and occupations of their parental units. They enter the information in a statistical package, Mystat, and run regressions to determine how much race, gender, and class affect earnings.

Lab Twelve—Explaining Earnings Differentials

This lab builds upon the previous lab. Students are shown how to decompose the observed earnings differential into its various components; the amount of the earnings differential attributed to the differential market valuation of the human capital characteristics of men and women, the amount of the earnings differential attributed to men and women having different human capital characteristics, and the amount of the earnings differential unexplained. The lab is intended to demonstrate that the market does not value the educational levels of men and women the same and that forces other than just those in the market are at work. The personal nature of the data brings the point home.

Lab Thirteen—Putting It All Together

This lab shows students how to bring all the information obtained, calculated, and presented in previous labs together into a complete economic brief on the economic worth of their client. The lab discusses presentation of the information and documentation. Students are asked to take the time to begin organizing their presentation and to write out an outline of their presentation.

Lab Fourteen—A Discussion of Findings

Students come to class with their finished economic briefs and discuss the similarities and differences between their cases. This is a time for them to acknowledge what they and others have accomplished and to display their work. The lab gives students a sense of completion and accomplishment.

The laboratory component of this class is vital to students' understanding of the forces at work in the labor market. The differences in DPVs that are generated by the different socioeconomic characteristics of the students helps them understand that the sources of economic difference and how they are affected. The wrongful death briefs are one way to make these points up-close-and-personal and to show students how to put economics to work.

What Occurred in Spring 1995

Two-thirds of the way through the course, a local attorney approached the instructor to be an expert witness in a divorce case. The case was for a women who was a full-time homemaker with four children. She was seeking the divorce. The instructor did not have the time to devote to the case. However, the instructor volunteered her class if the class would agree to take on the case and the client would agree to the experiment. The students were informed by the instructor about the possibility of doing a divorce case and were asked if they wanted to stop the course for two weeks and take on the project. The class was eager to do so. The attorneys explained to the plaintiff that the class would develop the economic brief for her case (with her approval) and the instructor would testify on their behalf. All services rendered would be gratis. She agreed and all the appropriate documents were purged of any identifying names (now referred to as John and Jane Doe) and account numbers and handed over to the students.

In addition, the lawyers wanted the students to try a new way of calculating the moneys owed the plaintiff and her four children. Rather than prepare the standard list of assets and debts that usually are divided in half and then add on the child support payment prescribed by Ohio law, the attorneys wanted the students to equalize each party's pre- and post-divorce standard of living. They were given a workshop presentation by Stephan Renas, an economic consultant. His work (1995) is based on the work of Weitzman (1985). The latter work examines the impact of divorce on the standard of living of men and women relative to the poverty level. Renas set up a framework to examine the intact family's standard of living relative to the appropriate poverty level to that of the separated family's.

Since it was the students' case, they were given the responsibility of determining how to proceed. After much discussion on the first Monday, the class decided to stay in their teams and have each team develop a strategy for presentation. The next class each team came prepared to argue over which vital statistics to use—which inflation rate to use and which W-2 of the husband was reflective of his earning power. They discussed whether the defendant's last year's salary was the right one to use even of it was significantly lower than the previous year's wages. He was a truck driver and received higher pay the more he delivered in a day. Was the decline coincidentally related to his new interest in another woman, or were there economic reasons for fewer deliveries? Was it better to average his salary over the past three years? With regard to the plaintiff's financial situation, the students had to determine the value of her in-home seasonal daycare services. Another discussion ensued over how to calculate the inflation rate for compounding his and her wages into the future. The instructor acted as a facilitator of these discussions.

Over the next few class periods the teams went to the library and found information on poverty levels and how they are calculated. They discussed whether it was a good measure and its shortcomings because surely the defense attorney would. During the last class of the two week period, the attorneys for the plaintiff visited the class for the students' presentation of the case. The students argued forcefully based on sound economic reasoning their method for determining the relevant calculations. During finals week five students were chosen to accompany the instructor for the official presentation of the case before the judge.

The case was basic. The wife wanted a divorce from her husband who said he was not happy in the marriage and had been seen in the company of another woman. The wife filed for divorce. The husband earned $49,774 as a truck driver and the wife earned $4,500 as a babysitter. She had never worked outside the home during their fifteen-year marriage. The students calculated that the intact family's standard of living was 2.5 times the poverty level for a family of six (two adults and four children). They then separated John and Jane into a family of five with one adult and four children and a family of one with one adult and recalculated each family's standard of living. Her standard of living was .26 times the poverty level for a family of five with one adult and his standard of living was 5.88 times the poverty level for a family of one adult. The question was how much money did John have to transfer to Jill in order for their resultant standards of living to be the same after the separation. John had to transfer $30,000 per year yielding an annual income for her and the children of $34,500 or 1.98 times the poverty level. John would be left with $15,274 annually or 1.98 times the poverty level for a family of one adult. Obviously, everyone was made worse off—both of the reassembled households were living at a standard of living 21 percent below their previous level.

Although the defense attorney had been presented with the students' economic brief prior to the testimony, she obviously had not taken it seriously and asked only a few questions of the instructor during her court appearance. The judge, in comparison, took the presentation very seriously and asked several questions about the poverty rate and how it was calculated. He seemed particularly taken by the fact that most persons in poverty are children. The plaintiff's lawyers felt the presentation went well.

Unfortunately, the fate of the case was not determined before the students had to leave for summer or permanent jobs. In fact, the case is on appeal. The judge wrote a fifty-four-page divorce decree. He ordered the usual division of property and child support. In addition, he ordered the husband to pay $150/week for the next five years to help the plaintiff finish her undergraduate degree and to remain at home until her fourth child entered first grade. Rehabilitative, spousal support, or alimony as it was called before no-fault divorce is not always given in divorce cases. When it is given, it depends on the judge before whom the case is argued. Note, however, that $150/week is not nearly as much as was argued for based on the students' calculations. Never before in Ohio had a formula for child and spousal support been argued with a formula based on pre- and post-divorce relative standards of living. The judge obviously had taken the students' case seriously and awarded the plaintiff more than the customary child support. The defense attorney has appealed the decision and the judgment is still pending.

The instructor evaluated the input of each student by averaging the student's own evaluation of his or her work with the average of that of other team members. Students used a 1 to 4 scale with 1 being little contribution to the case and 4 being a large contribution to the team effort. Interestingly, seventeen of the twenty-four students evaluated their own contribution within a half of a grade of the average of their teammates' evaluation of their contribution. Four students rated their contribution over one half a grade higher than their teammates did and three rated themselves over a half of a grade lower. The grades ranged from a 1.6 to 4.0. Four students earned 4.0. Nine students had 3.0 to 3.9. Nine students earned a 2.0 to 2.9 and one received a 1.64. The grade they gave one another and themselves was weighted equally and served as a test grade.

Student Reactions

In the next lab the instructor asked students to just reflect on this experience and write down any thoughts or reactions they had. The following quotes are instructive:

Male: I enjoyed the court case because it was something I had never been
    involved with before. It was exciting to actually be working on a real

case helping to solve Jill's financial difficulties. I was astonished to discover that the number-crunching that we had done has never been done in this area. What really surprised me, however, was the amount of money that John should give Jill. From a male standpoint, I had never thought that women deserved to get so much money from their ex. Although, after doing this case, I now realize that women get the short end of the stick in divorces, especially if they keep the children.

Male: Basically, this case taught me that breaking up a marriage is serious business. That in this case and in most cases children are the people hurt the most. The children were the ones who would lose their accustomed standard of living.

Male: The fact that the man does not want to take care of his own children really makes me sick. This fact itself deserves some sort of punishment. This kind of thing is what ruins kids' chances to survive and succeed in the world today. I feel that even if we do not get the full award that we have asked for, we have helped the woman and her children a great deal.

Female: From an economic perspective, this exercise allowed the class to work together to reach a common goal. Applying the fundamental economic principles and formulas we have learned over the course of our Denison career, has allowed us to come up with an economic analysis we felt the wife deserved. In addition to economic knowledge gained, I realized how divorces truly alter the lives of families. This case clearly proves that divorced women account for the largest amount of welfare recipients.

Spanish Male: The fact that we were capable of doing something real has been fascinating to me. I never imagined that I was going to do anything like this while I was at school. By making our economic analysis of the situation of each of the spouses before and after the divorce, we have learned about the real consequences of gender discrimination.

Male: And, even though I felt she was getting a lot of money, albeit justified, I was even more shocked to hear the opinion of the lawyers in that she probably wouldn't get anything close to that—$35 a week per child? I would also have liked to be able to go to court and explain "our" alimony argument. I don't think it's difficult to understand. I'm sorry that we aren't "qualified."

Male: With the lawyers and Jill counting on the quality of work, I believe most students took this on as a challenge. It was important to me, as I'm sure everyone else, that the project was done meticulously. I like splitting up the class into groups that worked independently from one another. This allowed for several analyses of the same project— giving us a good representation and allowing us to choose the best one or combination of reports.

Male: The interesting areas that left an impression on me were as follows: First, the attention to detail and proofreading the case to find any little detail and avoid the opposing lawyers' discrediting was a surprisingly long process. This lengthy process of polishing the report took just as long to finish as compiling the information in the first place. Second, the basic idea that there were real people depending on the quality of the work that we were to do, lead to better work by us—first as individuals, then collectively as a class.

Greek Female: In the beginning the whole thing seemed to me like working on a lab, we inflated figures to estimate current values and those in the future, we calculated salaries, all sorts of capital (houses owned, stocks, bonds), calculated the poverty needs of each person prior and after the divorce, the wife's with children before and after the age of eighteen. It was amazing to think that a college class was able to handle the case (the economic procedures), of a couple filing a divorce. Once we met the lawyers, I realized how serious and important our work was, more than just a lab!

Female: My group was very bright and we worked through many problems together that probably would have taken a long time for me to figure out alone. Working in a group was encouraging. We all received the chance to show what we could do and the result we can accomplish with each other's help.

Male: Many of the things we study as undergraduate students are not practical and have no relevance to the outside world that most of us will be entering shortly. It was good to do something that could be applied outside the classroom. This assignment was also helpful in that we had to work together with our classmates to come up with the answers. This is good practice for future employment when you have to work in small groups to get projects done.

Female: When the opportunity was first presented to us, I wanted to take part without any hesitation. However, as we began to look at the information and understand that there were 4 children who were depending on our work to make their standard of living above the poverty level, I was apprehensive and worried that our limited (or so I thought) skills would not be sufficient enough for the case. But as time went on and we all worked together to put our side of the case together, I became more confident and reassured that we were able to handle the situation. It made me finally understand what a crucial role Denison has played in preparing me for the world I am going to face come May 7th. For the first time, I am confident that I will contribute a great deal to my future employer.

Male, who discussed the monotony of most courses: When presented with something that is going to make a difference in this world, most college students are motivated to work at their full capacity. I am one of the students who is motivated by real-life work, work that makes a difference ... This case gave the class an opportunity to work as a group, very much like the work I have done in past internships. We accomplished the best learning, and that is learning with peers with outside guidance. I mean guidance, not hand holding. We were given a good deal of responsibility and I think we responded.

Female: Having centered the entire lab component of this course on a simulated death case, the chance to actually defend a client in a divorce case using a similar analysis to our lab reports really put a real-life scenario to our class.

Male: I recently had an interview in Chicago and was asked to discuss one class activity that I benefited from the most. I immediately went into a full discussion of what skills were used, and, most important, what I learned throughout this court case.

Conclusion

Using a more inclusive course content and pedagogy moves students away form the passive learning environments found in most economics courses and into more active learning environments—ones that include their peers and the broader community within which they live. The content of this course ensured that students understood the different sources of labor market discrimination in the United States and saw how it affected the lives of Jane and John Doe. The team learning component ensured that students had experience working in groups to accomplish a task and to develop personal and group communication skills. The laboratory format gave students familiarity with data and manipulating it so that they could put their economic skills to work. The divorce case—the judge's response to their brief, the evaluation of their own efforts, and their reflections—are qualitative pieces of evidence of the potential effectiveness of designing more inclusive courses.

Economics courses can be vehicles for students to develop the skills and capabilities to approach the challenges of life both in and outside of the traditional classroom. Student responses suggest how important developing these skills along with economic skills are to students. Students developed computer skills, personal skills, and, more important, self-confidence with the court case. In addition, by putting their knowledge to work, they made a difference. Making the course content and pedagogy of economics course more inclusive, as evidenced by the student responses, benefits all students.

NOTES

The author would like to thank her spring 1995 Economics 325 (Women in the Labor Force) students for their willingness to take a chance and help out another human being with the knowledge they had acquired in the class.

1. The course requirements for a major in economics are introductory economics, intermediate microeconomics and macroeconomics, econometrics, and three upper-level courses, one of which must have a laboratory component. The three core courses—intermediate microeconomics, intermediate macroeconomics, and econometrics—all have laboratory components. Courses with laboratory components usually, but not always, use the computer lab in the department. These exercises consist of a variety of activities—collecting data, inputting data, analyzing data with an appropriate statistical package, and writing reports. Most of the upper-level courses have laboratory components. The curriculum is highly tiered. All upper-level courses have either intermediate micro- or macroeconomics as a prerequisite.

2. For more information on the significance of cooperative learning groups for student understanding, see Johnson, Johnson, and Smith 1991; and Meyers and Jones 1993. Team structures are being used widely in the corporate world (see the work of Peter Senge et al. 1994). In addition, CNN reported that students who have had experience learning on teams are getting better jobs than those that have not.

3. Teams can be formed in a variety of ways from having students engage in ice-breaking exercises to having students fill out Post-it notes with their course objective on it and put up on the wall. In the first instance students can identify other students with similar interests and form teams. Post-it notes with similar course objectives on them are grouped together, and students form their own teams based upon similar interests. Some instructors assign teams based on academic similarities, however, given the nature of the grading, voluntary group formation on some common interest or goal is preferable. Ice-breaking exercises are used in this case.

4. Copies of the laboratory manual and the Leslie Doe exhibits are available upon request form the author.

REFERENCES

Anderson, James A., and Maurianne Adams. 1992. "Acknowledging the Learning Styles of Diverse Student Populations: Implications for Instructional Design." In *Teaching for Diversity*, no. 49, ed. Laura Border, and Nancy Van Note Chism, 59–69. San Francisco: Jossey-Bass.

Bartlett, Robin L. 1996. "Discovering Diversity in Introductory Economics." *Journal of Economic Perspectives* (spring): 141–53.

———. 1995a. "Attracting the Otherwise Bright Students." *American Economic Review* 85 (May): 362–66.

———. 1995b. "A Flip of the Coin—A Roll of the Die: An Answer to the Free-Rider Problem in Economic Education." *Journal of Economic Education* 26 (spring): 131–39.

———. 1995c. "Team Learning and the Confidence Gap." Paper presented at the International Association of Feminist Economics, Tours, France, July.

———. 1995d."An Introductory Lecture in Macroeconomics: Integrating the New Scholarship on Women." Paper presented at the American Economic Association Meeting, New York, NY, December.

Bartlett, Robin L., and Paul G. King. 1990. "Teaching Economics as a Laboratory Science." *Journal of Economic Education* 21 (spring): 109–12.

Belenky, Mary Field, Blythe McVicker Clinchy, Nancy Rule Goldberger, and Jill Mattuck Tarule. 1986. *Women's Ways of Knowing: The Development of Self, Voice, and Mind.* New York: Basic Books.

Cooper, James L., Pamela Robinson, and Molly McKinney. 1994. "Cooperative Learning in the Classroom." In *Changing College Classrooms: New Teaching and Learning Strategies for an Increasingly Complex World,* ed. Diane Halpern et al., 74–92. San Francisco: Jossey-Bass.

Davis, James R. 1993. *Better Teaching, More Learning: Strategies for Success in Postsecondary Settings.* Phoenix, AZ: Sage Publications. 1993.

Ginorio, Angela B. 1995. *Warming the Climate for Women in Academic Science.* Washington, DC: Project for the Status and Education of Women, Association of American Colleges.

Jacobsen, Joyce. 1994. *The Economics of Gender.* Cambridge, MA: Blackwell Publishers.

Johnson, David W., Roger T. Johnson, and Karl A. Smith. 1991. *Cooperative Learning: Increased College Faculty Instructional Productivity,* ASHE-ERIC Higher Education Report no. 4. Washington, DC: George Washington University, School of Education and Human Development.

Kolb, David A. 1981. "Learning Styles and Disciplinary Differences." In *The Modern American College: Responding to the New Realities of Diverse Students and a Changing Society,* ed. Arthur Chickering et al., 232–55. San Francisco: Jossey-Bass.

Light, Richard. 1990. *The Harvard Assessment Seminars: Explorations with Students and Faculty about Teaching, Learning, and Student Life, First Report.* Cambridge, MA: Harvard University Press.

Meyers, Chet, and Thomas B. Jones. 1993. *Promoting Active Learning: Strategies for the Classroom.* San Francisco: Jossey-Bass.

Musil, Caryn Mctighe. 1992. "Collaborative Learning and Women's Ways of Knowing." *Students at the Center: A Feminist Assessment,* 55–57. Washington, DC: Association of American Colleges.

Nieves-Squires, Sarah. 1991. *Hispanic Women: Making Their Presence on Campus Less Tenuous.* Washington, DC: Project for the Status and Education of Women, Association of American Colleges.

Renas, Stephen M. 1995. "Measuring the Economics Impact of Divorce." *Compleat Lawyer: The Magazine of the ABA General Practice Section* 12 (winter): 52–55.

Sandler, Bernice, Lisa A. Silverberg, and Roberta M. Hall. 1996. *The Chilly Classroom*

Climate: A Guide to Improve the Education of Women. Washington, DC: National Association for Women in Education.

Schoem, David, et al., eds. 1993. *Multicultural Teaching in the University.* Westport, CT: Praeger.

Senge, Peter M., Art Kleiner, Charlotte Roberts, Richard B. Ross, and Bryan J. Smith. 1994. *The Fifth Discipline Fieldbook: Strategies and Tools for Building a Learning Organization.* New York: Doubleday.

Smith, Donna, and David A. Kolb. 1985. *User Guide for the Learning-Style Inventory.* Boston: McBer and Co.

Tobias, Shelia. 1990. *They're Not Dumb, They're Different: Stalking the Second Tier.* Tucson: Research Corp.

Treisman, Uri. 1992. "Studying Students Studying Calculus: A Look at the Lives of Minority Mathematics Students in College." *College Mathematics Journal* 23(5): 362–72.

U.S. Department of Commerce, Bureau of the Census. 1993. *Poverty in the United States: 1992.* Washington, DC: USGPO.

Weitzman, Lenore J. 1985. *The Divorce Revolution: The Unexpected Social and Economic Consequences for Women and Children in America.* New York: Free Press.

Contributors

April Laskey Aerni has been teaching economics, women's studies, and freshman seminar at Nazareth College in Rochester, New York, since 1987. She received her Ph.D. degree in economics from the University of Cincinnati and her undergraduate degree from George Washington University. She worked in Washington, DC, at a consulting firm and then for the City of Cincinnati Planning Department, before beginning to teach. She was one of the founding members of the International Association for Feminist Economics (IAFFE) and has been investigating, experimenting with, and writing about integrating feminist issues into economic classes since she began teaching.

Robin L. Bartlett is the Laura C. Harris Chair and a Professor of Economics at Denison University in Granville, Ohio. She has taught Intermediate Macroeconomics, Money and Banking, and Women in the Labor Force at Denison since 1974. Her research has taken several twists and turns. She has authored articles on the determinants of executive compensation, on the determinants of the earning differentials between men and women, and on the effects of different pedagogical techniques on student learning. Her simulations of the Council of Economic Advisors staff meetings is the signature of her Intermediate Macroeconomics course. Her pedagogical interest has led her to develop the lecture/laboratory curriculum in the Economics Department and to incorporate team learning in all her classes. Currently, she is Chair of the American Economic Association's Committee on the Status of Women.

Eleanor Brown was born in 1954 and raised in southern California. She received her B.A. degree in economics from Pomona College in 1975 and continued her economics education at Princeton University, receiving her M.A. degree in 1977 and her Ph.D. degree in 1981. Her early work focused on unemployment insurance design and its effects on short-term unemployment. Her current research agenda centers on individual philanthropy in the United States. She has authored several papers on the impact of the federal income tax on charitable activity, including volunteer labor. She has taught at the University of Florida and at Princeton University and is currently Professor of Economics at Pomona College in Claremont, CA, where she lives with her husband and two children. Professor Brown is also a deputy editor of *Nonprofit and Voluntary Sector Quarterly* and a member of the grant advisory board of the Aspen Institute.

Amy McCormick Diduch is Assistant Professor of Economics at Mary Baldwin College in Staunton, Virginia. She received her Ph.D. degree in economics from Harvard University in 1995. Her research interests encompass a variety of labor-related topics, including international variations in strike activity and issues related to poverty and inequality.

Susan F. Feiner is an Associate Professor of Economics and Women's Studies at the University of Southern Maine, Portland. Professor Feiner received her Ph.D. degree in economics from the University of Massachusetts at Amherst. As Project Director for National Science Foundation and Ford Foundation grants, she has promoted faculty development to improve economic education. She is editor of volumes on race and gender, radical economics, and feminist economics. Her research has appeared in the *American Economics Review, Cambridge Journal of Economics, Gender & Society,* and *Journal of Economic Education.*

Marianne Ferber is Professor of Economics and Women's Studies Emerita at the University of Illinois at Urbana–Champaign and was the Horner Distinguished Visiting Professor at Radcliffe College from 1993 to 1995. Within the broad field of the economic status of women, she has concentrated on the standing of women in academia, the family as an economic unit, international comparisons in the position of women, and, recently, feminist theory. She is also currently doing research on the impact of nonstandard employment on the well-being of workers. She is coauthor, with Francine D. Blau and Anne Winkler, of *The Economics of Women, Men, and Work;* coeditor, with Brigid O'Farrell, of *Work and Family Policies for a Changing Work Force* (1991); coeditor, with Julie A. Nelson, of *Beyond Economic Man: Feminist Theory and Economics* (1993); coeditor, with Jane W. Loeb, of *Academic Couples: Problems and Promises* (1997); and editor of *Women in the Labor Market* (1998). She has published extensively in economics, sociology, women's studies, and education journals.

Mary Hirschfeld is Associate Professor of Economics at Occidental College, Los Angeles, CA.

Emily P. Hoffman is a Professor of Economics at Western Michigan University. She earned her Ph.D. degree in economics from the University of Massachusetts at Amherst in 1975. She previously taught at the University of Missouri in Rolla, the University of North Carolina at Chapel Hill, and Douglas College at Rutgers University. Her dissertation provided conclusive evidence of the underpayment of female faculty members there, which sparked a lawsuit, the settlement of which resulted in substantial equity adjustments. Since then her research has concentrated on the empirical analysis of large data sets in the areas of labor market discrimination, unemployment, and poverty.

Joyce P. Jacobsen is an Associate Professor of Economics at Wesleyan University in Middletown, Connecticut. She has published mainly in the area of labor economics, including articles on sex segregation, migration, and the effects of labor force intermittency on women's earnings. She is the author of *The Economics of Gender* (2d ed., 1998).

Maureen J. Lage is an Associate Professor of Economics and an Affliate of the Women's Studies Program at Miami University, where she has been employed since 1990. Her professional areas of interest include economic education, applied econometrics, health economics, and gender economics.

Margaret Lewis is an Associate Professor of Economics at the College of Saint Benedict, where she teaches the political economy of gender and race, industrial organization, quantitative methods, and introduction to economics. She holds a B.A. degree from the College of William and Mary and Ph.D. and M.A. degrees from the University of Maryland. Her interest in feminist pedagogy grows out of the College of Saint Benedict's emphasis on gender and the liberal arts, her belief that learning economics creates a more informed citizenry, and her scholarly work on the interplay between institutional economics, feminist economics, and rhetoric.

KimMarie McGoldrick is an Associate Professor of Economics in the Robins School of Business at the University of Richmond in Virginia. She has taught Principles, Statistics, Industrial Organization and Public Policy, The Economics of Poverty and Discrimination, and Women and Gender Issues in Economics since she began teaching as a graduate student in 1990. Her innovation in applying teaching techniques, including the incorporation of service learning, has earned her two teaching awards (one as a graduate student and more recently at the Robins School of Business in 1996). Her research on compensating wage differentials and pedagogical issues earned her the Outstanding Research Award at the Robins School of Business in 1997.

Robert L. Moore has been teaching at Occidental College since 1978. Prior to that time he was an Assistant Professor of Economics at Harvard University, in charge of Harvard's Principles of Economics course. He was the editor of the "Teaching Tools" section of Economic Inquiry from 1987–97. He has published numerous journal articles in the areas of labor economics, personnel economics, public finance, and economic education as well as three supplemental textbooks, including *Microeconomic Principles in Action* (with James Whitney [1990]) and *Readings, Issues, and Problems in Public Finance* (with Eleanor Brown [1995]).

Janice Peterson is an Associate Professor of Economics at the State University of New York, College at Fredonia. Her current research interests include institutional and feminist economics, poverty and social welfare policy, and economics education. She has published work on these topics in a variety of journals and book collections.

Meenakshi Rishi has been teaching economics at the College of Business Administration, Ohio Northern University, since September 1993. She earned her Ph.D. degree from the Department of Economics at the University of Massachusetts, Amherst. Her research interests are in the areas of development economics and pedagogy. Her publications in the latter field include articles in *Feminist Teacher* and *College Teaching*. She is actively involved in curriculum transformation projects and recently served as a project staff member at a faculty development conference on strengthening economics education at historically black colleges and universities.

Bruce B. Roberts is Associate Professor of Economics at the University of Southern Maine, Portland. Professor Roberts received his Ph.D. degree in economics from the University of Massachusetts at Amherst. His publications have appreared in the *Cambridge Journal of Economics, Review of Radical Political Economy, History of Political Economy,* and *American Economic Review.*

Jean Shackelford is a professor in the Economics Department at Bucknell University, Lewisburg, Pennsylvania. She is the founding president of the International Association for Feminist Economics and continues to serve as the Executive Secretary of the association. Her research and teaching interests include feminist pedagogy, economic principles, and early women in the history of economic thought. She is a coauthor of *Economics: A Tool for Critically Understanding Society* (1998).

Myra H. Strober is a labor economist and Professor at the School of Education at Stanford University. With Agnes Chan, she is the coauthor of *The Road Winds Uphill All the Way: Gender, Work, and Family in the United*

States and Japan. She is also the author of numerous articles on occupational segregation, women in the professions and management, the economics of childcare, feminist economics, and the teaching of economics. Myra is currently on leave from Stanford and is serving as Program Officer in Higher Education at Altantic Philanthropic Services. Myra was the founding director of the Stanford Center for Research on Women, the first chair of the National Council for Research on Women, President of the International Association for Feminist Economics, Vice President of the NOW Legal Defense and Education Fund, and associate editor of *Feminist Economics* and of the *Journal of Economic Education.*

Dennis Sullivan is Professor of Economics at Miami University in Oxford, Ohio. His research on topics in income distribution and redistribution has led to articles in journals such as *Public Choice, National Tax Journal,* and *Economy Inquiry.* His current research focuses primarily on the comparative data in the Luxembourg Income Study.

Michael Treglia is Senior Health Economist at Eli Lilly and Company. Besides economic education, his research interests include health economics and topics in microeconomics. He is currently examining the impact of technology on economic education, with particular attention to gender implications.

Mary E. Young is an Associate Professor of Economics at Southwestern University, a liberal arts college in Georgetown, Texas. She was a founding member of the International Association for Feminist Economics (IAFFE) and has been an active member of its Pedagogy Committee. Among her additional research interests are the economics of abortion in the United States, forensic economics, and the economics of discrimination.

Andrea L. Ziegert is an Associate Professor of Economics at Denison University. She received B.S. and M.A. degrees in economics from Miami University (Ohio) and a Ph.D. degree in economics from the University of North Carolina–Chapel Hill. Her current research and teaching interests include public policy issues surrounding market failure and market distribution including environmental economics, access to health care, and poverty and income distribution.

Index